ISBN: 978129036537

Published by:
HardPress Publishing
8345 NW 66TH ST #2561
MIAMI FL 33166-2626

Email: info@hardpress.net
Web: http://www.hardpress.net

Heroes of History

EDITED BY

Evelyn Abbott, M.A.
FELLOW OF BALLIOL COLLEGE, OXFORD

FACTA DUCIS VIVENT, OPEROSAQUE
GLORIA RERUM.——OVID, IN LIVIAM, 265.

THE HERO'S DEEDS AND HARD-WON
FAME SHALL LIVE.

SIR PHILIP SIDNEY

SIR PHILIP SIDNEY.

FROM AN ENGRAVING, BY H. ROBINSON, OF ZUCCHERO'S PORTRAIT AT PENSHURST.

Heroes of History

SIR PHILIP SIDNEY

TYPE OF ENGLISH CHIVALRY IN THE ELIZABETHAN AGE

BY

H. R. FOX BOURNE

AUTHOR OF "THE LIFE OF JOHN LOCKE," "ENGLISH SEAMEN UNDER THE
TUDORS," "ENGLISH MERCHANTS," ETC., ETC.

NEW YORK

G. P. PUTNAM'S SONS

27 & 29 WEST 23D STREET

[Subscription Department]

Electrotyped, Printed, and Bound by
The Knickerbocker Press, New York
G. P. PUTNAM'S SONS

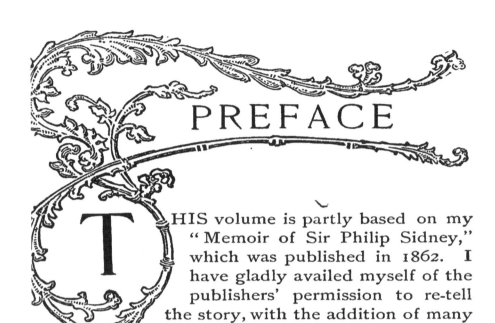

PREFACE

THIS volume is partly based on my "Memoir of Sir Philip Sidney," which was published in 1862. I have gladly availed myself of the publishers' permission to re-tell the story, with the addition of many details which the researches of others during the past quarter of a century have brought to light, or which I have myself been fortunate enough to come across. But, while what had already been said in terms that did not call for alteration has been reproduced, this is substantially a new book. Some matters previously enlarged upon have been lightly dealt with; much fresh information has been presented; and the book has been written throughout on lines consistent with the general plan of the "Heroes of the Nations" series.

The effort has been to bring into prominence, and to keep always in view, but without exaggeration or distortion, the chivalrous aspect of Sir Philip Sidney's life, and its relations in that aspect with the history of his time and country, with the contemporaries among whom he moved, who influenced him and who were influenced by him. Had space allowed, some biographical incidents of minor importance here passed by or briefly disposed of would have been more closely handled, and much more would, perhaps with advantage, have been said about Sidney's surroundings. But I have endeavoured to draw a true and not incomplete picture ✓ of him as a type of English chivalry in the Elizabethan age.

I am anxious to retract, and make such amends as I can for, one grave fault in the earlier volume. Careful thought and investigation have led me to repudiate the view there taken of the "Astrophel and Stella" episode; that is, of Sidney's connection with Lady Penelope Devereux, afterwards Lady Rich, and of the circumstances in which she became the heroine of his sonnets. A blunder in noting down a wrong date, and consequently supposing that Lady Penelope's betrothal and marriage to Lord Rich took place in 1580 instead of 1581, partly misled me. This is all the more to be regretted because some critics and biographers, who were not aware of my error as to the date, appear to have been led thereby to overstep the conclusions I drew from it.

In a volume like the present it would be pedantic to vouch in footnotes for every statement made. But, in justice both to myself and to the reader, precise references have been made to the sources of actually fresh information about Sidney's life; and it will be seen that the references are not few or unimportant. For the rest, my principal authority is the "Memoir" already mentioned, in which the

voucliers for details are carefully given ; but I grate-
fully acknowledge indebtedness to several authors
and editors who have incidentally contributed to the
elucidation of episodes and connections in Sidney's
life.   The books that I have found most helpful are
included in the subjoined list.

H. R. FOX BOURNE.

LONDON, 17 October, 1891.

LIST OF PRINCIPAL AUTHORITIES (EXCLUSIVE OF MS. COLLECTIONS), IN ORDER OF CHRONOLOGY.

" Holinshed's Chronicles," vol. iii. (containing brief memoirs of Sir Henry Sidney, Lady Mary Sidney, and Sir Philip Sidney), 1587.

" The Procession at the Obsequies of Sir Philip Sidney," by Thomas Lant, 1587.

" The Countess of Pembroke's Arcadia," written by Sir Philip Sidney, 1590.

" Sir P. S.; his Astrophel and Stella," 1591.

" The Defence of Poesy," by Sir Philip Sidney, 1595 (another edition in the same year, entitled " An Apology for Poetry ").

" The Life of the Renowned Sir Philip Sidney," by Fulke Greville, Lord Brooke, 1652.

" Letters and Memorials of State, Written and Collected by Sir Henry Sidney, the Famous Sir Philip Sidney, and his Brother Sir Robert Sidney . . . also Memoirs of the Lives and Actions of the Sidneys," edited by Arthur Collins, 1745.

" Langueti Epistolæ ad P. Sidneium," edited by Lord Hailes, 1776.

" Memoirs of the Life and Writings of Sir Philip Sidney," by Dr. Thomas Zouch, 1808.

" Royal Progresses of Queen Elizabeth," edited by John Nichols, 1823.

" The Miscellaneous Works of Sir Philip Sidney," edited, with a prefatory memoir, by William Gray, 1829.

" Sidneiana," edited by Bishop Butler, for the Roxburgh Club, 1837.

" Queen Elizabeth and Her Times," edited by Thomas Wright, 1838.

" Correspondence of Robert Dudley, Earl of Leicester, in 1585 and 1586," edited by John Bruce, for the Camden Society, 1844.

" The Correspondence of Sir Philip Sidney with Hubert Languet," translated and edited, with a prefatory memoir, by S. A. Pears, 1845.

" Lives and Letters of the Devereux, Earls of Essex," by the Hon. W. B. Devereux, 1853.

" The Ulster Journal of Archæology," vols. ii., iii., v., and viii. (containing " Sir Henry Sidney's Memoir of his Government of Ireland," edited by Herbert F. Hore), 1854–1860.

" Calendar of State Papers, Domestic Series, of the Reigns of Edward VI., Mary, and Elizabeth," edited by Robert Lemon and Mary Everett Green, vols, i., ii., vii. and xii., 1856–1872.

" Calendar of State Papers Relating to Scotland," edited by Markham John Thorpe, vol. i., 1858.

" Calendar of State Papers Relating to Ireland," edited by Hans Claude Hamilton, vols. i.–iii., 1860–1865.

" Calendar of State Papers, Foreign Series, of the Reign of Elizabeth," edited by Joseph Stevenson and Allan James Crosby, vols. i.–ix., 1863–1880.

" Calendar of the Carew Papers," edited by J. S. Brewer and William Bullen, vols. i. and ii., 1867, 1868.

" Appendices to Reports of the Historical Manuscripts Commission " (especially those describing the MSS. in the possession of Lord de L'Isle, the Marquis of Salisbury, the Duke of Rutland, and the Marquis of Bath), 1873–1889.

CONTENTS.

CHAPTER I.

ILLUSTRATIONS.

St. James' Palace

SIR PHILIP SIDNEY:

TYPE OF ENGLISH CHIVALRY IN THE ELIZABETHAN AGE.

CHAPTER I.

PRELIMINARY.

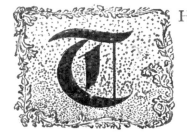

THE chivalry that grew up in Europe as part of the feudal system, giving it much of its strength and most of its adornment, was never so firmly established in England as in France or in some other countries. And among Englishmen the mediæval institution was broken down during the Wars of the Roses, about a century before Sir Philip Sidney was addressed by Edmund Spenser, and honoured by all whose honour was worth having in his day, as

> the president
> Of nobless and of chivalry.

The chivalry of the Elizabethan age, of which Sidney was the most complete and conspicuous type, was in some respects out of date, in others immature. It strove to conform to traditions and to follow methods unsuited to the altered and altering arrangements of society in sixteenth-century England. Adapting itself as best it could to these arrangements, it found or sought its ideals in the past ; yet all its dignity came from the efforts of its heroes to help on the great change from mediæval to modern ways of thought and action, and to reshape the old ideals in forms proper for the future. Its successes and failures, its illusions and exploits, are as distinctly characteristic of the transition period in English history during which it showed itself as were the political and religious crises, the intellectual and literary upheavals, contemporary and intimately connected with it.

The earlier chivalry was the crown of feudalism. The military service that sovereigns claimed as a mere matter of duty from their tenants and vassals was in it supplemented by the like or the more laborious and more ennobling service that knights and courtiers voluntarily rendered, in excess of loyalty to their masters or of fondness for martial deeds and for the fame thus won.

The knight's devotion to his immediate lord was the first motive, and thereby kingdoms and principalities were set up and enlarged, or crippled and overturned. In England, all that chivalry did in this direction was to maintain and expand the power of the Norman and Plantagenet monarchs, to aid them in their invasions of Wales, Ireland, Scotland, and France, and their occasional crusading to more distant lands, until, after nearly four centuries, the feud between Yorkists and Lancastrians arose, and, giving a death-blow to mediæval systems, prepared the way for Tudor rule. But in France and the neighbouring countries, where there were almost constant rivalry and struggle for supremacy among the fragments of the Holy Roman Empire and of Charlemagne's dominion, chivalry had a busier and more variable part to play ; and instances are numberless of English knights, without sufficient occupation under their own sovereigns, taking temporary service in foreign lands, and, in humble ways, anticipating and striving to emulate the achievements of the Chevalier Bayard, the greatest and among greater men the latest of the heroes of mediæval chivalry.

✓   Religion was, of course, closely mixed up with chivalry ; and chivalry itself became a religion. This we see not only in the memorable crusades against the Saracens, by his participation in which Richard Cœur-de-Lion earned all his title to renown, but also in the history of the Knights Templars, the Order of St. John, and other old fighting guilds.

An aspect of chivalry not to be forgotten, moreover, and much to its credit, was the respect that, in its better days, it caused to be paid to the female sex. The homage rendered to women, under its rules, may have been often spurious and superficial; but it had notable effect in advancing social progress.

And with gallantry towards women went other refinements of life. There was not much tenderness or humanity towards inferiors. The world of mediæval chivalry was narrow and selfish. The base multitude had no acknowledged claim to generous treatment, and the many were supposed to exist only as chattels for the benefit of the few. The vulgar herd gained little by the civilisation that was introduced in courts and castles. But it gained something and the world gained more.

If in the encouragement given to tyranny, cruelty, lasciviousness, and much else, there was an ugly side or a yet uglier background to the fabric, the better side or the agreeable front appears in the great advance made between the twelfth and fifteenth centuries in those notions of loyalty and courtesy, the duty of keeping faith with princes and comrades and of avoiding all unknightly vices, which rendered it possible for Europe to emerge from the dark ages and to enter on the broader path of progress which has been opened up in modern times. The records of Froissart and Sainte Palaye, the epics and romances and ballads and lays of famous and of unknown writers, show us much to deride and condemn, but also much to admire and reverence, in the institution that Cervantes justly mocked at when it had ceased to be of use.

In England the traditions of mediæval chivalry chiefly survived under the Tudors in the jousts and tournaments that were favoured by Henry the Eighth, and yet more by Queen Elizabeth ; and they gave a tone and colour to serious pursuits, as

well as pastimes, when there was no mimic warfare
to be engaged in at Court and in baronial halls.
But knight-errantry was not extinct. We shall see
Sidney pining for it, and it was freely practised by
Raleigh and many others in his day. One of the
problems that Sidney and his peers had to solve, if
they could, was how to give new form and fresh
dignity to knight-errantry; how to develop a chivalry which should be true to the old traditions, and
yet, retaining the old virtues of loyalty and courtesy,
courage and justice, should be serviceable to the
England that was called upon, as the champion of
Protestantism and all the political, social, and intellectual revolts incident to the Protestant rebellion,
to take a bolder position than heretofore among the
nations of Europe.

It is by viewing him as the type of such chivalry
as was aimed at and was possible in the Elizabethan
age that we shall best understand Sir Philip Sidney's
character, and most truly comprehend not merely
the projects and ambitions, the achievements and
the disappointments of his own short life, but also
the conditions of success and of failure to which
others in his day, more or less resembling him or
differing from him, alike in temperament and in
circumstances, were subjected.

Sidney, it must be noted, was barely four years
old when Elizabeth became queen of England.
Elizabeth had been nearly seventeen years on the
throne before he took a man's place at her Court;
and after his death she reigned through nearly seventeen other years. It was only during the inter-

mediate term of less than a dozen years, from 1575 to 1586, that he moved in and out of her presence as the foremost representative of English chivalry at that time, all the more its representative because his years of service were years of thraldom. Whatever he did for good was done in spite of the courtly chains imposed upon him. Posterity may be grateful to Queen Elizabeth for her administration of English affairs during nearly half a century; for coincident with that administration, if not consequent upon it, was a vast increase of power and prosperity to England. But if her rule was favourable to the chivalrous movements of the day, they were not favoured by her.

To know what Sidney was as an Elizabethan courtier, and what were the restraints laid upon him in his compulsory courtiership, we must review not merely the events of his own early career, but also some matters preliminary to any information we have about him beyond the bare date of his birth.

Among the minor statesmen of Henry the Eighth's reign were two grandfathers of Sir Philip Sidney. The one was Sir William Sidney, born in 1482, and descended from another William Sidney, who came over from Anjou with Henry Plantagenet in 1154, and was the founder of a worthy family of knights and squires. The other was John Dudley, born in 1501, who claimed descent from Robert de L'Isle, a partisan of the barons in their opposition to King John. Lady Elizabeth Grey, sister of a Baron de L'Isle, had married the Edmund Dudley who was

Richard Empson's colleague in assisting Henry the Seventh's reckless appropriations of other people's wealth, and of whom Bacon said that " he was an eminent man, and one who could put hateful business into good language." This Dudley was beheaded, and his estates were forfeited, in 1509. But his son John, only eight years old at that time, grew up to win for himself wealth and rank and royal favour—and ultimate disgrace. " I am a Dudley in blood," Philip Sidney wrote, in 1585, with excess of courtliness, " and do acknowledge—though, in all truth, I may justly affirm that I am, by my father's side, of ancient and always well-esteemed and well-matched gentry—yet I do acknowledge, I say, that my chiefest honour is to be a Dudley." There was less honour in being a Dudley than in being a Sidney.

All through the reign of Henry the Eighth Sir William Sidney was a zealous servant of the State; and during a large part of it he held office as the King's chamberlain. He was one of the commanders of an English force sent in 1510 to aid Ferdinand of Spain in his war with the Moors; and he was off Brest in the squadron that made havoc of the great fleet of France in 1513. Knighted for his share in that sea-fight, he was next employed on land. In the same year he commanded the right wing of the army which was victorious on Flodden Field. Much other work, as warrior, diplomatist, and courtier, fell to him during the ensuing forty years, and the last of the many rewards bestowed upon him was a grant by Henry the Eighth's son, in 1552, of the old castle and lands of Penshurst, in Kent, famous in the hands of his descendants.

But Sir William Sidney's progress, though surer and more honest, was less rapid and brilliant than that of John Dudley, his associate in King Henry's service, and his junior by nineteen years. John Dudley so successfully pushed his fortunes under Henry that in 1543 he was made Baron de L'Isle and Lord High Admiral of England; and in 1547 he was appointed one of the executors under the King's will, to administer the affairs of the realm during Edward's minority. Of the other executors Lord Hertford was chief, and when Hertford contrived to be made Lord Protector and Duke of Somerset, Dudley aided his ambitious schemes on condition that he also should be raised in rank and invested with much arbitrary power. Dudley was created Earl of Warwick. How his show of friendship with Lord Protector Somerset soon gave way to open feud and desperate intrigue, until by Somerset's overthrow he acquired absolute control in 1550, and made himself Duke of Northumberland in 1551, need not be detailed. Here it mainly concerns us to remember that for a while he was the most powerful man in England, labouring most unscrupulously for his own aggrandisement and, in so far as selfish ambition left room for fatherly affection, for the advancement of his sons and daughters.

Of these, besides one who died young, there were seven—John, Ambrose, Robert, Guildford, Henry, Mary, and Catherine—whose ages in 1547 ranged from nineteen to eleven. Edward the Sixth was not yet ten when in that year he became king. His sister Elizabeth was fourteen, and the other sister, Mary, was one-and-thirty. Henry the Eighth's younger children and the children of Dudley had been playmates; and close friendship continued after the change of monarchs, especially, it would seem, between little Lady Mary Dudley, who was to be the mother of Sir Philip Sidney, and the Princess Elizabeth. There was yet closer intimacy between this princess's brother and Philip's other parent.

Sir Henry Sidney, who was born on the 20th of July, 1529, tells us that at the age of nine he was appointed henchman to King Henry, and he adds: " I was by that most famous king put to his sweet son, Prince Edward, my most dear master, prince and sovereign; my near kinswoman being his only nurse, my father being his chamberlain, my mother his governess, and my aunt by my mother's side in such place as, among meaner personages, is called a dry-nurse—for, from the time he left sucking, she continually lay in bed with him, so long as he remained in women's government. As the prince grew in years and discretion, so grew I in favour and liking of him." Henry Sidney's mother, it may be noted, was Anne, a daughter of Sir William Pagenham, who died in 1543. Henry was the only son, but he had four sisters, all of whom married well. Mary, the eldest, became the wife of Sir William Dormer. The husbands of the other three, Lucy, Anne, and Frances, were Sir James Harrington, Sir William Fitzwilliam, and Thomas Ratcliffe, Lord Fitzwalter, who became third Earl of Sussex in 1542. It was this Earl of Sussex's widow, Henry Sidney's sister, who by bequest founded Sidney Sussex College at Cambridge in 1598.

Sir William Sidney, who died at Penshurst in February, 1554, at the age of seventy-two, appears to have spent his last few years in retirement; but his son prospered as he rose to man's estate amid the political and religious squabbles, the personal ambitions, and the base intrigues which harassed England while Edward bore the title of king, and which gave place to worse troubles when the crown passed to Mary.

Soon after Edward's accession Henry Sidney was appointed one of the four principal Gentlemen of the King's Bedchamber—partly, according to the quaint report in Holinshed's Chronicle, on account of his royal friend's affection for him, partly because, "by reason of his comeliness of person, gallantness of spirit, virtue, quality, beauty, and good composition of body," he was reputed "the only odd man and paragon of the Court." In favour with Lord Protector Somerset, he lost nothing by Somerset's overthrow. In 1551 he was knighted in company with William Cecil, afterwards Lord Burghley, who was by nine years his senior. In that year, and again in 1552, he was sent on special missions to France; and on another occasion he went as ambassador to Scotland. Among the less onerous offices bestowed upon him were those of chief cupbearer to the King and of royal cypherer, the latter entitling him to an annual stipend of £33 6s. 8d.

"The only odd man and paragon of the Court" in Edward the Sixth's day was thought well of, not merely as a courtier, but also as a rising statesman. There is particular evidence of this in the fact that the unscrupulous Duke of Northumberland chose him, or at any rate accepted him, as a husband for his eldest daughter. On the 29th of March, 1551, when she was about sixteen years old, and he not yet two-and-twenty, Lady Mary Dudley was married to Sir Henry Sidney. The ceremony appears to have been then private, as it is recorded that the marriage was "afterwards most publicly and honourably solemnised in Ely Place, Holborn, in the Whitsun-holidays next following." *

In all the records we have of the union which thus began, and which lasted during thirty-five years, we find no trace of discord, nothing but tender affection on both sides, mutual help and mutual admiration ; and, as the two must have been well acquainted with one another for a long while before the wedding, we may suppose that it was partly a love-match. But it was evidently sanctioned by the Duke of Northumberland, if not ordered, on grounds of expediency. Soon afterwards Northumberland married his other daughter, Catherine, to Lord Hastings, son of the Earl of Huntingdon, and in May, 1553, in furtherance of his

* A MS. Psalter of Sir Henry Sidney's, now in the Library of Trinity College, Cambridge, from which the above and other extracts were communicated by Mr. W. Aldis Wright to "Miscellanea Genealogica et Heraldica," part i. (April, 1870). This authority, in important particulars correcting some hitherto accepted dates, will in future be referred to as "Sir Henry Sidney's Psalter."

criminal project for retaining the mastery of English affairs, he made his son, Lord Guildford Dudley, husband of Lady Jane Grey. He would not have taken Sir Henry Sidney for son-in-law had he not deemed it prudent to attach firmly to the Dudley faction King Edward's cherished companion. As for Sir Henry, it is but reasonable to assume that the charms of Lady Mary were rendered all the more acceptable by the fact that her father was the mightiest statesman of the day. But the immediate issues to him, as courtier and politician, were none the less disastrous because there may have been included in them such increase of social and official dignity as his father-in-law could procure for him during the brief remainder of Edward the Sixth's lifetime.*

Throughout this period young Sidney appears to have been one of the dupes or willing tools of the wily but self-ruining Northumberland. A curious document, dated the 18th of May, 1553, just a week before Lord Guildford Dudley's marriage with Lady Jane Grey, authorised Sidney, in the King's name, to put in livery fifty gentlemen and yeomen as retainers in his service, and also forgave him "all his trespasses, forfeitures, penalties, outstanding debts, and whatsoever else amiss was by him done or perpetrated since King Edward's coronation day." The King's illness had warned Northumberland that

---

* On 25 July, 1552, the Duke of Northumberland wrote from Carlisle to Sir Henry Sidney, bidding him "make haste to Court before you go home to your wife," important business having to be attended to.—State Papers, Domestic, Addenda, vol. iv., No. 8.

unless he could prevent the accession of the Princess Mary, next heir to the crown under Henry the Eighth's will, he would soon be driven from power ; and at this time he was busily plotting against Mary. On the 21st of June he persuaded Edward to sign letters-patent transferring the inheritance to Lady Jane Grey. In the long list of signatures to that document is included the name of Sir Henry Sidney,* who may have considered that in joining company with all the privy councillors and prelates and judges, he was but performing a duty to his dying friend—the friend who a fortnight later died in Sir Henry's arms, with this prayer on his lips, " Oh, my Lord God, defend this realm from papistry, and maintain thy true religion ! " But whatever were Sidney's motives or excuses for taking part in the scheme against Mary, he soon repented. The proclamation of Lady Jane as queen on the 10th of July having been followed on the 20th by proclamation of Mary's queenship, he was one of the seven who, on the 21st, took the lead in tendering submission to the new sovereign, and in seeking and obtaining pardon for having attempted to injure her.†

Thus avoiding ruin by action that, if allowable, was hardly praiseworthy, Sir Henry Sidney had to look on while others suffered for the folly or the crime he had been led to countenance. On the 25th of July his father-in-law and four of his brothers-in-law—John, who had been made Earl of Warwick,

---

* " Chronicles of Queen Jane and Queen Mary " (Camden Society), p. 10.

† *Ibid.*, p. 13.

Lord Ambrose Dudley, Lord Robert Dudley, and Lord Guildford Dudley—were imprisoned in the Tower of London. Northumberland was beheaded on the 22d of August, and on the 12th of February, 1554, the same fate befell Guildford Dudley and his young wife, the one blameless victim in the tragedy. The other Dudleys obtained forgiveness after more than a year's imprisonment, but the eldest died on the 21st of October, 1554, within three days of his liberation. In the previous February, moreover, Sir William Sidney had died at Penshurst, in taking possession of which at such a time, Sir Henry and his fair wife can have had small happiness.

But Sir Henry Sidney had made his peace with the new sovereign, and although, as he tells us, "neither liking nor liked as he had been," he continued in the service of the State. On the 14th of March, 1554, not long after he had buried his father, he started for Spain as companion of the Earl of Bedford, on an embassy to King Philip, "to fetch him into this realm."* The task was accomplished in time for the wedding of Queen Mary and King Philip to take place at Winchester in the following July, and doubtless Sir Henry was present at the ceremony. By a charter dated the 8th of November in the same year, all his former offices and honours were confirmed to him, and it was partly through his influence and intercession that his brothers-in-law were released from the Tower.

---

* " Chronicles of Queen Jane and Queen Mary." p. 62.

Penshurst · Birth Place of Sir Phillip Sidney

CHAPTER II.

DURING PHILIP SIDNEY'S BOYHOOD.
1554–1568.

PHILIP SIDNEY was born at Penshurst on Friday the 30th of November, 1554, being christened Philip in honour of the husband of Queen Mary, whom his father had escorted to England a few months before. King Philip was himself one of the godfathers, the other being John Russell, Earl of Bedford; and for godmother the boy had his lately widowed grandparent, "the most virtuous Lady Jane, Duchess of Northumberland." *

Pleasantly situated in the valley of the Medway, and but a few hours' ride from London, Penshurst was as restful a place as might be found for Sir

---

* Sir Henry Sidney's Psalter. The date always hitherto given for Philip's birth is the 29th of November; but the entry in the Psalter is authoritative. According to it the event occurred at "a quarter before five in the morning."

Henry Sidney to retire to when he could be spared from Court or was not on business farther away; a place in which, his young wife might shake off her troubles in looking after their little son, and a little daughter, Margaret, who was born eighteen months later, but did not live to be two years old. Although

> That taller tree, which of a nut was set
> At his great birth where all the muses met,

no longer stands on the Dryad-haunted mount in the romantic grounds

> Where Pan and Bacchus their high feasts have made,
> Beneath the broad beech and the chestnut shade,

it is safe to guess that Philip, tenderly nurtured and wisely trained, passed his baby days in and about the fourteenth-century castle, of which, even after it had been enlarged and adorned by Sir Henry Sidney in 1580, Ben Jonson said,

> Thou art not, Penshurst, built to envious show
> Of touch * or marble, nor canst boast a row
> Of polished pillars or a roof of gold ;
> Thou hast no lantern, whereof tales are told,
> Or stair, or courts, but stand'st an ancient pile,
> And—these grudged at—art reverenced the while.
> Thou joy'st in better marks of soil, of air,
> Of wood, of water ; therein art thou fair.

All those "marks" the poet's verse helps us to see as they were three centuries ago, and as they are with very little change to-day ; the undulating ex-

---

* " Touch " was a costly stone, hard and black, used as " touch-stone " in testing gold.

PENSHURST PLACE, KENT, AS SEEN FROM THE GARDEN.

THE STATUE IS OF LATER DATE THAN THE PERIOD OF THE BIOGRAPHY.

panse in which woods and copse were stocked with deer, in which the "lower land" was stored with sheep and kine and horses, and through which the "high-swoll'n Medway" gracefully curved. Then, as he added,

> Then hath thy orchard fruit, thy garden flowers,
> Fresh as the air, and new as are the hours ;
> The early cherry, with the later plum,
> Fig, grape, and quince, each in his time doth come ;
> The blushing apricot and woolly peach
> Hang on thy walls that every child may reach—

with little Philip as one of the children ;

> And though thy walls be of the country stone,
> They 're reared with no man's ruin, no man's groan ;
> There 's none that dwell about them wish them down,
> But all come in, the farmer and the clown,
> And no one empty-handed, to salute
> Thy lord and lady, though they have no suit. *

Sir Henry and Lady Sidney had four other children, besides an infant, apparently the first-born, who seems to have died too soon to be even christened, and Margaret, who died and was buried at Penshurst in 1558. Another daughter, Ambrosia, who lived to be fifteen, was born at Hampton Court in October, 1560, and had Queen Elizabeth for her godmother.† Yet another, Mary, afterwards Countess of Pembroke, was born at Ticknell, near Bewdley,

---

* The lord whom, with his lady, Ben Jonson honoured was not Sir Henry Sidney, but his younger son Robert, afterwards Earl of Leicester. Yet the praise was perhaps more appropriate to Sir Henry and his good wife than to their son and daughter-in-law.

† State Papers, Foreign, Elizabeth ; Henry Killigrew to Throckmorton, 10 October, 1560.

on the 27th of October, 1561. There were two sons
who outlived Philip: Robert, destined to perpetuate
the family name, who was born on the 19th of November, 1563; and Thomas, born on the 25th of March,
1569, of whom very little is known.*

We have no record concerning Philip's early childhood, but the first few years, it may be assumed,
were passed at Penshurst with his nurses and his
tutors, his little sisters, and his parents now and
then. His father can rarely have been at home, and
his mother, after 1558, at any rate, was often kept
away by court duties.

In the summer of 1556 Sir Henry was sent to
Ireland with a convoy of treasure and munitions of
war for the assistance of his brother-in-law, the Earl
of Sussex, then Lord Deputy†; and he remained
there throughout the second and worse half of
Mary's reign. In Ireland, if he had some ugly work
to do as sharer in blundering efforts to crush violence by violence, he was free from personal contact
with the more cruel and hateful business then being
done in England under a pretence of zeal for religion. The office to which he was appointed was
that of Vice-Treasurer and Governor-General of the
Royal Revenues in Ireland ; but he also, as he said,
"had the leading of both horsemen and footmen,
and served as ordinarily with them as any other private captain did there." On one occasion, as commander of a force sent against the rebellious Scots
of Ulster, he slew with his own hand their leader,

---

* Sir Henry Sidney's Psalter.

† "Historical Manuscripts Commission Reports " ; vol. v., p. 343.

James McConnell.   When, in 1557, the Earl of Sussex returned to England for a holiday, Sir Henry was promoted to be a Lord Justice, acting for the Lord Deputy in his absence ; and his holding of that post was ratified, in November, 1558, on Elizabeth succeeding Mary as queen.   Thereafter, as well as before, moreover, he enjoyed other offices or sinecures, one of the more curious, granted as a compliment or by way of attaching him to the English Court, being that of Sergeant of Her Majesty's Otter Hounds.   For serving in this capacity he drew a stipend of £28 2s. 8d. a year.*

Queen Mary's death, delivering England from many grievous evils, brought speedy and important change to Sir Henry's wife and some of her kinsfolk.   In 1557 she lost another of her brothers, Lord Henry Dudley, who was killed at the battle of St. Quentin.   The two who survived, Lord Ambrose and Lord Robert Dudley, though they had been pardoned for their share in the attempt to place Lady Jane Grey on the throne, and had obtained some employment under the Catholic sovereign and her husband, had not been regarded by them with much favour.   Immediately after Elizabeth's accession both brothers, and their sister too, were summoned to Court.

All three had been the new queen's playmates in the lifetime of her father, and her intimate friends during her brother's reign ; Ambrose being about three years, and Robert about one year her senior,

---

* " Historical Manuscripts Commission Reports," vol. viii., **part i.**, p. 94.

and Mary her junior by a year or so. They were not now forgotten. The royal grace shown to Lady Sidney was to consist chiefly in requiring her to give frequent and often irksome attendance on her old companion at Whitehall, Hampton Court, and elsewhere; but the brothers were to have more substantial rewards. Lord Robert Dudley, having special talent for self-advancement, used his influence over Elizabeth so well that on the 11th of January, 1559, he was appointed Master of the Horse, and on the 23d of April following was made a Knight of the Garter, and sworn into the Privy Council. Other honours ensued in quick succession, until the highest was reached by his elevation to the peerage as Baron Denbigh on the 28th of September, 1564, and as Earl of Leicester on the next day. Throughout the five years before and the five years after this date, nearly every year bringing a fresh grant of land and rich pension, he was openly talked of as the Queen's lover, only prevented by State reasons or her own whims from becoming her husband. Lord Ambrose Dudley was not so highly favoured; but he was made Master of the Ordnance in 1560, created Baron de L'Isle, and allowed to assume his brother John's lapsed title as Earl of Warwick in 1561, and invested with the Order of the Garter in 1563.

Sir Henry Sidney, being busy in Ireland, can have seen nothing with his own eyes of the boisterous gaiety with which all Englishmen—except those who were Catholics by conviction, and many even of them—welcomed the change from Queen Mary's

ROBERT DUDLEY, EARL OF LEICESTER.
FROM AN ENGRAVING IN " HEROOLOGIA ANGLICA. "

sombre and oppressive rule to the brilliance and the promise of beneficence that dazzled and intoxicated them when Queen Elizabeth, just twenty-five years old, rode up from Hatfield to be proclaimed and crowned in London. But Lady Sidney was within reach, able—and indeed compelled—not merely to look on at the spectacle and to join in the thanksgivings and rejoicings, but also to peer below the surface and discern some of the vanities and jealousies that were incident to even the coronation shows, and that gained strength in the following years. Her husband, also, was soon brought into contact with them.* His first term of service in Ireland ended early in 1560, when, returning to England, he was appointed Lord President of Wales, with jurisdiction over the adjacent English counties which were at that time, for purposes of government, joined to the old principality. Though he was frequently called off for employment elsewhere, especially in Ireland, he held the office of Lord President continuously for the next quarter of a century, with Ludlow Castle, in Shropshire, as his official residence ; and from Ludlow he often went to Court.

Of the uses to which this trusty servant of the State was put we have illustrations in 1562. In the

---

* Strange stories are told by Mr. Froude (" History of England," vol. vi., pp. 264–271, 452, 481, 487), on the authority of De Quadra, the Spanish ambassador in London, concerning the share taken by Sir Henry and Lady Sidney in Leicester's alleged plotting to acquire fresh and discreditable influence over Elizabeth ; but as I am not able to consult the Simancas MSS. from which Mr. Froude quotes, it is safer to leave the curious reader to draw his own conclusions from the historian's statements.

April of that year he was sent on a special mission to France, with instructions to attempt a reconciliation between Catherine de'Medici, regent during the minority of her son, Charles the Ninth, and Henry of Navarre—that is, between the Catholic and Protestant factions, whose quarrel already threatened to result in civil war. He was in Paris in May, when he did all that could be done in the way of pleasant speaking and the extracting of empty promises. Returning to London in June, he was next month despatched on another errand. This time the journey was to Edinburgh, and his business to visit Mary Queen of Scots, and arrange for postponement of a contemplated interview between her and Queen Elizabeth at York. Then other duties were assigned to him in assisting his brother-in-law, the newly made Earl of Warwick, who, as Master of the Ordnance, had to prepare for the little war in which, to befriend the Huguenots, Elizabeth now embarked against France. In October and November, 1562, he was at Dover, Rye, Newhaven, and other places, looking after the shipment of troops and the fortifications. Newhaven appears to have been his headquarters until May, 1563, when he was at Portsmouth, still busy about the defences of the English coast and arrangements for attacking the French.*

There is more interest for us in the fact of Sir Henry Sidney being thus variously employed, since

* State Papers, Foreign, Elizabeth ; letters dated 28 April, 8 and 28 May, 8 and 14 June, 15 and 25 July, 30 October, and 2 November, 1562, and 28 May, 1563.

it shows what value was placed on his services, than in the details of his occupations. Yet one detail in the family history, which must be referred to this time, is both important and pathetic. "When I went to Newhaven," he wrote twenty years later concerning his wife, "I left her a full fair lady, in my eyes at least the fairest, and when I returned I found her as foul a lady as the small-pox could make her, which she did take by continued attendance of her Majesty's most precious person, sick of the same disease; the scars of which, to her resolute discomfort ever since, remain in her face, so as she liketh solitariness, *sicut nicticorax in domicilio suo.*"

Others beside Sir Henry thought Lady Sidney "a full fair lady," one of the fairest in her day, before she fell a victim to the small-pox, caught in zealous attendance on Queen Elizabeth; and no physical affliction could spoil her mental and moral beauty. But the disaster had a cruel effect on her. Henceforth, as we are told by the dear friend and first biographer of her son Philip, "she chose rather to hide herself from the curious eyes of a delicate time than come upon the stage of the world with any manner of disparagement; this mischance of sickness having cast such a veil over her excellent beauty as the modesty of that sex doth many times upon their native and heroical spirits." *

Lady Sidney retired to Penshurst, where her husband, it may be taken for granted, visited her as often as he could turn aside from his duties as Lord

---

* Fulke Greville, Lord Brooke, " The Life of the Renowned Sir Philip Sidney."

President of Wales and in other capacities. At Penshurst their second son, Robert, was born in the following year, and their eldest boy was being prepared for training and occupation elsewhere.

For positive information about Philip, after the date and place of his birth, we have to wait till his tenth year; and then we have a strange glimpse of him. From a day-old infant he has developed into a clerk in holy orders, requiring only a few formalities to qualify him as rector of a parish church in Wales.

On the 6th of May, 1564, Philip Sidney, clerk, appointed one Master Gruff John, clerk, bachelor of laws, and rector of Skyneog, to appear as his proctor before Thomas, Bishop of St. Asaph, and, after excusing his absence and alleging the cause thereof, to claim, on his behalf, admission to and institution in and corporeal possession of the church and rectory of Whitford, in the county of Flint, and, also on his behalf, to renounce the jurisdiction of the Pope and take the oath of allegiance to Queen Elizabeth. On the 7th of May the Bishop of St. Asaph appended his signature and seal to a document preferring Philip Sidney, scholar, to the church aforesaid. On the 8th of May Philip Sidney, represented by his proctor, was duly admitted by the bishop's vicar to the church and rectory, the same being declared vacant through the just deprivation of Hugh Whitford, the former rector; and on the 4th of June the transfer was completed by the signing of an indenture between the Bishop of St. Asaph and Philip Sidney, son of Sir Henry Sidney, knight, whereby the said

LADY MARY SIDNEY.

FROM AN ENGRAVING BY E. HARDING.

Philip Sidney was collated to the said church of Whitford.*

This comical arrangement can be easily explained. Master Hugh Whitford, hitherto rector of Whitford, was evidently one of the thousands of Papists, who, loyal to Queen Mary, refused to adopt the Protestant ritual prescribed by Queen Elizabeth. More than five years had elapsed before his heresy was discovered, or before it was convenient to displace him. At length, Sir Henry Sidney—being Lord President of Wales, and anxious to make some provision for his son—followed a plan which looks strange and scarcely honest in the nineteenth century, but which was common enough in the sixteenth, and took advantage of Master Whitford's contumacy. From the time when Philip Sidney was nine and a half years old, he was lay-rector of Whitford. It appears from a proposed marriage settlement drawn up for him in 1569, when he was not yet fifteen, that his title to the living had then still sixty years to run, and, after all dues and all charges for performance of the work by deputy were deducted, yielded him an income of £60 a year.†

Philip having been made a clerk in holy orders, it was time for him to be sent to school. Under date of the 16th of November, 1564, his name is entered, along with that of Fulke Greville, in the register of Shrewsbury school. Shrewsbury, which Sir Henry often visited on public business, was within easy

---

* These four documents are among the MS. treasures at Penshurst.

† This document, dated 6 August, 1569, is among the Hatfield MSS., No. 1316.

reach of Ludlow Castle, his place of residence when he was able to attend to his presidential duties. "At this day," Camden said of Shrewsbury in 1586, "it is a fine city, well inhabited, and of good commerce, and by the industry of the citizens, and their cloth manufacture and their trade with the Welsh, is very rich ; for hither the Welsh commodities are brought as to the common mart of both nations. Its inhabitants are partly English, partly Welsh. They use both languages. And this, among other things, must be mentioned to their highest praise—that they have erected the largest school in all England for the education of youth ; for which Thomas Ashton, the first schoolmaster, a person of great worth and integrity, provided, by his own industry, a competent salary." As they had been contemporaries at Oxford, it is probable that Sir Henry Sidney and Master Ashton were old friends, and knew one another's merit. At any rate, the Lord President of Wales doubtless had excellent reasons for placing his son under the charge of the Shrewsbury dominie.

During some four years, between the ages of ten and fourteen, Philip was with Master Ashton. He evidently profited by the care bestowed upon him. In those days schooling began and ended sooner than it does now ; but Philip appears to have been more precocious than his comrades. "Of his youth," wrote Fulke Greville, who was a kinsman of Philip, and was born at Beauchamp Court, near Warwick, in the same year, " I will report no other wonder than this, that, though I lived with him and knew him from a child, yet I never knew him other than a man; with such staidness of mind, lovely and familiar gravity, as carried grace and reverence above greater years; his talk ever of knowledge, and his very play tending to enrich his mind, so that even his teachers found something in him to observe and learn above that which they had usually read or taught.   Which eminence by nature and industry made his worthy father style Sir Philip in my hearing, though I unseen, *lumen familiæ suæ.*"

Light of the household, indeed! There was good warrant for Sir Henry Sidney's pride in the boy. The view that Fulke Greville gives us of his schoolmate is confirmed and amplified by a letter which Sir Henry wrote when Philip can have been scarcely more than eleven years old, and which throws much welcome light on the father's character as well as on the son's—with some also on that best mood of thought in Queen Elizabeth's day which had Roger Ascham for one of its leaders.   Being, as he says, the first letter that the busy statesman had had leisure or occasion to send to the child he dearly loved, he tried to compress into a few sentences a whole code of manly duty.

SON PHILIP,

I have received two letters from you, one written in Latin, the other in French ; which I take in good part, and will you to exercise that practice of learning often ; for that will stand you in most stead in that profession of life that you are born to live in.   And now, since this is my first letter that ever I did write to you, I will not that it be all empty of some advices which my natural care of you provoketh me to wish you to follow, as documents to you in this your tender age.

Let your first action be the lifting up of your mind to Almighty God, by hearty prayer ; and feelingly digest the words you speak in prayer, with continual meditation and thinking of Him to Whom you pray, and of the matter for which you pray. And use this as an ordinary act, and at an ordinary hour ; whereby the time itself shall put you in remembrance to do that you are accustomed to do in that time.

Apply your study to such hours as your discreet master doth assign you, earnestly ; and the time I know he will so limit as shall be both sufficient for your learning and safe for your health. And mark the sense and the matter of that you do read, as well as the words ; so shall you both enrich your tongue with words and your wit with matter, and judgment will grow as years grow in you.

Be humble and obedient to your masters, for, unless you frame yourself to obey others—yea, and feel in yourself what obedience is, you shall never be able to teach others how to obey you.

Be courteous of gesture and affable to all men, with diversity of reverence, according to the dignity of the person. There is nothing that winneth so much with so little cost.

Use moderate diet, so as, after your meal, you may find your wit fresher and not duller, and your body more lively and not more heavy. Seldom drink wine ; and yet sometimes do, lest, being enforced to drink upon the sudden, you should find yourself enflamed. Use exercise of body, yet such as is without peril of your bones or joints : it will increase your force and enlarge your breath. Delight to be cleanly, as well in all parts of your body as in your garments : it shall make you grateful in each company—and otherwise loathsome.

Give yourself to be merry ; for you degenerate from your father if you find not yourself most able in wit and body to do anything when you are most merry.   But let your mirth be ever void of all scurrility and biting words to any man ; for a wound given by a word is oftentimes harder to be cured than that which is given by the sword

Be you rather a hearer and bearer away of other men's talk than a beginner and procurer of speech : otherwise you shall be accounted to delight to hear yourself speak. If you hear a wise sentence or an apt phrase, commit it to your memory with respect of the circumstance when you shall speak it.   Let never oath be heard to come out of your mouth, nor word of ribaldry : so shall custom make to yourself a law against it in yourself.   Be modest in each assembly, and rather be rebuked of light fellows for maiden-like shamefastness than of your sad friends for pert boldness.   Think upon every word that you will speak before you utter it, and remember how nature hath ramparted up, as it were, the tongue with teeth, lips—yea, and hair without the lips, and all betokening reins and bridles for the loose use of that member.

Above all things, tell no untruth ; no, not in trifles. The custom of it is naughty.   And let it not satisfy you that for a time the hearers take it for a truth ; for after it will be known as it is, to your shame.   For there cannot be a greater reproach to a gentleman than to be accounted a liar.

Study and endeavour yourself to be virtuously occupied.   So shall you make such a habit of well-doing in you as you shall not know how to do evil, though you would.   Remember, my son, the noble blood you are descended of by your mother's side ; and think that only by virtuous life and good action you may be an ornament to that illustrious family.   Otherwise, through vice and sloth, you may be counted *labes generis*—one of the greatest curses that can happen to man.

Well, my little Philip, this is enough for me, and too much, I fear, for you.   But if I shall find that this light meal of digestion nourish in anything the weak stomach of your capacity, I will, as I find the same grow stronger, feed it with other food.

Commend me most heartily unto Master Justice Corbet, old Master Onslow, and my cousin, his son.   Farewell !   Your mother and I send you our blessings, and Almighty God grant you His, nourish you with His fear, govern you with His grace, and make you a good servant to your prince and country !

Your loving father, so long as you live in the fear of God,

H. SIDNEY.

Thus worthily wrote the Lord President.   Then followed "a postscript by my Lady Sidney, in the skirts of my Lord President's letter."

Your noble careful father hath taken pains with his own hand to give you, in this his letter, so wise, so learned and most requisite precepts for you to follow with a diligent and humble, thankful mind, as I will not withdraw your eyes from beholding and reverent honouring the same—no, not so long as to read any letter from me. And therefore, at this time, I will write unto you no other letter than this ; whereby I first bless you, with my desire to God to plant in you His grace, and, secondarily, warn you to have always before the eyes of your mind these excellent counsels of my lord, your dear father, and that you fail not continually, once in four or five days, to read them over.

And for a final leave-taking for this time, see that you show yourself as a loving, obedient scholar to your good master, to govern you yet many years, and that my lord and I may hear that you profit so in your learning as thereby you may increase our loving care of you, and deserve at his hands the continuance of his great joy, to have him often witness with his own hands the hope he hath in your well-doing.

Farewell, my little Philip, and once again the Lord bless you !

Your loving mother,

MARY SIDNEY.

Neither letter nor postscript was dated. Both were probably written either shortly before or soon after Sir Henry Sidney's return to Ireland, whither he was sent at the close of 1565, and whither we must follow him to see something of his occupations while the little Philip was at school in Shrewsbury. Of Philip himself we have no further knowledge till his school days were over.

Sir Henry was thrice Lord Deputy of Ireland, and the work there done by him, as the ablest and worthiest of Queen Elizabeth's viceroys, occupies an important place in the history of this reign. But here only so much may be said about it as is necessary to explain some passages in his son's life.

He and Lady Sidney started for Dublin at the end of November, 1565, but more than six weeks were occupied in the journey. They were detained by contrary winds, and shipwrecked in crossing St. George's Channel. When the Lord Deputy was at length able to enter on his duties in January, 1566, other storms and troubles oppressed him. He had been selected for further service in Ireland, after nearly six years' interval, because he was considered the fittest man to repair some of the mischief caused by his brother-in-law, the Earl of Sussex. Sussex had not been able to control the lawless chiefs or to establish order among the persecuted people committed to his management as Lord Deputy of Ireland. He had blundered especially, and had thereby provoked a formidable rebellion, in his interference with Shane O'Neill, styled the Captain of Tyrone, and the most turbulent of the local despots at that time. Sir Henry Sidney's first business was to stamp out this rebellion, and this he only succeeded in doing after two tedious campaigns. Not till May, 1567, was O'Neill's head brought to him " pickled in a pipkin," as he reported, and the northern part of Ireland reduced to a semblance of subjection which lasted for a few years.

Sir Henry considered that he might have performed this task in much less time and with much more ease and credit had he been duly supported by Queen Elizabeth and her ministers in London. He had to make repeated and reproachful appeals for the supplies of money promised and absolutely required for payment of his troops. He was also sorely hampered by the conflicting orders sent from Court, and by the unreasonable demands made upon him at the instigation chiefly of Thomas Butler, the

SIR HENRY SIDNEY.
FROM AN ENGRAVING BY E. HARDING

tenth Earl of Ormond. This Earl of Ormond, one of the few Irish nobles resident in England, deemed that his courtly bearing in London authorised him to do anything he pleased with his own wild dominions in the neighbourhood of Waterford, and he used all his influence with Elizabeth towards gaining his wishes and procuring harsh treatment of his rival, the Earl of Desmond. Her suitor being a handsome man and a zealous flatterer, the Queen gave a ready ear to his appeals and sent preposterous instructions to the Lord Deputy. Sir Henry's fighting against O'Neill in the north had to be interrupted for several months in order that he might look after Ormond's interests in the comparatively peaceful south ; and, after O'Neill had been disposed of, he found it impossible to reconcile the claims of the two earls or to reduce their partisans to order. " Albeit they would inveigh against each other," he reported, "yet if any sentence passed for the advancement of the Queen's prerogative, or suppression of either of their tyrannies, straightway it was cried out of and complained to the Queen, specially by the Earl of Ormond, as injustice and oppression."

That state of things, lasting at intervals through a dozen years, must be borne in mind as explaining much in Sir Henry Sidney's whole career as a servant of the state and largely influencing that of his son Philip. The Lord Deputy's firm and honourable dealing, his self-sacrificing and far-seeing statesmanship, caused much misfortune to both father and son and to the rest of the family. There was evidence of this in the winter of 1566–1567. " I received,"

3

wrote Sir Henry, " many a bitter letter, which indeed tried me, and so perplexed my most dear wife as she fell most grievously sick upon the same, and in that sickness remained once in a trance above fifty-two hours ; upon whose recovery I sent her into England, where she lived till my coming over."

The Lord Deputy followed his wife in eight or nine months. In October, 1567, as he said, " I procured my revocation, being tired in body with my long and most painful travail, but more wearied in mind with the sharp and bitter letters which I almost weekly received out of England by the procurement of the Earl of Ormond."

Notwithstanding his weariness and chagrin, Sir Henry made a brave show when he reached Hampton Court one November morning, with about two hundred noblemen and gentlemen in his train. Chief among these was the Earl of Desmond, who came to state his case against the Earl of Ormond, in the hope of winning some favour from the Queen ; and with him were several other Irish leaders and their attendants, anxious, as Sir Henry declared, to behold with their own eyes " the high majesty of our sacred sovereign." That " high majesty," according to contemporary gossip, was looking out of a window when the quaintly attired company arrived. Asking what it meant, she was told that it was Sir Henry Sidney's party. " Ay, that it well may be," she exclaimed, " for he hath two of the best offices in England."

The visitors had crossed over at their own expense, and seeing that Sir Henry had had to provide a substitute during his absence from Wales, and found that he had been out of pocket more than £3,000 by his two years' Irish service, he was certainly not a pecuniary gainer by his double office-holding as Lord Deputy and Lord President. Nor was he recompensed even with thanks. For having rescued Ireland from the despotism of the Captain of Tyrone his praises were sung, it is true, in " The Mirror for Magistrates " and other popular verse ; but, as he complained, " when I came to Court it was told me it was no war I had made, nor worthy to be called a war, for that Shane O'Neill was but a beggar, an outlaw, and one of no force." And his other zealous work was condemned as well as slighted.

But his services could not be dispensed with for long, or limited to the easy duties of Lord President of Wales. Going back to Ludlow Castle in December, he was there dangerously ill, and in the following February he had to be operated upon for a disease attributed to the hard work and unhealthy living forced upon him in Ireland. The surgeon's report was that he could only hope to keep himself alive by careful dieting and avoidance of violent exercise. He was summoned to Court in May, however, and though he was then excused from immediate reinstatement as Lord Deputy, or kept back through the influence of the Ormond faction, it was in August deemed necessary that he should start at once, making it his first and chief business to put down disturbances that had broken out in Ulster since his departure.

His second viceroyship lasted until March, 1571. Through more than two and a half years he worked as zealously as before in Queen Elizabeth's service, and his labours met with the same reward. More than ever, as he averred, the Earl of Ormond was his "professed foe" and the chief cause of the harsh treatment he received. "According to his piquant speeches I had sour letters, which in truth to me were tortious; for when my designs were reasonable, my proceedings painful, and my success and the event both profitable and honourable, what should I say but *Miserere nobis, Domine!*"

Christ Church, Oxford, 16th Cent.

CHAPTER III.

UNDERGRADUATE YEARS.

1568–1572.

ITHIN a few months after Sir Henry Sidney's return from Ireland in November, 1567, and probably quite early in 1568, he removed his son Philip, who was then only in his fourteenth year, from Master Thomas Ashton's school at Shrewsbury, and placed him in Christ Church College, Oxford, where his education was continued during the next three years or more. The change was made at any rate before the 2d of August, 1568, when Sir Henry paid a visit to the university, partly to receive a complimentary degree as Master of Arts, and partly to see how Philip was advancing in his studies and to take him away for a short holiday at Ludlow.

About Philip's studies we are not told much ; but as, so far as actual schooling went, they ended before he was seventeen, and as afterwards he was considered a man of rare learning, he must have made good use of all the opportunities in his way; and we may credit the statement of an old writer, that in his case "an excellent stock met with the choicest grafts, nor could his tutors pour in so fast as he was ready to receive." "All sorts of learning," says this informant, "were so indifferently favoured by him that each of them might allege arguments that he most reflected in his dearness upon them, insomuch that those that were to make a meal of learning, and to have it for their fixed habitation, envied him who only took it *in transitu*, and, as it were, in complement in his passage to higher designs."

At Christ Church he had the best teaching that Oxford could then give, and his first tutor there, Dr. Thomas Thornton, appears to have been a man of exceptional worth. Of Thornton it was said in his day that he was "the common refuge of young poor scholars of great hopes and parts"; and so proud was he of his share in the training of Philip Sidney, that when he died he left directions that the fact should be recorded on his tombstone. Another of Philip's tutors was one Master Robert Dorset, who was afterwards tutor to Philip's brother Robert, and was in due time made Dean of Chester, doubtless through Sir Henry Sidney's influence.

Of Philip's college companions at least three rose to eminence. One was Richard Carew, of Antony, the first English translator of Tasso. Another was Richard Hakluyt, famous as a voyager and more

Philippus Sidneius

From a letter to Sir William Cecil, written in Latin on March 12, 1569 (æt. 14).

Your honors humble at comaudement Philip Sidnei

From a letter to Sir Francis Walsingham, written on December 17, 1581 (æt. 27).

Your Lps humble at commandment Ph Sidnei

From a letter to Lord Burghley, written on May 15, 1585 (æt. 30).

SIGNATURES OF SIR PHILIP SIDNEY.
FROM THE ORIGINALS IN THE RECORD OFFICE.

famous as the editor and chronicler of other men's voyages. A third was William Camden, the foremost of England's historians. Both Hakluyt and Camden maintained friendship with Philip in later years, and looked up to him as a patron. But his most intimate Oxford friend was Fulke Greville, who had been at school with him at Shrewsbury, and was a student, not of Christ Church, but of Broadgates, now Pembroke, before passing to Trinity College, Cambridge.

Philip's uncle, the Earl of Leicester, was Chancellor of Oxford University, and during his visits there he appears to have taken some care of the youth, one instance of which appears in a letter addressed by him to Archbishop Parker, soliciting " a license to eat flesh during Lent, for my boy Philip Sidney, who is somewhat subject to sickness." Philip, however, was more steadily looked after by Sir Henry's old friend, Sir William Cecil, at this time Chancellor of Cambridge University. Leicester and Cecil, never good friends, were now as much at feud as their fear of offending Queen Elizabeth permitted. In Cecil's eyes Leicester was always the Queen's evil genius, leading her into frivolities and extravagances, and directing to his own use too much of the income of the State which the prudent minister wished to see employed in the country's service. In Leicester's eyes Cecil was a churl, treacherous and grasping in furtherance of his own interests, and puritanical in his views on public affairs. But Sir Henry Sidney, perhaps with the help of some jesuitry, was generally on good terms both with his unscrupulous, loose-living brother-in-law, who was yet in his poor way chivalrous and even generous, and with the discreet Secretary of State, presently to become Baron Burghley and Lord High Treasurer, who never neglected his personal advantage while honestly and skilfully holding the Queen's purse. In his own way Cecil was a faithful friend to the Lord Deputy and to his family. Lady Sidney, too, had been intimate from girlhood with Lady Cecil—the Mildred Cooke who had been one of Roger Ascham's favourite and most talented pupils, along with Princess Elizabeth and Lady Jane Grey. The boy Philip was Sir William Cecil's pet.

On the 8th of August, 1568, six days after Sir Henry, as we have seen, had gone to visit his son at Oxford and to take him back to Ludlow, we find him reporting to Leicester that he had turned aside on the road to pay a visit to Kenilworth, which Queen Elizabeth had given to her favourite just five years before. "I could not come so near your fair and ancient castle as my way led me to do," he wrote, "and leave it unseen, but thither I went"; and there, he added, he was fitly entertained by the people in charge, who "knew me to be your lordship's well-beloved brother." "I was never more in love with an old house, nor never new work could be better bestowed than that which you have done." Philip's name is not mentioned in this letter; but we may be sure that he shared his father's admiration for the famous building he now visited for the first time.

At the end of a letter written to Cecil on the same

8th of August, Sir Henry said, "Most heartily I recommend unto you my wife, myself and my boy, and I beseech you recommend me humbly to my lady your wife "; and that letter was crossed by one which Cecil addressed to Sir Henry from Court on the 9th of August, and in which he sent his compliments to Lady Sidney and "the darling Philip." "The darling Philip" remained with his father till the end of the month, when the Lord Deputy started for Ireland.   Another letter from Cecil, written in a playful mood, on the 3d of September, followed Sir Henry across the Channel.   "There is one thing that is heavy for you to bear," he said, "considering you have therein offended many.   You carried away your son and my scholar from Oxford, not only from his books, but from the commodity to have been seen of my lords, his uncles, and to have been approved by me, and to have pleasured both me and my wife.   I think, indeed, either you forgot the Queen's progress to be so near Oxford, or else you have some matter of necessity to allege for your taking him from Oxford, and for your detaining him so long in wild Wales."

As he was not to see his father again for more than two years, there was good reason for Philip's being detained three weeks or so in Wales, or rather in Shropshire, and there was doubtless more wholesome pleasure for him in this holiday than he would have found in the bustle of Queen Elizabeth's "progress" in August, 1571, which included visits to Lord Grey of Wilton, a friend of the Sidneys, at Whaddon, and to Earl Pomfret, another friend of the

Sidneys, at Easton Neston, in Northamptonshire. This letter reminds us, however, that Philip was already, in his fourteenth year, not merely an Oxford scholar, but in training for the courtly life in which he was soon to shine.

Other correspondence between Sir William and Sir Henry, and Sir Henry's son also, throws welcome light on Philip and his surroundings, and introduces us to what might have been a very memorable incident in his career.

The Lord Deputy had not long been absent from England, or his wife long settled at home, before the Secretary of State found time to run down to Penshurst.* "I most heartily thank you," Sir Henry wrote on the 29th of November, "for your courteous visitation of my wife; and I pray you sometimes hearken of our boy, and be working how to get home the father." And the letter ends with "most hearty commendations to yourself, my lady, and my sweet jewel, your daughter." The "sweet jewel," was Anne, the elder of the two surviving daughters of Sir William and Lady Cecil, three others having died in infancy. She was about two years younger than Philip Sidney, having been a baby at the close of 1557, when Sir Philip Hoby wrote to invite Lady Cecil to come and spend Christmas with his wife, and to bring "little Tannykin" with her. "Little

* On the 5th of November Cecil, in a letter to Sir Henry Sidney, informed him, evidently with a touch of scorn, that "my lord of Leicester" was "at dice and merry" in his (Cecil's) apartments in the Savoy, "where he hath lodged these two nights." On the 15th of December Cecil tells Sidney that he "chides" Leicester for not helping as he should in Sidney's affairs.—State Papers, Irish.

Tannykin " had now grown to be a sprightly maiden, praised for her sweet looks, as well as for her ready wit and graceful ways; and she had much to do with the intimacy which at this time was closer than usual between Philip's parents and hers.

Ten days before the date of the letter just quoted, Sir William had written to tell Sir Henry that he expected Lady Sidney to arrive next Monday on a visit to his wife at Hampton Court. There Lady Sidney probably kept Christmas, and, if so, she met Philip, who spent his holidays with the Cecils and joined the crowd of Elizabeth's courtiers. "Your Philip is here," wrote Sir William to Sir Henry on the 6th of January, 1569, at the end of a long letter, in which he complained of the "tub full " of troublesome business in which he was immersed—"your Philip, in whom I take more comfort than I do openly utter for avoiding of wrong interpretation. He is worthy to be loved, and so I do love him, as he were mine own."

Those words, or some other communication to Sir Henry, which has not been preserved, prompted him to send from Ireland a proposal, also not on record, of which the purport is indicated in Sir William's cautious reply. "I thank you," Cecil wrote on the 2d of February, " for your free offer made to me by your letters concerning your son, whom truly I do so like for his own conditions and singular towardness in all good things as I think you a happy father for so joyful a son. And as for the interest that it pleaseth you to offer me in him, I must confess, if the child alone were valued without the natural good that dependeth of you his father, I could not but think him worthy the love I bear him, which certainly is more than I do express outwardly, for avoiding of sinister interpretation. For, as for the account to have him my son, I see so many incidenties as it sufficeth me to love the child for himself, without regard therein of my daughter, whom surely I love so well as, so it be within my degree or not much above it, I shall think none too good for her. Thus you see a father's fondness, which to a father I dare discover, and so for this time it sufficeth."

Through Sir William Cecil's strained and diplomatic phrases his meaning may be clearly seen. He would like Philip for a son-in-law, and would always love him as though he were his own son; but his daughter's husband must be rich enough to keep her in a dignified position, and he was evidently not satisfied as to Philip's prospects, nor willing himself to make any large provision for the young couple. Thereupon doubtless followed more letters than we now know of. The next extant is one from Sir Henry Sidney, written on the 7th of April, 1569, deploring that he was, for his station, a poor man, and not able to do as much as he would like. At the same time, he said, "let me know what you would have me do, and you shall find me ready. For, before God, in these matters, I am utterly ignorant, as one that never made a marriage in his life. But I mean truly, loving your daughter as one of my own, regarding her virtue above any *dot*, and your friendship more than all the money you will give. And for my boy, I confess if I might

have every week a boy, I should never love none
like him, and accordingly have dealt with him, for I
do not know above £100 a year I have not assured
to him." *

Sir William appears to have still thought that
Sir Henry—perhaps with help from the Earl of
Leicester—should provide a larger income for Philip
than that letter gave promise of ; but he did not at
this time reject the proposal. He continued to be
on as intimate terms as heretofore with the Sidneys,
and in June he was godfather to Sir Henry's
youngest child, born while he was in Ireland.† Negotiations for the proposed marriage were continued,
and they went so far that on the 6th of August
settlements were actually drafted. In these Sir
Henry Sidney, or rather the Earl of Leicester, on
his behalf, undertook, out of lands in his possession,
valued at £1,140 3s. 4d. a year, to secure to Philip
and his heirs a reversion of £840 4s. 2d. a year, and
to assign to him on the day of his marriage an
income of £266 13s. 4d., to which were to be added
other sums after the decease of Sir Henry and of
Lady Sidney respectively ; besides which, it is noted,

---

* Hatfield MSS., No. 1289. The authorities for the previous
letters on this subject, and most of those which follow, are given in
my " Memoir of Sir Philip Sidney."

† State Papers, Irish : Sir Henry Sidney to Sir William Cecil,
30 June, 1569. In this letter Sir Henry thanked Cecil for helping
to " make a Christian" of his little son, adding that, before he left
England he had given orders that, " if it were a boy it should have
been a William, if a woman a Cycill." But Cecil seems to have
thought he already had namesakes enough, and to have preferred to
name the child Thomas instead of William.

Philip would have the £60 a year derived from his Whitford rectory. On Sir William Cecil's part, it was stipulated that his daughter should receive £500 on her wedding day, £500 more within half a year after; also that she and Philip, if they chose, should have food and lodging in his house for two years, and that on his death he should leave Anne an annuity of £66 13s. 4d. The agreement included other provisions, conditional on the deaths of various persons. No more was assured to the couple, however, than £1,000 to start with, and about £330 a year until other sums gradually fell in.* This, even at the value of money in Queen Elizabeth's day, was not a large fortune; but it was, of course, assumed that Philip, as soon as he grew to man's estate, would acquire other property by his own deserts or Queen Elizabeth's favour.

It does not appear that Leicester, whom the Queen had loaded with gifts of lands and sinecures, offered to contribute anything to his nephew's maintenance, but he heartily approved the match, and, Sir Henry being in Ireland, he arranged the details with Sir William. " I have been pressed with such kind offers of my Lord Deputy's, and with the like of my lord of Leicester's," Cecil wrote in a matter-of-fact memorandum, " as I have accorded with him upon articles that if P.S. and A.C. hereafter shall like to marry, then shall H.S., the father of P.S., make assurances, etc., and then shall also W.C., the father of A.C., pay, etc. What may follow I know not, but as I wish P.S. full liberty, so surely shall A.C. have

---

* Hatfield MSS., No. 1316.

it, and in the meantime I will omit no point of friendship." The document was taken to Dublin by John Thomas, the Lord Deputy's treasurer, who on the 24th of October wrote to Sir William : " My Lord Deputy doth very well like every of the articles, and is ready to perform it in such sort as by yourself shall be thought meet. I moved him also touching the marriage-money, to know whether he would receive it himself or else bestow·the same upon your two children, for so I promised your honour I would do. He is very well contented the money shall be employed to their commodity, and that he will receive no part of it himself." And two days later Sir Henry wrote to Lady Cecil, expressing his joy at the betrothal of their children, and praying her to make much of his dear daughter—that is, of Anne—to whom he sent his " loving and father's kiss." *

Yet the scheme was abandoned. As late as the 24th of February, 1570, Sir Henry, in a letter to Sir William, spoke affectionately of Anne Cecil as " *our* daughter Anne." But the same letter shows that obstacles were already in the way of her becoming his daughter-in-law. " I am sorry," he there said, " that you find coldness anywhere in proceeding, when such good liking appeared in the beginning. For my part, I was never more ready to perfect that matter than presently I am. If I might have the greatest prince's daughter in Christendom for him, the match spoken of between us, on my part, should not be broken." Sir Henry seems to have vexed his friend by not returning the articles of settlement sent

---

* Hatfield MSS., No. 1393.

to him for signature. He had " well allowed " them, he wrote in this letter; " but where they be, God knoweth : the paper I cannot find." " This, for troth, Sir," he added, " I was never more joyous of the match than I am ; but how and which way never confer with me while I am here, without special direction ; for I neither can care nor consider, while I here dwell, for wife, child or myself." The poor Lord Deputy was now in the thick of his troubles, shattered in health by overwork, and distracted by Queen Elizabeth's treatment of him, which he evidently thought might be different if Sir William Cecil took his part more zealously. As Philip was not yet sixteen and Anne only about thirteen, neither of them arrived at years in which it could be expected that they would " like to marry," he doubtless considered that the signing of the marriage articles might wait awhile. The project fell through, however, either because there had been delay in completing the document, or because, even had that been done, obstacles arose that would have caused Cecil to cancel it.

In the spring of 1571 Sir Henry Sidney came back from Ireland, and all through that year as well as for some time longer he was out of favour at Court. Meanwhile Sir William Cecil was created Baron Burghley, and henceforth his position as the Queen's chief adviser on matters of business, a courtier too shrewd and too honest to be dispensed with, was firmer than ever. We need not blame him very much, especially as the change could have caused no heart-breaking to the boy and girl betrothed in their

teens, for consenting to a better match for his daughter, so far as show went, than the one about which
Sir Henry Sidney thought there need be no hurry.

There were several promising suitors for the hand
of pretty little Anne Cecil. One, perhaps not very
eager, was Edward, third Earl of Rutland; another
was Edward, seventeenth Earl of Oxford, a rich
ward of Lord Burghley and, like the other earl, considerably older than Philip Sidney, besides being now
almost the prime favourite at Court. " There is no
man of life and agility in every respect in Court but
the Earl of Oxford," wrote one correspondent of the
Earl of Rutland in June, 1571 ; and another reported
in July that " the Earl of Oxford hath gotten him a
wife, or at least a wife hath caught him—that is,
Mistress Anne Cecil ; whereunto the Queen hath
given her consent. The which hath caused great
weeping, wailing and sorrowful cheer of those that
hoped to have had that golden day. Thus you may
see that, whilst some triumph with olive branches,
others follow the chariot with willow-garlands."
And in August Lord Burghley himself offered some
apology to the Earl of Rutland in terms implying
that, though satisfied with his son-in-law, he would
have preferred the other suitor had he been ready
and at hand. " Truly, my lord," he said, " after I
was acquainted of a former intention of a marriage
with Mr. Philip Sidney, whom I always loved and
esteemed, I was fully determined to have of myself
moved no marriage for my daughter until she
should have been near sixteen years old, that with
moving I might also conclude "—that is, that there
4

might be no long interval between the betrothal
and the wedding days. "And yet I thought it not
inconvenient, in the mean time, being free, to
hearken to any motion made by such others as I
should have cause to like." And he added, after
more worldly-wise talk, in words that can scarcely
have been genuine, coming as they did from so keen
an observer of character as he was : " Now that the
matter is determined betwixt my lord of Oxford and
me, I confess to your lordship I do honour him as
much as I can any subject, and I love him so dearly
from my heart as I do mine own son, and in any
case that may touch him for his honour and weal, I
shall think mine own interest therein. And surely,
my lord, by dealing with him I find that which I
often heard of your lordship, that there is much
more in him of understanding than any stranger to
him would think." *

The friendship between the Sidneys and the
Cecils was not weakened by the failure of the marriage arrangements between Philip and Anne, and
there is nothing to show that the young people took
the matter much to heart. It was clearly a match
not of their own making, but planned by their parents and guardians. Three letters sent by Philip
to Sir William Cecil while the project was being
discussed, which are extant, contain no mention of
Anne, and merely give us a little pleasant insight into
the relations between the young Oxford student and

---

* Belvoir MSS., in the possession of the Duke of Rutland ; George
Delves to the Earl of Rutland, 24 June, 1571 ; Lord St. John to
the same, 28 July, 1571 ; Lord Burghley to the same, 15 August, 1571.

the sage statesman who took a fatherly interest in his education. In the first, written in Latin, on the 12th of March, 1569, Philip says: " To speak truthfully, and not without heavy grief, I must confess that I can in no way satisfy either your expectation or my desire "—as regards his progress in book work, and declares " with what grateful memory I recall your kindness towards me, about which I shall ever think as I do now." " The duties and respect which I owe to you, and which I wish most heartily to fulfil," he rather stiffly adds, " will bind me closely to you all life long, and always I shall set before myself, ever more and more eagerly, to find my happiness in deserving well of you." In the next letter, written in English, on the 8th of July, Philip thanks Sir William for his favours to his father and himself, and says he would write more and oftener, but that he knows not whether the busy Secretary of State cares for long letters. And on the 27th of February, 1570, Philip asks that the canonry of Christ Church may be given, as it had previously been promised, to his sometime tutor, Dr. Thomas Thornton, he being entitled to that advancement " by his desert towards me and the worthiness of his life and learning."

But though no hearts were broken by the abandonment of the proposed match between Philip and Anne Cecil, it seems a pity that they were not allowed to be married when they were old enough. Philip might have gained much by union with this lovable woman, and might have received from her wifely encouragement in his efforts to live an

altogether heroic life. And it certainly would have
been far better for Anne had she been mated to a
husband worthy of her, willing and able to protect
her amid the rough conditions of attendance on
Queen Elizabeth. The Earl of Oxford was well-
nigh the gayest and well-nigh the most brutal of
Elizabeth's courtiers. Treason in politics often
estranged him from his sovereign, and treason in
morals often estranged him from his wife; but his
fine outside and the fact that he was not, as we have
seen that his father-in-law discovered, quite such a
fool as he looked, obtained for him, in either case,
as often as there was need, a woman's pardon.*
When he was young he killed his cook. When he
was old, and had squandered his immense patrimony, he persuaded Thomas Churchyard to be
surety for his lodgings, and then ran away, leaving
the poor poet to hide himself till he could scrape
together silver enough for payment of the bill.
While he was at the height of his renown, as will be
noted in a later chapter, he played the coward, and
was charged with trying to play the murderer, in a
quarrel with Sir Philip Sidney.

---

* It appears from a MS. at Hatfield, dated 12 June, 1576, that
Lord Burghley had then to protest against Oxford's conduct in sepa-
rating himself from his wife and secluding her in the country.
Burghley, "in conclusion, desires that his lordship will yield to her,
being his wife, either the love that a loving and honest wife ought to
have, or otherwise to be so used that all hard and vain speeches of
his unkindness to her may cease, and that, with his favour and permission, she may both come to his presence and be allowed to come
to do her duty to her Majesty, if her Majesty shall be therewith content ; and she shall bear as she may the lack of the rest."

In following the story of young Sidney's first matrimonial project we have passed beyond the years of his residence at Oxford. In the early months of 1571 a terrible plague raged in that city. The townsmen died in great numbers, and the schools were closed, the students being sent to read with their tutors in country houses, or allowed to return to their own homes. There is an unvouched tradition that Philip took refuge at Cambridge, whither his friend Fulke Greville had already gone or then went. But there is no record of his doing this, or of his taking any degree either at Oxford or at the sister university; and it is most probable that, his father having just now returned from Ireland, he passed the next few months partly at Ludlow with his parents and the brothers and sisters from whom he had long been parted, partly at Kenilworth, with his uncle, the Earl of Leicester, and partly at Penshurst, amid the haunts of his boyhood, but mainly at Court, for service wherein he was to be further trained. We have no certain knowledge as to his movements until the spring of 1572.

Of the parents, at this period there is almost as little trace as of the son. Nearly all we can be sure of is that, resuming his office as Lord President of Wales in March, 1571, Sir Henry Sidney was usually resident there for some time to come. The duties performed by him, however, must have now and then taken him to Court, where also, as we know, there was occasional occupation for him in winding up his Irish accounts and defending himself from the charges of his enemies. He appears to have gradually regained the moderate place in royal favour from which he was too useful a public servant to be long excluded, though he never received the hearty thanks or the substantial recompense which he deserved; and, wherever he and his son may have been, his wife was evidently much with the Queen during these years. It being Elizabeth's fancy to exact handsome New Year's gifts from those about her, Lady Sidney presented to her on the 1st of January, 1572, according to the Court inventory, "a ring of gold, with a mount of diamonds containing a lozenge diamond on the top, with three diamonds on either side of the ring." This is the first compliment of the sort from Lady Sidney of which we have record; but we read of others in future years. They were tokens either of revived friendship with the Queen or of desire to win her favour.

Lady Sidney was at Court on the 2d of May, 1572, at any rate, and on that day she wrote a noteworthy letter to Lord Burghley. The Queen, it seems, had offered Sir Henry Sidney a peerage, and had even pressed it upon him, but had not proposed to accompany it with any such grant of land or fat pension as she was fond of bestowing on the Earl of Leicester or any of her other special favourites. To Lord Burghley, therefore, Lady Sidney appealed in her and her husband's "hard distress," as she explained, "considering our ill ability to maintain a higher title than that we now possess, since titles of greater calling cannot well be wielded but with some amendment at the prince's hand of a ruinated state, or else to his discredit greatly that must take them upon him." "Truly, my lord," she said, "I do find my lord my husband greatly dismayed with his hard choice which is presently offered him, as either to be a baron, called in the number of many far more able than himself to maintain it withal, or else, in refusing it, to incur her Highness's displeasure." And unless Lord Burghley could induce the Queen to couple a substantial gift with the proffered honour, which clearly would have been welcome to Lady Sidney, and doubtless also to her husband, she implored him to add to all his other kindnesses to the family by "staying the motion of this title to be any further offered." The prayer was so far answered that Sir Henry Sidney was never made a peer.

Three weeks after the date of Lady Sidney's letter, her son went abroad to learn lessons that were to help him in making a career for himself, and henceforward we shall be able to follow his course much more precisely than has thus far been possible. But before we cross the sea with him, it will be convenient to break through the order of chronology in order to note a mysterious reference to him in a letter written seventeen months after he had started on his travels.

On the 26th of October, 1573, Messrs. Nicholas Poyntz, Richard Berkeley, Thomas Throckmorton, and Giles Poyntz wrote thus to Lord Berkeley: "Because you are over-resolutely determined to have your daughter to inherit your land, and not to give the same to any heir male of your house, which is great pity, we think it necessary for you, upon reasonable conditions, to accept the offer of Mr. Philip Sidney, if the same be again made. If also a further offer be made by Mr. Robert Sidney for one of your daughters, we likewise hold the same nothing necessary for you to refuse." *

As to the grounds for this formal notification of the second marriage project that was made for Philip Sidney before he was nineteen years old, or of the similar project for his little brother Robert, who was now only ten, we are not informed ; nor do we know anything either of the antecedents of the proposal or threat of Lord Berkeley's four plain-speaking correspondents, or of its sequel, save that neither Philip nor Robert married a daughter of his lordship. Lord Berkeley, the twelfth peer of the name, was a somewhat eccentric person. His chief pleasure in life was hunting. Queen Elizabeth visited him at Berkeley Castle in 1563, when he was about thirty, and her courtiers made such havoc of his deer-park, that, in his wrath at the mischief they had done, he cleared out all the deer that remained and turned it into pasture-land. Thereupon her Majesty sent him word that he must be careful as to his behaviour, seeing that my lord of Leicester greatly desired to include Berkeley Castle among his possessions.

---

* This document is among the MSS. in the possession of Lord Fitzhardinge at Berkeley Castle.

S Philipp Sidney

S Rb Sidney

PHILIP SIDNEY AND HIS BROTHER ROBERT AS YOUTHS.

FROM AN ENGRAVING, BY O. LACOUR, OF THE PAINTING AT PENSHURST.

Massacre on St. Bartholomews Day.

CHAPTER IV.

A VISIT TO PARIS.

1572.

N the last week of May, 1572, the Earl of Lincoln, at the head of a brilliant company, left London for Paris on a special mission from Queen Elizabeth to King Charles the Ninth of France. In his party was, according to the wording of the passport issued in the Queen's name, "her trusty and well-beloved Philip Sidney, Esquire, licensed to go out of England into parts beyond the seas, with three servants, four horses, and all other requisites, and to remain the space of two years immediately following his departure out of the realm, for his attaining the knowledge of foreign languages."

The young traveller took with him a letter of introduction from the Earl of Leicester to Mr. Francis Walsingham, her Majesty's regular ambassador at the Court of France. "I have thought

good," wrote Leicester, " to commend him by these
my friendly lines unto you, as unto one I am well
assured will have a special care of him during his
abode there. He is young and raw, and no doubt
shall find those countries, and the demeanours of
the people, somewhat strange unto him ; in which
respect your good advice and counsel shall greatly
behove him for his better directions, which I do
most heartily pray you to vouchsafe him, with any
other friendly assistance you shall think needful for
him." Philip Sidney, in his eighteenth year, was
certainly young and raw, and in need of direction
and assistance from his seniors amid the strange
demeanours of the people he was presently to visit ;
but he had had some experience of court life, and
was already an apt observer and shrewd critic of the
political complications as well as of the courtly
arrangements of his day.

The purpose of the Earl of Lincoln's mission was
to forward a fresh project that was on foot for providing Queen Elizabeth with a husband. All through
the past thirteen years of Elizabeth's reign it had
been the constant prayer of her subjects that she
would marry, and thus afford reasonable hope of a
peaceful succession to the throne ; and in these
years she had had suitors enough and to spare. If
she had ever gravely thought of marrying Lord
Robert Dudley, whom there can be small doubt she
would have preferred to anyone else, that thought
had been finally abandoned about the time when she
made him Earl of Leicester, and all other plans had
been quickly discarded. Now, however, fresh

reasons on the score of policy were urged for her marrying someone, and her own whim harmonised with the weighty advice of her counsellors in favour of her mating, at the age of thirty-eight, with a lad of nineteen—the Duke of Alençon, youngest brother of King Charles of France, and son of Catherine de' Medici, the real ruler of the country. Overtures were made as early as the autumn of 1570, when Walsingham wrote home urging the union, and reporting how well it was thought of by the Queen-Mother and the whole French Court; and it was highly commended by Burghley, Leicester, and others from whom the Queen was sometimes willing to ask guidance. It was one of the grounds on which a treaty of amity between Elizabeth and Charles was signed at Blois on the 19th of April, 1572, and to further the negotiations an interchange of special embassies was arranged for the following month. The Duke of Montmorenci was sent with a large suite to London, but, being delayed on the way, he only arrived on the 9th of June, his lateness in coming being, as Lord Burghley informed one of his correspondents, a cause of much annoyance to all the husbands, whose wives were put to great expense in waiting at Court to take part in the gorgeous reception. Meanwhile, the Earl of Lincoln, with Philip Sidney under his charge, had reached Paris.

The ambassador and his party, quitting London on the 26th of May and taking ship from Dover, entered the French capital on the 7th of June. They were there gaily entertained during a fortnight, in the course of which the Treaty of Blois was ratified, and on the 20th of June they started on their way back to England.

Young Sidney did not, of course, return with them. He stayed on in Paris for nearly three months, and on the 9th of August the King, " desiring well and favourably to treat him on account of the good and commendable knowledge which was in him," bestowed on him the title of Baron, and appointed him by a formal document to be a Gentleman-in-Ordinary of the Royal Bedchamber. Hence we may infer that he was more or less in residence at Court, though he appears to have lived generally with Walsingham, his firm friend henceforth through life, and eleven years later his father-in-law.

Walsingham's age was now six and thirty. Educated at Cambridge, and a Protestant by conviction, he had lived abroad throughout Queen Mary's reign, using the time well in studying the languages and institutions of the countries of Western Europe. On Elizabeth's accession he had returned to England, and in 1561 he had entered the service of the Crown. Since August, 1570, he had been ambassador in Paris, and his courtly bearing, his extensive learning, and his sound practical wisdom must have made his society very welcome to the young traveller confided to his care.

Of other society, which may have been yet more welcome to him, Philip Sidney saw plenty at this time. In Paris there was just now one blaze of enjoyment. The old strife between Catholics and Huguenots seemed to have ceased, and everywhere there was show of peace-making, in which men, like Walsingham, trained to watch for guile, could detect none. King Charles, or their mother, had offered a year before to give his sister Margaret in marriage to Henry of Navarre, and the young king had come to claim his bride. In his company were all the Huguenot leaders, with many, if not all, of whom Sidney made acquaintance. Henry of Navarre, we are told by Fulke Greville, accepted him as a friend and treated him as an equal.

In honour of the approaching marriage of Henry and Margaret there were jousts and dances, banquets and triumphal shows while Sidney remained in Paris after the Earl of Lincoln had gone back to London. Men who before had met in stern battle now broke lances together for sport. Men who had cursed each other for apostates and idolaters now joined hands and thanked heaven that there was once more peace in the land.

The 18th of August was the great day of pacification. On it two stately processions entered the Church of Nôtre Dame. The one included King Charles and the Queen-Mother and all the great officers of state,—the newly-made and youthful " Baron " Sidney being of the number, doubtless,— who brought with them the Princess Margaret, pale and haggard, in bridal apparel. The other was led by her intended husband, the young King of Navarre, with whom were Coligni and a brave company of Huguenots. Joint Catholic and Protestant rites were performed, in the course of which one incident must have arrested Sidney's notice and appeared to him strange indeed. When Margaret was asked whether she would take Henry for her husband, she made neither answer nor bow; so Charles had to place his hand on the back of her head and push it forward in forced token of assent, she declaring afterwards that, having pledged herself to the Duke of Guise, Navarre's sworn foe, she did not assent.

This was an idle protest. The marriage had been performed, and Henry might take away his bride as soon as the concluding festivities were over.

Presently the Duke of Guise came with armed men into Paris, and by his evil presence threw a gloom over the gaiety. But what was to be done? The King took counsel with Admiral Coligni, the recognised head of the Huguenot party. He could not send his kinsman away, he said; yet he feared there might be some small disturbance. Did not the Admiral think it would be prudent to bring a few more troops into the city? The Admiral saw no harm, and the Protestants believed that care was being taken for their safety.

Coligni was wounded by the shot of an assassin. It was a bad omen. But it was arranged that the culprit should be caught and punished. And the pleasant sports went on for three days more.

The 23d of August was Saturday, the eve of the festival of Saint Bartholomew. The city seemed asleep when, an hour and a half after midnight, the palace clock gave an unwonted sound. In an instant lights were placed at every window. Soldiers emerged from hitherto dark corners, and thousands of men, armed and muffled, with the mark of the cross on their sleeves, streamed out of the houses and joined in the cry, " For God and for the King ! " Then all was confusion ; half naked men and women rushing out to be slaughtered ; a ghastly mingling of prayers and curses, of laughter and wailing. In most places there was indiscriminate butchery of all Huguenots. Here and there little parties of murderers did their work in orderly manner. One such party was headed by the Duke of Guise. He hastened to the house of Coligni, and sent one of his men to force an entrance. The fellow made his way to the Admiral's couch and stabbed him. " Is it done ? " asked the Duke from below. " Yes," was the answer. " Let us see the body," shouted the leader. So the quivering corpse was thrown out of the window. The Duke looked closely at the face, and when he knew that it belonged to his old enemy, he kicked it again and again. Then he hurried off, exclaiming merrily : " Come, comrades ! On with your work ! God and the King command it ! "

Many such scenes occurred. Sidney, lodging with Walsingham, was safe ; but there were sights sad and horrible enough to swim in his eyes for a lifetime. Had he looked next morning from the ambassador's house to the palace, he might have seen the King, who a fortnight before had assigned him a post in his household, standing at his bedroom window, with a broken arquebuse in his hand, trying in vain to fire towards the Faubourg Saint-Germain, where Protestants mostly congregated, and screaming, " Kill ! Kill ! "

They did kill. It was reckoned that at least five

thousand Huguenots were murdered in Paris, and about a hundred thousand in the provinces. For seven days the slaughter lasted, and through that time blood flowed in the streets like rain.

This was the Massacre of Saint Bartholomew. Having seen it, Sidney must have felt that he had seen enough of Paris. Had he wished to remain, however, the fears of his friends and kindred would have driven him away. On the 9th of September, almost immediately after the news of the massacre had reached London, a letter, signed on behalf of Elizabeth's Privy Council by Burghley and Leicester, was written to Walsingham, thanking him for the protection he had afforded to the young Englishmen in Paris, and desiring him with all speed to procure passports and safe conduct out of the country for Philip Sidney and his comrades. That was done, and before the end of the month the travellers were on their way to Lorraine, under the care of Dr. Watson, the Dean, and afterwards Bishop, of Winchester.

Sidney paid no second visit to Paris, and henceforward kept clear of France. But his experience of the " demeanours of the people " during his fifteen or sixteen weeks' residence among them, somewhat stranger even than Leicester had anticipated, made a lasting impression on his character. It quickened and hardened his Protestantism, and, among other things, induced him to regard with special aversion Queen Elizabeth's project for marrying the Duke of Alençon, which, necessarily lapsing for a time, was renewed seven years later.

Arcade of the Doge's Palace · Venice

CHAPTER V.

FOREIGN SCHOOLING.

1572–1575.

IDNEY'S foreign schooling, of which such memorable commencement was made in Paris, was to be continued, with great advantage to him, through two and a half years.

Of his occupations in the first half year we know little. In Lorraine, though it was a province of France, he was in safe Huguenot company, and he seems to have remained there some time, probably with Dean Watson, learning French and pursuing other studies. Thence, apparently without his guardian, he went to Strasburg and down the Rhine, through Heidelberg, to Frankfort, where we find him in March, 1573, writing at any rate two letters to the Earl of Leicester.* In one, of small

---

* Philip Sidney to the Earl of Leicester, 18 and 23 March, 1573; among the Marquis of Bath's MSS. at Longleat.

importance, he informs his uncle that the bearer is taking to England some choice articles which he has arranged that the Earl shall have the option of buying. In the other he asks his uncle to return the courtesy he has received from the bearer, who has employed his credit in helping him, Philip, out of the straits for money to which he was driven. This second letter also reports that he had spent last Thursday with Count Lewis of Nassau, and with a German gentleman named Schomberg, whose acquaintance, as well as the Count's, he had made at the French Court. We may assume that Sidney was drawn to Frankfort by some of the better friendships which he had started in Paris, and he was here to meet with the best friend of all.

At Frankfort he lodged, during three or four months, at the house of Andrew Wechel, a printer renowned both for his careful reproducing of Greek and Hebrew books and for his generous bearing towards the studious men who visited this great centre of sixteenth-century culture. With Wechel was also lodging Hubert Languet.

Languet, born in 1518, was a native of Viteaux, in Burgundy, but a true cosmopolitan. In 1547 he was a professor of Civil Laws at Padua. Two years later, being at Wittenberg, he met with Melancthon, who taught him to be a Protestant, and to whom he became so attached that he resigned his Italian chair in order that he might sit at the feet of his amiable and heroic tutor. His great learning and greater shrewdness soon secured for him a prominent place among the men who carried on, with more or less purity, the work begun by Luther and Melancthon. He was the friend of nearly every leading Protestant, especially of Philip du Plessis-Mornay, and the trusted adviser and agent of the princes who, aiming at advancement of the reformed religion, had need of help from one whose clear intellect saw through the mazes of European politics and made him master of the plots and counter-plots in which the friends and foes of his party were mixed up. He it was, most likely, who wrote the famous "Vindiciæ contra Tyrannos," laying down the doctrine that kings who despoil the Church of God and the inheritance of his saints, who sanction idolatries and blasphemies, may and should be deposed by the open revolt of their subjects, though not by the private hands of assassins; a book much read by Englishmen in Cromwell's day. He had found some warrant for his argument in the St. Bartholomew massacre, which he watched from a hiding place with Du Plessis-Mornay in Paris.

Sidney did not meet Languet in the French city; but at Frankfort a rare and beautiful friendship grew up between the two. The ripened scholar and politician of fifty-four found an exquisite freshness in the youth of eighteen who was vigorously learning to apply in life the lessons of the schools. The youth was gladly strengthened by the experienced and lettered talk of one who knew nearly everything of note then happening in the Christian world, and could tell more than most men would ever hope to read about byegone times. Thus, in his "Arcadia," —writing nine years later, under pastoral image, and

speaking of himself as Philisides singing to his sheep,
—Sir Philip Sidney acknowledged his debt :

> The song I sang old Languet had me taught—
> Languet, the shepherd best swift Ister knew
> For clerkly rede, and hating what is naught,
> For faithful heart, clean hands, and mouth as true,
> With his sweet skill my skill-less youth he drew
> To have a feeling taste of Him that sits
> Beyond the heaven, far more beyond our wits.
>
> He said the music best those powers pleased
> Was jump concord between our wit and will,
> Where highest notes to godliness are raised
> And lowest sink not down to jot of ill.
> With old true tales he wont mine ears to fill,
> How shepherds did of yore, how now they thrive,
> Spoiling their flock, while 'twixt themselves they strive.
>
> He likèd me, but pitied lustful youth :
> His good strong staff my slippery years upbore :
> He still hoped well because I lovèd truth :
> Till, forced to part, with heart and eyes even sore,
> To worthy Coridon he gave me o'er.*

The final parting was not till 1581 ; but earlier and
temporary separations caused sore heart and eyes to
Languet who, austere bachelor though he was, soon
came to feel for Philip Sidney a sort of lover-like
tenderness as well as the devotion of a father to a son.

They were together at Frankfort for three months
or more. Then, when Languet's business took him
to Vienna early in the summer of 1573, Sidney
went thither with him, to see with his friend's vision

---

* It would be interesting to have a portrait of Languet, but the
only one I am acquainted with, that at Penshurst, is evidently
untrustworthy.

whatever was worth seeing at the Court of the Emperor Maximilian the Second, to be introduced to all the learned and devout people there, and to be watched over with more solicitude than at that time he was as grateful for as he should have been.

At their first parting Sidney seems to have resorted to a pardonable trick for slipping away from his mentor and acquiring in his own way some of the experience he had been sent from England to obtain. In August or September he left Languet in Vienna, proposing only to make a three days' journey to Presburg. But, once on the move, he stayed away for a few weeks, visiting other parts of Hungary. "Like a bird that has broken out of his cage," Languet wrote half-complainingly, "you make merry, unmindful, perhaps, of your friends, and heedless of the host of dangers incident to such a mode of travelling. I am sorry that you have no one with you who might discourse to you in the course of your journey, or instruct you about the manners and institutions of the people you visit, conduct you to learned men, and, if need be, serve as your interpreter. I could have procured you such a companion, had you told me what you were going to do."

Returning to Vienna in October, Sidney spent about another month with Languet, and then he started on a longer journey. He wanted to see Italy, and was not deterred by his friend's unwillingness to lose sight of him or fears as to the dangers he might meet with. But it was arranged that they should write to one another every week. Languet appears to have kept to the bargain. Sidney was

not so regular a correspondent, and many of the
letters which he did write have been lost.   Those we
have—of course in Latin—give valuable evidence of
the workings of his mind and of the influence of
outside events upon it at this important stage of his
career.

He was in Italy some eight months, having with
him at least one Englishman besides the three attendants he was licensed to take to France in 1572.
Through part of his travels he was accompanied by
Thomas Coningsby, a youth of his own rank, who
afterwards, but not in Sidney's lifetime, married
Sidney's cousin Philippa Fitzwilliam.   One of the
servants in his train was Griffin Madox, who was
Sidney's faithful henchman through life, and to
whom he bequeathed a legacy of £40 a year; and
another member of the party, of higher station
in life, was Lewis Brysket, afterwards Clerk to the
Council in Dublin under Sir Henry Sidney and one
of Sir Henry's successors, Lord Grey of Wilton.
Brysket, too, was faithful to the last.   Writing an
eclogue on the death of Sir Philip Sidney in 1591,
he recalled their adventures in 1573 and 1574, and
asked himself,

> Where is become thy wonted happy state,
> Alas, wherein through many a hill and dale,
> Through pleasant woods, and many an unknown way,
> Along the banks of many silver streams,
> Thou with him rodest, and with him didst scale
> The craggy rocks of the Alp and Appennine,
> Still with the muses sporting, while those beams
> Of virtue kindled in his noble breast
> Which after did so gloriously forth shine ?

Sidney went first to Venice, and soon after his arrival the Council of Ten granted him license to bear arms in that city, and in all other cities, towns, and places in the dominion which he might visit for purposes of study, and to be accompanied by Lewis Brysket, his " gentleman attendant," and by three other servants.* In Venice he passed most of his time while in Italy. He could not have chosen better headquarters. The Queen of the Adriatic was then at the height of her glory. Older than most of her neighbours and rivals, she had quietly worked her own way through centuries, caring little for the political struggles that went on around her. Neither Guelf nor Ghibelin, she had watched with but languid interest the Florentine disputes that made Dante an exile, and the Roman struggles towards liberty under Rienzi. Now, indeed, in Sidney's day, when all other Italian states were sunk in the worst degradation, there were signs of political life in Venice, and forces were silently preparing for one staunch battle in the cause of freedom. But Shakespeare's picture was true. The Rialto was the heart of Venice, and Antonios and Shylocks made up the body of her citizens. Hither came men from all parts of the world, chiefly on errands of merchandise, though, being assembled, they knew how to secure other advantages of intercourse. Adepts in science and letters found here fellow-workmen with whom they could sympathise, and from whom they could learn. Arts, newly risen to unrivalled eminence, here had better patrons and

---

* Calendar of Venetian State Papers, vol. vii., No. 583.

more genial critics than were known elsewhere. Students of theology here received kindlier regard than could be met with in other parts; and here they were able, without fear of persecution, to set forth what opinions they chose.

There were less worthy marks of freedom which Venice shared with Naples and the other Italian cities, and in which, according to Roger Ascham, she surpassed them all. Halting but nine days in Venice, Ascham avers that in that time he there saw "more liberty to sin than ever he heard tell of in our noble city of London in nine years." But for the vices which other moralists of the time, as well as Ascham, denounced, and which caused the ruin of many, Sidney had no liking. It was he who translated the proverb, " Inglese italianato è diavolo incarnato," into

> An Englishman that is Italianate
> Doth lightly prove a devil incarnate.

He preferred the society of men of letters and politicians, to several of whom Languet had introduced him by letter. Such were Arnaud du Ferrier, the French ambassador, and François Perrot, a French resident in Italy; neither of them strictly Protestants, but zealous champions of religious liberty, and associates with Henry of Navarre. Another was Count Philip Lewis of Hanau, a young man not much older than Sidney, but with a reputation for zeal and courage on behalf of the reformed faith which had already spread throughout Europe; and there were many others of the same school of thought with whom the young traveller was acquainted. Then there were the painters. Sidney may not have gained access to Titian, at this time more than ninety years old; but he was intimate with Titian's greatest pupils, Tintoretto, now about sixty, and Paul Veronese, whose age was forty. Finally, there were the rich men. His English connections secured for him the favour of haughty senators, and he sat at the tables of splendid merchants. "Yet I would far rather have one pleasant chat with you, my dear Languet," he wrote, "than enjoy the magnificent magnificences of all these magnificoes."

In Venice, as elsewhere during his travels, he busied himself as much with his books as with the places and people. "Just now," he informed his friend in 1573, "I am learning astronomy, and getting a notion of music. I practise my pen only in writing to you; but I find that practice does anything but make perfect. The more I write, the worse I write. Do pray send me some rules about composition; and at the same time put in those bits of advice which you said you would keep till you see me again; for I know that your counsel can never be exhausted, and there are faults enough in me to deserve endless admonitions." In this letter he asked Languet to send him a French translation of Plutarch, and offered in return to forward some books he had had special pleasure in reading. Among these were a history of the world and two histories of Venice, a collection of letters by "thirteen illustrious men," of whom Boccaccio was one, and a treatise on mottoes by Ruscelli, a friend of Tasso. He was evidently making himself master of Italian history and literature, with special attention to the antiquities of the town in which he lodged.

Some of Languet's "bits of advice" must be quoted, as their recipient evidently paid heed to them. "You ask me how you ought to form a style of writing," Languet said. "In my opinion, you cannot do better than give careful study to all Cicero's letters, not only for the sake of the graceful Latin but also on account of the weighty truths they contain. Nowhere is there a better explanation of the way in which the Roman republic was overthrown." Languet went on to say that for all the money in the world he could not buy a French version of Plutarch, though perhaps he might borrow one. "But when you begin to read Cicero's letters, you will hardly need Plutarch. I approve of your giving some study to astronomy; for those who are ignorant of it cannot understand cosmography, and they who read history without knowledge of cosmography seem to me to be just groping in the dark."

"You have done well," Languet wrote in another letter, "in learning the rudiments of astronomy, but I do not advise you to work much more at that science, since it is very difficult, and will be of small value to you. I know not whether you are wise in turning your attention to geometry. It is a fine study, and well deserves thoughtful application. But you must consider what are your prospects, and how quickly you will have to abandon this literary ease ; and consequently you ought to give to those matters which are absolutely needful all the little time you have. I call those things needful of which it is discreditable for a man of high rank in life to be ignorant, and which, by and by, will perhaps serve you for ornament and resource. Geometry, it is true, may be of great use to a general in fortifying and investing towns, in measuring camps, and in every kind of construction. But a great deal of time is needed to acquire enough knowledge of it to be really helpful ; and I think it very foolish to get a smattering of all sorts of subjects, for show and not for use. Besides, you have too little fun in your nature, and this is a study which will make you still more grave. It requires close application of thought, and thus wears out the lively parts of the mind, and greatly weakens the body. And you know that you have not a morsel too much health."

" I must admit," Sidney replied, " that I am more sober than my age or business requires. But I have always found that I am never so little troubled with melancholy as when my weak mind is employed about something particularly difficult." Languet had repeatedly to warn his young friend against overwork. " A brain too much taxed," he reminded him, " cannot live long, and a healthy mind is good for nothing unless lodged in a healthy body."

Partly as a rest from his studies, partly in order to see more of Italy, Sidney went to Padua in the middle of January, 1574, and he spent six weeks in the quiet university town. He was in Venice again

before the end of February, when he sat to Paul
Veronese for his portrait, to be sent as a present to
Languet. After that he visited Genoa, and in the
middle of April he returned to Padua for a few
weeks. The last two months of his Italian residence
were probably passed wholly in Venice, much to
Languet's discontent, who thought the young man
had had enough, and more than enough, of Venetian
sights.

It was not that the blunt reformer altogether
objected to sight-seeing. He was very anxious that
Sidney should join with him in witnessing one ceremony of unusual splendour. This was on the occasion of the French King's eldest brother, the Duke
of Anjou, being installed as King of Poland. Wonderful preparations were made for the business, and
Languet urged his friend to be present, both for the
pomp and glitter he would see and for the opportunity he would thus have of widening his acquaintance
with great men. But Sidney preferred to stay in
Italy, strengthening his friendship with those men
he already knew, and especially with Count Philip
Lewis of Hanau. His journeys from one part of
Italy to another seem to have been in company with
the Count, and his chief reason for loitering so long
near the Adriatic was that he might enjoy this
friend's society.

Languet disliked the loitering. He was eager to
renew companionship with his pupil, his son, his boy
—as he variously called Philip. He was also full of
fears that harm might come to Philip, lest his health
should be ruined by the climate, or his life endan-

gered through the hatred of all devout Catholics to the English, or his moral and religious principles poisoned by the evil influences surrounding him. This was the burden of many of Languet's letters. Sometimes he wrote playfully and in coaxing terms; at other times his words were stern and reproachful. " If I thought that my counsel had any weight with you," he declared when he heard that Philip had gone to Genoa, " I should urge you, as I have done over and over again, to keep clear of those places which are under Spanish rule; for the Spaniards, with good cause, hate the English, and Genoa is so bound up with Spain that you cannot possibly be safe there. But I suppose you find pleasure in seeing so many vessels being made ready for war; or else there is sweet music for you in the clank of the chains of the poor galley-slaves; or is it that you wait in hope of seeing this Don John of Austria as he passes back into Spain ? "

Don John, it may be noted, the half-brother of King Philip of Spain, had a few years before been appointed captain-general of the combined forces despatched by Spain, the Pope, and the Venetian republic on a crusade against the Turks. In 1571 he had won the battle of Lepanto, the greatest sea-fight of the century, but not great enough to crush the Ottoman power, and he was now carrying on the war in Tunis and Morocco.

Sidney's letters in the second half of his stay in Italy show that he was at this time taking too much interest in politics to have much leisure for studying music or geometry, or adding Greek to the Latin,

French, and Italian languages of which he was already master. His political information was incomplete, and some of his judgments were crude ; but his remarks on these subjects reveal more knowledge and wisdom than could have been looked for in a youth of nineteen. He was watching with keen eyes, and greater hopefulness than the more experienced Languet could feel, the working out of some of the most momentous problems that have ever been played on the political chessboard of Europe—problems in which the craftiest, if not the skilfullest, player was his own god-father, Philip of Spain.

Being in Italy, he was nearest to the contest in which King Philip, as the champion of Catholic Christianity, was engaged with the followers of Mahomet ; but he recognised the greater importance of the other crusade that the same champion was carrying on against Protestantism. This more vital struggle was not newly begun. It had been growing for some fifteen years, and, with the Duke of Alva for chief persecutor in the Netherlands, had caused the deaths of thousands upon thousands. Now, however, it was receiving fresh impulse. The Spanish forces employed against the Netherlanders having been strengthened after the retirement of the Duke of Alva, formidable preparations to meet them had been made under the wise guidance of William of Orange and his brother Lewis of Nassau. With Count Lewis, Sidney had made acquaintance in Paris and he had renewed it in Frankfort. It was a special shock to him, therefore, to hear of the defeat of the Protestant army by the Spanish General D'Avila at Nimeguen on the 15th of April, 1574, when Lewis and his younger brother Henry, with Christopher, the son of the Elector Palatine, and other German allies were killed.

Though hardly any of them can now be traced, Sidney appears at this time to have written many letters to his friends in England, besides those to Languet, on political events. Early in May, as he reported, he sent to the Earl of Leicester a full account of the state of opinion in Italy produced by the recent victory of the Spaniards. "Perhaps some good may come of my letter," he said ; " at any rate I would rather be blamed for too little wisdom than for lack of patriotism." To him it seemed strange and wrong that England did not go to the assistance of the Prince of Orange and his brave associates in their grand battle for liberty and for principles that should be as dear to all honest men elsewhere as they were to the Netherlanders ; and he blamed the German Protestants yet more for their cowardice and apathy. All save the Elector Palatine, he complained, seemed resolved to ruin their people and disgrace themselves. Some of these unworthy princes cared for nothing but moistening their throats ; others threw their time away on idle hunting-parties ; others squandered wealth in such foolish work as altering the course of rivers.

In another letter he checked himself in the midst of some playful talk. " My dear Languet, what are we doing ? Jesting in times like these ! I cannot think there is any man, possessed of common understanding, who does not see to what these storms are driving, by which Christendom has been agitated these many years. If there is anyone who sees what is to follow, and is not moved by it, I say that such a man should either take his place among the gods, or be classed with the brutes." Yet he found warrant in philosophy and precedent for being merry in misfortune. " Refreshing of the mind consists, more than anything else, in that seemly play of humour which is so natural, and so ingrafted, as it were, in the characters of some of the wisest men that neither Socrates nor our own Sir Thomas More could lose his jest even in the hour of death."

Sidney took life more seriously than is common with young people in their teens, and the desire to join in the great fight for civil and religious liberty against the tyranny of Spain and Rome was already strong in him ; but he evidently contrived to enjoy himself. Soon after arriving in Venice he talked of going on to Constantinople. He was much more anxious to see Rome before he left Italy. Languet, however, dissuaded him from both projects.

As it was, Languet scolded him for remaining in the south so long. " I fear you will suffer harm from the great heat," he wrote in the middle of June, 1574, "since you are of such tender constitution, and knowing, as I do, how eagerly, almost intemperately, you eat all sorts of fruit. I warn you of fever and dysentery if you stay in Italy during the summer." Nor was the warning quite unnecessary. In July Sidney was seriously ill, suffering from severe pains in the head which threatened to issue in pleurisy, and which were thought to be the result of drinking too much water. " This I foresaw and dreaded," Languet wrote. " If you love me, show some care for your health. If any mischance befel you, I should be the most wretched man in the world; for there is nothing to give me the least pleasure save our friendship, and the hope I have of your manhood. The misfortunes of my native land, and the calamities that have lately overtaken all my friends but you, make life a great deal worse to me than death."

Languet often wrote in this strain. Philip, he thought, with the prospect of many active years before him, was bound to be hopeful and to use every nerve in fitting himself for manly service in the world; but what had he to hope for? " My life is of no good to anyone, and death will only rid me of my miseries. What can be more wretched for a man who has any feeling of humanity in him than to be haunted by such crimes as have through the last ten or twelve years been committed, and are still being committed, in my ill-fated France, and in the Netherlands ? " Sidney's reply was characteristic. " This last letter of yours has troubled me much. I can hardly collect my thoughts to answer it. Oh, my dear Languet ! can it be that *you* are unhappy— you whom all with a spark of virtue in them love and honour? As for me, if any service of mine can help you at all, you know how I shall rejoice to do it ; for I have nothing that is not more rightly yours than mine."

The service Languet most desired was rendered

6

at the end of July, when Sidney went back to Vienna. There, he was detained for some time by illness. After that, he accompanied Languet on a trip to Poland, and he was in Vienna again, still "not in a very good state of body," before the end of November. This much we learn from letters that he wrote home to the Earl of Leicester and Lord Burghley. The letter to the Lord High Treasurer was, he said, one of his "scribbles," sent rather in obedience to his lordship's commands than for anything worth reading in it. It contained, however, a long and graphic account of the state of politics as viewed in Vienna, and of the recent proceedings of the Grand Turk.* As the two years' leave of absence from England that had been allowed to him was more than run out, and as he was now old and experienced enough for his reports on public affairs to be considered worth having, it was probably a condition of his being allowed to stay abroad for another year that Sidney should furnish Queen Elizabeth's ministers from time to time with "news-letters" of the sort that were indispensable in the days before newspapers. Unfortunately very few of them are extant.

For three months or so he was in Vienna lodging in the same house as Hubert Languet, who was now in the service of the Emperor Maximilian the Second. Sidney also appears to have held some sort of office at Court, corresponding more or less perhaps to that of secretary of legation or *attaché* in

* State Papers, Foreign, Elizabeth ; Philip Sidney to Lord Burghley, 17 December, 1574.

modern times; and for companion in his diplomatic duties, such as they were, he had Edward Wotton, an elder brother of the better known Sir Henry Wotton. Maximilian, though he was father-in-law both to Philip of Spain and to Charles of France, was a peace-loving monarch, tolerant towards Protestants and willing that his subjects should be prosperous. In his present surroundings, Sidney had good opportunity of seeing Catholic monarchy in its more agreeable phases; and the lull in persecution elsewhere—consequent on the temporary inability of the Netherlanders to continue their resistance to Philip, and on the death of Charles, who was succeeded by his brother Henry, a yet more contemptible king of France—made the study of Catholic politics less painful, but not less instructive, than they had been of late.

Sidney had time and inclination in Vienna for healthy pastime, and for acquiring some of the lighter arts proper to the making of a gentleman. The opening sentences of his " Defence of Poesy " contain a lively account of the teaching he received from John Peter Pugliano, esquire of the Emperor's stables, to whom he and Wotton " gave themselves to learn horsemanship." " He," says Sidney, " according to the fertileness of the Italian wit, did not only afford us the demonstration of his practice, but sought to enrich our minds with the contemplations therein which he thought most precious. But with none, I remember, mine ears were at any time more laden than when, either angered with slow payment or moved with our learner-like admiration, he exercised his speech in praise of his faculty. He said soldiers were the noblest estate of mankind, and horsemen the noblest of soldiers. He said they were the masters of war and ornaments of peace, speedy goers and strong abiders, triumphers both in camps and courts. Nay, to so unbelieved a point he proceeded as that no earthly thing bred such wonder to a prince as to be a good horseman: skill of government was but a pedantry in comparison. Then would he add certain praises by telling what a peerless beast a horse was, the only serviceable courtier without flattery, the beast of most beauty, faithfulness, courage, and such more that, if I had not been a piece of a logician before I came to him, I think he would have persuaded me to have wished myself a horse."

Having learnt from Master Pugliano to be one of the best horsemen of his day, and something else besides, Sidney rode out of Vienna near the end of February or the beginning of March, 1575, in the train of the Emperor Maximilian, who then went to Prague to preside at the meeting of the Bohemian Diet. Thither also went Languet; and soon after the opening ceremony the friends parted company.

Sidney had been somewhat hurriedly called home; partly, it would seem, because an unreasonable report had reached England that he was becoming a Catholic. Walsingham, who since we saw him in Paris had returned to England, and had been made Secretary of State, wrote to Languet on the subject, and the sturdy Huguenot had to employ all his eloquence in persuading the English minister that his fears were entirely groundless. As a further help towards righting him in the opinion of his kindred, Languet advised Sidney to cultivate more than he had done the society of Protestant pastors. On his way home, he said, he would meet several who were learned and sensible men.

Whether in search of sensible pastors or for some other reason, Sidney travelled home by a very zig-zag route. Quitting Prague early in March, he passed through Dresden, and then turned round for an excursion to Heidelberg, whither he bore a letter of introduction to Count Lewis of Wittgenstein, holding high office under the Elector Palatine. There he made acquaintance with the renowned Doctor Zacharius Ursinus, who marked his covetousness of time by labelling on his doorway these words: "My friend, whoever you are, either go away or give me some help in my studies." From Heidelberg he went farther south to Strasburg in order to visit Doctor Lobetius, with whom he had been long intimate, a man held in high honour by the Protestants of that time. Then he turned back and proceeded to Frankfort, whither Languet also came to spend a few weeks with his beloved pupil.

In a letter written by the old reformer after his return to Prague there is an interesting reference to this meeting, as well as to the portrait of Sidney which Paul Veronese had painted a year before, and of which, unfortunately, we have now no trace. "All the while I could feast my eyes with the sight of you," said Languet, "I took small heed of the picture which you gave me, and for which, by the bye, I never thanked you half as much as so splendid a gift deserved. But as soon as I came back to Frankfort my longing for you induced me to have it framed and hung up in a conspicuous place. That done, it looks to me so beautiful and true a likeness of you that I feel there is nothing in the world I prize so much. I think, though, that the artist has made you appear too sad and thoughtful : I should have liked it better if your face had had a merrier look when you sat for the painting."

From Frankfort Sidney made his way to Antwerp ; but he fell ill on the road, and his return home was thus further delayed. He reached London early in June, 1575. "On the last day of May," he said in a letter to Count Lewis of Hanau, "fair winds conveyed me to this island nest of ours. I found all my kindred well, and the Queen, although she is certainly advancing in years, still in excellent health. To us she is just like that brand of Meleager, which, should it be extinguished, would take from us all our quietness."

"CROWN" OF QUEEN ELIZABETH

CHAPTER VI.

WITH QUEEN ELIZABETH'S COURT.

1575–1576.

ETURNING to England in his twenty-first year, Philip Sidney found himself in an altogether different position from that he had held when, at the age of seventeen and a half, he had gone out, " young and raw," to gain experience of the world. Young he still was, even among the Elizabethan courtiers and politicians, for whom manhood and manliness began— if they ever did begin—at least two or three years earlier than is now usual; but raw he certainly was not.

He had had rare opportunities of studying life abroad and the conditions of healthy and unhealthy living either abroad or at home, and he had made rare use of them. He was now quite prepared to join the group of Queen Elizabeth's favourites from which he was seldom absent during the next ten years.

He had already formed opinions as to the political duties incumbent on him and on others like him ; and he was soon to find himself hampered in his efforts to perform those duties by the courtiership imposed upon him.   In the remainder of his life, failing in some respects, yet achieving much, he was nearly always struggling and striving towards realisation of ideals that must have been strong and clear before he came back to London.   It behoves us therefore here to take some account of the affairs in which he was henceforth to be involved.

Throughout the three years of Philip's residence abroad, his father, Sir Henry, was usually at Ludlow, quietly and honestly filling his office as Lord President of Wales ; but he had often to be at Court on matters of business, and Lady Sidney was much oftener in attendance on the Queen.   Little as Sir Henry was thanked for his services to the State, these could not be dispensed with, and at the time of his son's return plans were being made for sending him once again as Lord Deputy to Ireland, there for the third time to undo some of the mischief made by other and less skilful viceroys.

Elizabeth was not able to quarrel outright with her faithful officer ; and now and then she was kind to him, at any rate in words.   A gracious, albeit pompous, letter was written by her when she heard that her god-child, Ambrosia Sidney, had died, at the age of fifteen, on the 23d of February, 1575, while Philip was on his way home from Vienna. "Good Sidney," it began, "although we are well assured that, with your wisdom and great experience of worldly chances and necessities, nothing can happen unto you so heavy but you can and will bear them as they ought to be rightly taken, yet, for as much as we conceive the grief you yet feel thereby, as in such cases natural parents are accustomed, we would not have you ignorant, to ease your sorrow as much as may be, how we take part of your grief upon us." Thereupon followed an offer in the nature of a command. "God hath left unto you the comfort of one daughter of very good hope," wrote the Queen, "whom if you shall think good to remove from those parts of unpleasant air into better in these parts, and will send her unto us before Easter, or when you shall think good, assure yourself that we will have a special care of her, not doubting but, as you are well persuaded of our favour towards yourself, so will we make further demonstration thereof in her."

There was no great generosity in thus proposing to find lodgings at Court, her father doubtless being left to provide clothing, for the beautiful and sprightly Mary Sidney, now in her fourteenth year. Elizabeth liked to have handsome and clever women and girls about her, never deeming that her own appearance was not made more attractive by proximity to others of her sex, even if they were younger and better-looking than herself. She was only jealous when they thought of marrying the courtiers in whose compliments and admiration she claimed a monopoly; and she was not unwilling that some of them should be mated with the courtiers for whom she had no special affection. In promoting Philip Sidney's only surviving and dearly loved sister to be one of her maids of honour, and soon afterwards in helping to put a rich husband in her way, the Queen meant and acted kindly. The change was doubtless welcome to Mary, and we may be sure that it rendered the Court life on which he was about to enter much more agreeable to Philip.

Their uncle, the Earl of Leicester, was still the chief courtier. Leicester, like the Queen, was never jealous of younger courtiers, provided they did not venture to thwart him; and it had been his policy from the first to help forward promising aspirants to Elizabeth's favour in order that he might strengthen his own position at Court. Some of his early foes, like Lord Hunsdon and the Earl of Arundel, had died or been finally disgraced in the course of the seventeen years through which he had been playing his showy, and, on the whole, successful, but by no means dignified or praiseworthy, game as prime flatterer and cajoler of the Queen. But others had taken their places. One was the Earl of Oxford, husband of the young lady whom it had been at one time intended that Philip Sidney should marry. Another was Sir Christopher Hatton. Hatton had owed to the Earl of Leicester his introduction to royal favour; but that favour had so turned his head and aroused his ambition that he had come to be one of Leicester's principal rivals, and he was disliked accordingly. Fresh recruits for the Leicester party at Court had to be brought forward, and one of these, a few years older than Philip Sidney, and therefore a few years earlier in the field, is especially interesting to us. He was Edward Dyer, an old friend of the Sidney family, and soon to become one of Philip's most intimate and cherished companions.

A gossiping letter that young Gilbert Talbot wrote in May, 1573, to his father, the Earl of Shrewsbury, gives curious insight into the court plotting of the day. The Earl of Oxford was in great liking with the Queen, Talbot reported, and so was Sir Christopher Hatton ; but Hatton was very ill and unable to attend upon her Majesty. " Now," he went on to say, " is their devices—chiefly by Leicester, as I suppose, and not without Burghley's knowledge—how to make Dyer as great as ever Hatton was ; for now, in this time of Hatton's sickness, the time is convenient. It is brought thus to pass. Dyer lately was sick of a consumption, in great danger, and, as your lordship knoweth, he hath been in displeasure these two years. It was made the Queen believe that his sickness came because of the continuance of her displeasure towards him, so that unless she would forgive him he was like not to recover ; and hereupon her Majesty hath forgiven him, and sent unto him a very comfortable message."

After this trick, Dyer seems to have steadily made way, but with too much self-respect ever to be a rival of his patron, the Earl of Leicester. He was also a staunch ally of Leicester's sister, and of her husband. From Chiswick, where she had gone for rest and change of air after a serious illness, Lady Sidney, writing on the 1st of September, 1574, to Sir Henry's secretary, Edmund Molyneux, said :

" In all your proceedings in my lord's cause, take the wise, noble Mr. Dyer's friendly counsel, who, I know, doth most dearly tender my lord's honour and well-doing, as much as a faithful friend may do." In the same letter Lady Sidney sent messages to two of her friends and companions in attendance on the Queen. " Tell them I would write to them, but I have nothing to tell them but of my unhealthy, unrecovered carcase."

It is not pleasant to think of our Sidney's unworthy uncle being his chief patron and promoter at Queen Elizabeth's Court. But we must take facts as we find them ; and if we cannot quite excuse Philip Sidney for attaching himself as closely as he did to the Earl of Leicester, and for apparently regarding him with unstinted admiration, we may well be astonished that his own temperament and bearing were so unlike those of the man on whom he mainly depended for advancement in life. Large allowance must be made, too, for the exigencies of Philip's position ; and it should never be forgotten that the standard of morals in the sixteenth century, even with the austerest moralists, differed widely from that of the nineteenth. " Remember, my son," Sir Henry Sidney had written when Philip was a small schoolboy, " the noble blood you are descended of by your mother's side, and think that only by virtuous life and good action you may be an ornament to that illustrious family." It seems never to have occurred to either father or mother or son that the family of which the Earl of Leicester was now head could be other than illustrious, with

virtuous life and good action as its proper ornaments ; still less, that virtuous life and good action
could be crippled or contaminated, or could be in
any risk of being injured, by association with and
dependence on such a head. Of Leicester Elizabeth once said, on receiving from him a letter asking
pardon for having offended her, and praying to be
reinstated in her favour, that he " did mistake the
chameleon's property, who doth change into all
colours, according to the object, save white, which
is innocency." Leicester's vices were notorious,
and though they may have been exaggerated by
his enemies, they could not but be patent to his
friends ; yet people of much purer life and much
finer taste than Queen Elizabeth forgave him and
ignored them.

If Philip Sidney suffered strangely little, moreover, from a moral point of view, through dependence on his uncle, and if this uncle was in many
ways very helpful to him in his progress as a
courtier, we must not lose sight of the fact that his
relations with Leicester did not in all respects con-
duce to his worldly advantage. It certainly cannot
have been on the score of virtuous life or good
action that Lord Burghley preferred to Philip Sidney, as a husband for his daughter Anne, the Earl
of Oxford, notorious as a libertine and a scoundrel
even in 1571, when he was but one-and-thirty.
But at that time and always Burghley disliked and
mistrusted Leicester, was constantly on the watch
for his downfall, and, as a matter of State interest,
was not unwilling to assist it on occasion ; and we

may be sure that if he thought the son of his self-sacrificing and impoverished friend Sir Henry Sidney no equal match for his daughter, he objected yet more to have Philip for a son-in-law because he was nephew of the self-seeking and vainglorious man who was always encouraging the Queen in her vanities and extravagances, and so hindering the prudent and prosaic building up of England's prosperity which the Lord High Treasurer advocated.

In Philip and Philip's parents Lord Burghley always took as kindly an interest as his unemotional temperament and his many public cares allowed. Philip also now had another and in some respects a more estimable friend on that side of the Court which was not given up to frivolities. Francis Walsingham, recalled from France in April, 1573, had then been knighted and appointed Secretary of State. If in statecraft he was not Burghley's equal, he was, to say the least, as patriotic, and in his new office, and others connected with it, he put to good use the intimate knowledge of foreign affairs which he had acquired by long and varied experience abroad. Less grave or less pompous than Burghley, he was a courtier of the best type, too honest and self-respecting to compete with men like Leicester, Hatton, and Oxford, in the line of courtiership most approved by Queen Elizabeth. The mutual liking that arose between him and Philip Sidney when the young man was under his protection in Paris lasted and grew; and in the absence of his own father, and of Languet too, Philip perhaps had truer help and guidance from Walsingham than from anyone else.

SIR FRANCIS WALSINGHAM.

FROM AN ENGRAVING, BY J. HOUBRAKEN, OF ZUCCHERO'S PORTRAIT.

Of Elizabeth's Court at its gayest Philip had experience as soon as he returned from his travels. Preparations were then on foot for the most memorable of all the royal progresses for which this reign is famous, its main incident being a visit paid by the Queen to the stately mansion of Kenilworth, which thirteen years earlier she had granted to the Earl of Leicester. The party, which included Philip and his parents, having left London a few days before, reached Kenilworth on the 9th of July, and the next eighteen days were given up to entertainments more gorgeous, if the chroniclers are to be believed, than subject had ever yet provided for his sovereign.* Every sort of spectacle and festivity that could be devised was furnished in most lavish style. There was bear-baiting, much to the Queen's fancy, on one day, and on another there were wrestling and Italian feats of skill. There were splendid hunting excursions. There was a play performed by the men of Coventry. There were masques, and allegorical processions of gods and goddesses, nymphs and satyrs. Music and dancing filled up the intervals between more novel amusements in the daytime, and at night there were fireworks. At one " most delicious and ambrosial banquet " three hundred different kinds of dishes were set on the tables. When her Majesty rode out of the grounds, Deep-Desire, as the central figure in a pleasure-provoking but grief-pourtraying pageant, uttered this dirge :

---

* Readers of Sir Walter Scott's " Kenilworth " need not be reminded of the brilliant account there given of these entertainments, but must be cautioned against accepting as facts the main portions of the novel.

Come, muses, come and help me to lament ;
  Come, woods ; come, waves ; come, hills ; come, doleful dales ;
Since life and death are both against me bent,
  Come, gods ; come, men ; bear witness of my bales !
Oh, heavenly nymphs, come help my heavy heart
With sighs to see Dame Pleasure thus depart !

" The princely pleasures of the Court at Kenilworth," as they were styled by George Gascoigne, one
of the poets of the occasion, in his collection of the
" verses, proses, or poetical inventions," specially
prepared for them, being over on the 27th of July,
the Queen and her courtiers next went to Lichfield,
where they occupied eight days in other entertainments. Thence they proceeded to Chartley Castle,
the seat of Walter Devereux, Earl of Essex, who
was in Ireland, but whose wife was a sufficient host
in his absence. After that Stafford, Dudley, Worcester, and other places were visited in succession,
and on the 11th of September Elizabeth reached
Woodstock, the scene of her girlish confinement,
where she was again the Earl of Leicester's guest.

His three months of holiday-making in Warwick-
shire and the neighbouring counties, as one of the
youngest but not the least approved of her courtiers, must have given Philip Sidney a full taste, if
not for the time a surfeit, of the gay life on which
he was entering.

His brief stay at Chartley may have had peculiar
interest for him. Here, doubtless, he first saw the
maiden whom he afterwards made famous under the
name of Stella. Lady Penelope Devereux was now
only about twelve years old, and, even if we are to

believe that all the love he professed for her in later days was real, it would be absurd to suppose that at this time he regarded her with stronger feelings than any beautiful damsel, just budding into womanhood, might arouse in the susceptible heart of a young man of twenty who was privileged to dance and frolic with her in her own home. But as barely a year elapsed before there was talk of a marriage contract between them, it is fair to assume that even at this early stage in their intimacy impressions were started which took shape hereafter.

At Chartley Philip had other matters to think of besides courtly gaieties and the youthful charms of Penelope Devereux. There, on the 5th of August, Sir Henry Sidney received the patent under which he was again appointed Lord Deputy of Ireland, and a week later the father and son, who had spent about two months together after being separated for three years, parted company for another year. While the Queen was being entertained at Dudley Castle, Sir Henry, " taking leave of her Majesty and kissing her sacred hand with most gracious and comfortable words from her," started on his journey, leaving his wife and elder son and daughter to continue in attendance.

The Earl of Leicester's London residence, known in his time as Leicester House, and much enlarged by him, but formerly styled Exeter House, and afterwards Essex House, was a stately building, on the south side of the Strand and west of the Temple gardens, with its own gardens stretching down to the Thames. It was within easy reach,

7

either by land or by water, of Whitehall, where the Queen kept Court when she was in the metropolis ; and here, probably, with occasional visits to Penshurst, Philip passed most of the autumn and winter months in which he was becoming an adept in courtly ways.

From London, early in November, he wrote the only letter that he sent this year to Languet, except a short one announcing, in June, his safe return from the continent. Poor Languet complained of this tardiness. " I am more than distressed by your obstinate silence," he said in November, before the second letter reached him ; " since for five or six months I have received nothing from you, although I have often written to you, and you have written to others. Surely in all that time you could have spared one hour to your old friend." When the long-looked for letter arrived, Languet was scarcely mollified. " At the cost of one dance a month," he urged, " you could have done all that was expected of you. Last winter you spent three or four months with me. Just think how many eminent authors you studied in that little time, and what good came to you in reading them. If in so brief a space you could learn so many things which would be helpful to you in the proper conduct of life, could not that hinder you from burying yourself in foolish pleasures?" But the stern Huguenot softened as he went on. " You see," he added, " how unkindly I am answering your letter, so full of kindness. I do thank you for it, although I cannot suffer you to run the risk of squandering your powers in idleness. I never doubted that you would at once secure the admiration of all your friends, and of all the noblest men about you. In this particular your letter tells me nothing of which I was not sure before ; but I am very glad indeed to be told it."

It is a pity that Sidney's few letters to his plain-speaking friend are not preserved to give us detailed information about his occupations at this time. Languet's replies, however, show us something of their purport. In a former letter he had joked with Sidney about marriage, and commended to him the example of Edward Wotton, who had just taken a wife. Sidney appears to have sent back vehement protestations in favour of bachelorhood. Languet answered : "What you say in jest about a wife, I take in earnest. I think you had better not be so sure. More cautious men than you are sometimes caught ; and for my part I am very willing that you should be caught, that so you might give to your country sons like yourself. But, whatever is to happen in this matter, I pray God that it may turn out well and happily. You see how nobly our friend Wotton has passed through the trial. His boldness seems to convict you of cowardice. However, destiny has a good deal to do with these things. Therefore you must not suppose that by your own foresight you can manage so as to be always happy, and to have everything according to your wishes." True enough always, and especially true in Sidney's case.

That Sidney was at this time winning favour at Court, with Queen and subjects, is clear. But we

can only guess at his movements during several
months ; and if he continued to be as well dressed
and as merry as any of the richer and more experienced courtiers with whom he associated, it was not
without difficulty. His father was obliged to spend
more than his salary in performing his duties in
Ireland. His mother was hard pressed to keep up
the dignity necessary to her position in the Queen's
household. " My present estate is such, by reason
of my debts," she wrote in plaintive terms to Lord
Burghley, " as I cannot go forward with any honourable course of living." Yet go forward she must,
" for that I had, by her Majesty's commandment,
prepared myself to attend the Court." " Seeing it
hath pleased her Majesty to hold this hard hand
towards me," she added, " I am again thus bold to
trouble your lordship for your comfortable direction
how I may best in this case deal with her Majesty.
I am presently greatly to seek what else to do than
sorrow much at her Majesty's unkindness towards
me, because it brings me in no small disgrace among
such as are not determined to wish me well."

Sidney had his own debts to meet as best he
could. In August, 1575, he gave a bond for £42 6s.
to Richard Rodway, " citizen and merchant tailor of
London." Somewhat later he had to send a boot-
maker's bill for £4 10s. 4d. to his father's steward,
saying, " I have so long owed this bearer this expressed sum of money, as I am forced, for the safeguard of my credit, to request you to let him have
it presently, and this shall be your sufficient discharge
to be received at Midsummer quarter,"—when,

doubtless, the steward would have an instalment of his allowance to hand him, or might be collecting the tithes of his Flintshire living.

Among the courtly friends with whom he must have been especially intimate at this time, as well as afterwards, were his kinsman and schoolfellow Fulke Greville, of his own age, and Edward Dyer, his senior by a few years ; but concerning their relations in 1575 and 1576 there is no record, and of Greville he cannot have seen much, as the latter then held some office in Wales.   The only friend, indeed, with whom we know that Sidney was in frequent inter-course, was the Earl of Essex.   Their acquaintance began in the autumn, when Essex, after nearly two years' absence in Ireland, came to pass a few months at Durham House, his residence by the Thames side, just below Charing Cross, and it was destined to be short-lived ; but it was close while it lasted.

Essex, thirteen or fourteen years older than Sid-ney, stands out as the most conspicuous and attrac-tive type of chivalry, with all its ambitions and all its infirmities, in the earlier stage of Elizabeth's reign during which Sidney was growing up to follow and surpass him.   Too honest to succeed as a courtier, he was of too restless and reckless a disposition for suc-cess to come to him in any other line of life.   Hav-ing inherited from his grandfather the title of Lord Hereford in the year of Queen Elizabeth's acces-sion, and having given some offence three or four years later by marrying the Queen's cousin, he had in 1572 been made an earl for his services as a sol-dier, and soon after that he had sought and obtained

Elizabeth's permission to plant an English colony in Ulster.

At his own cost Essex equipped the small army with which his experiment was commenced in August, 1573 ; but he had not means or prudence enough for carrying it on, and, though Queen Elizabeth helped him with a loan of £10,000, at good interest, both this money and the £25,000 that he raised by mortgaging and impoverishing his estates were wasted. Had Sir Henry Sidney been then Lord Deputy, controlling and assisting the project, the event might have been different. But Sir Henry's successor and brother-in-law, Sir William Fitzwilliam, utterly unable to keep order in Ireland and consenting to be the tool of others, readily lent himself to the parsimonious and meddling policy that the Queen dictated. He neither restrained Essex's impetuosity nor left him free to work out his own plans. Essex was insulted and hampered, and the melancholy issue of his experiment was the massacre of the Scots at Rathlin in July, 1575, for which but partial excuse can be found in the general opinion of the day, that no mercy whatever was due to enemies, especially if the enemies were rebels in Ireland or Spanish foes. Sir Henry Sidney, more humane and chivalrous than most, sanctioned and applauded indiscriminate slaughter, and Queen Elizabeth was of the same way of thinking. Essex's cruelty, as it would now be regarded, in no way shocked her. She was only prompted by it, in this instance, to condole with him on the misfortune he had brought on himself, and to send him one of the

graciously worded letters which often did duty for
solid help or real consolation from her. " If you knew
what comfort we take to have a subject of your
quality to grow in this time when the most part of
men give themselves over, as it were, a prey unto
delicacy," she wrote from Dudley Castle, where the
news reached her in August, " you should then acknowledge that care and hazard and travail bestowed
in the service of a prince maketh as thankful accep-
tation of the same from me as from any other prince
that liveth." A week before, while being entertained by the Countess of Essex at Chartley, she
had written more prettily and also more meaning-
lessly : " If lines could value life, or thanks could
answer praise, I should esteem my pen's labour the
best employed time that many years hath lent me.
But to supply the want that both these carrieth, a
right judgment of upright dealing shall lengthen
the scarcity that either of the other wanteth. Deem
therefore, cousin mine, that the search of your
honour, with the danger of your breath, hath not
been bestowed on so ungrateful a prince that will
not both consider the one and reward the other."

While Sir Henry Sidney was beginning a new
term of service in Ireland, Essex came home to seek
some of the reward and consideration thus promised
him, at any rate to the extent of being enabled to
continue the exploit on which his heart was set.
In 1574 Elizabeth had promised to make him Earl-
Marshal of Ireland, but the appointment had never
been confirmed. " I assure myself," he wrote in
January, 1576, " that your Majesty that hath uttered

so honourable speeches of me and my service—that hath stopped my course on your own motion, not without some blemish to my credit—who might have prevented with your only commandment both your charge and mine in the beginning—will now so deal in the end as may increase my duty and prayer for you, and enlarge your own fame for cherishing your nobility and rewarding of true service." That was plainer language than the Queen liked to hear, and Essex received no favourable answer from her till May.

Meanwhile he lived, in something like disgrace, at Durham House, visited only by the few friends who cared to be friendly to him through his misfortunes, and with Philip Sidney for one of his most frequent visitors. Strong liking grew up between the two. To Essex, well-nigh exasperated by the many indignities he had received, and full of scorn for the fair pretences that had been made to him, the sympathy of the young courtier, who was resolved to be much more than a courtier, was welcome. In Sidney admiration for the brave enthusiast who had suffered so much left no room for discernment of his faults, which few at that time would regard as faults. There were more profit and more interest for him in the converse he had at Durham House than at Leicester House, or at Whitehall—except with his mother and sister,—or anywhere else, it may be. We have seen, and shall see again, that he had no great fondness for gorgeous gatherings and scenes of splendid idleness. He was never loth to dance with the fine ladies or to tilt with the fine gentlemen whom Eliza-

WALTER DEVEREUX, FIRST EARL OF ESSEX.

FROM AN ENGRAVING IN LODGE'S "PORTRAITS."

beth collected about her.   But at heart he preferred
the quiet company of friends he could trust, older
men like Languet and Walsingham and Essex, as
well as others nearer his own age like Greville and
Dyer.

Nor was there only male society for him at Durham House.   We hear of no intimacy between him
and Lettice, Countess of Essex.   This lively lady,
the daughter of the worthy Sir Francis Knollys,
whose wife was a niece of Anne Boleyn, and therefore first cousin to Queen Elizabeth, had never been
among the foremost favourites at Court ; and there
were already whispers about the too close attention
paid to her by the Earl of Leicester, who was certainly no friend to her husband.   Philip may not
have admired her ; but we may be sure that the
pretty frolicsome ways of her elder daughter, now
thirteen years old, were not distasteful to him.   Half
girl, half woman, Lady Penelope Devereux was just
old enough to begin exercising pleasant tyranny,
and doubtless liked well to be tyrannical.   Whatever
Philip thought about her at this time, or she about
him, it is important to note that the Earl of Essex
had begun to call him his son by adoption.

The Durham House meetings came to an end in
May, when Essex received his long-promised appointment as Earl-Marshal of Ireland, Leicester, it
was said, procuring this favour for him, not out of
kindness, but to get him away from England.   Soon
after that he went down to Chartley, and there, as
though anticipating the doom that was before him,
made careful arrangements for the disposal of his

estates.   He left Holyhead on the 22d of July, and
reached Dublin next day.   In the same month Philip
also went to Ireland on a visit to his father ; and
there can be no doubt that he travelled in company
with his friend.

"Good my lord, send Philip to me," Sir Henry
had written to the Earl of Leicester from Dundalk,
on the 4th of February ; "there was never father had
more need of his son than I have of him."   But the
Lord Deputy had to wait six months for his son's
visit, which then only lasted for a few weeks.   He
was busy in Connaught, suppressing a rising of the
people in the west which had been provoked by the
Earl of Clanricarde and his family, when he heard
that the Earl of Essex was on his way to Ireland,
bringing Philip with him.   He hurried up to Dublin
in August, there spent a few days in entertaining the
Earl of Essex and in formally investing him with his
office as Earl-Marshal, and then hastened back to the
rebellious district.

Philip accompanied his father to Athlone, where
they were on the 4th of September, and on to Galway.   He had a month's rough experience of the
work in which Gilbert, Raleigh, and many others
who were afterwards his friends passed some years
as soldiers in the service of Sir Henry and the viceroys before and after him.   To the young courtier it
must have been interesting to contrast and compare
the condition of affairs he had studied during his
foreign travels with the practical difficulties incident
to the plan, or almost planless vigour, with which
Ireland was being administered as an alien territory

under English domination. But on the 20th of September he was unexpectedly recalled to Dublin.

Immediately after the Sidneys, father and son, had left the Irish capital, the Earl of Essex had been taken suddenly and mysteriously ill. He had been seized with violent pains on the 20th of August, and these had continued and steadily increased through thirty days. No medicine the doctors provided was of any service to him. His body was racked with agonies that he bore with manly resignation, and his body wasted away. "The only care he had of any worldly matter," wrote one who watched him from first to last, probably Edward Waterhouse, a faithful follower of both Essex and Sir Henry Sidney, "was for his children, to whom often he commended his love and blessing, and yielded many times, even with great sighs and most devout prayers, unto God, that He would bless them and give them His grace to fear Him. For his daughters also he prayed, lamenting the time, which is so vain and ungodly, as he said, considering the frailness of women, lest they should learn of the vile world." He talked much, too, of the state of England, and grieved over it. "For they lean all to policy and let religion go," he complained; "would to God they would lean to religion and let policy go!"

On the 21st of September he died, not many hours after Philip Sidney had for the first time heard of his friend's illness, and of his "being most earnestly wished and written for" by him. "Oh, that good gentleman!" Essex had exclaimed two days before his death, and when he had lost hope of the young

man's coming to him in time—" Oh, that good gentleman! Have me commended unto him. And
tell him I sent him nothing, but I wish him well—so
well that, if God move their hearts, I wish that he
might match with my daughter. I call him son—he
so wise, virtuous, and godly. If he go on in the
course he hath begun, he will be as famous and
worthy a gentleman as ever England bred."

The message was delivered to Philip as he stood
weeping over the dead body of Essex. Sir Henry
Sidney, busy in Galway, did not hear the sad news
till some days later. " I left him," he wrote, " a
lusty, strong, and pleasant man ; but before I returned his breath was out of his body, his body out of
this country, and undoubtedly his soul in heaven."

The suddenness of Essex's illness, and the un-
natural pains he had endured, inclined many to the
suspicion that he had met his death by foul means.
The Lord Deputy promptly instituted a careful in-
quiry as to the circumstances of the case, but without result. No proof of poisoning could be found.
Still less was there anything to point out a probable
or possible poisoner. Eight years afterwards the
Lord Deputy's own brother-in-law, the Earl of Leicester, was anonymously accused of the crime, as he
had been previously accused of murdering his first
wife, Amy Robsart. The jealousy with which Leicester had regarded Essex, still more his unworthy
passion for Lady Essex, gave colour to the charge.
But there is no reasonable ground for admitting it.

Equally unfounded, as it seems, were the current
imputations against the fair fame of the Countess of

Essex. She may not, in these last years, have had much love for her slighted husband, who is not reported to have made any mention of her on his deathbed, and who was far too good a man for her to value at his worth ; and perhaps even before his death she may have had some evil affection for the Earl of Leicester. It is certain that she was married to Leicester two years after becoming a widow, and it is likely that she had been united to him long before by private rites. These were her offences. We can charge her with none greater.

Almost immediately after his good friend's death Philip Sidney returned to England and to Court ; in fulfilment, it would seem, of arrangements made with his father before he left Galway. We find him at Greenwich, where the Queen was staying, on the 4th of November. Somewhat later the Earl of Essex's remains were conveyed to Wales by Edward Waterhouse, and on the 29th of November they were deposited at Carmarthen, where he had held property.

By the Earl's death the fortunes of his family were improved in appearance and as far as standing at Court was concerned. Robert, the new earl, a pretty clever lad just ten years old, was already a favourite with the Queen, and he was taken under the protection of Lord Burghley, in whose household, from the beginning of the new year, he resided. " I protest unto your lordship," Waterhouse wrote on the 14th of November to Sir Henry Sidney, " that I do not think there is at this day so strong a man as the little Earl of Essex, nor any man more lamented than his father since the death of King Edward." Every one wished well to the children, he reported; "and all do expect what will become of the treaty between Mr. Philip Sidney and my Lady Penelope. Truly, my lord, I must say to your lordship, as I have said to my lord of Leicester and Mr. Philip, the breaking off from their match, if the default be on your parts, will turn to more dishonour than can be repaired with any marriage in England."

That enigmatic remark shows us that in Philip's twenty-second year there was a serious project for his being married to Lady Penelope Devereux. Had Penelope's father lived, the match—which he anxiously desired—would probably have been made. It was broken off, however, though with what dishonour is not apparent. Whatever pleasure Philip may have found in Penelope's society, it is likely that he was not himself very eager to be formally contracted to a damsel, not yet fifteen, who could scarcely become his wife for at least two or three years. While he was waiting her guardians deemed it better to find for her a wealthier husband, and there was nothing left for him to do but praise and worship her in sonnets.

LADIES' HEAD-DRESSES OF THE SIXTEENTH CENTURY

Prague

CHAPTER VII.

WORK AS AMBASSADOR.

1577.

OW Philip Sidney passed the three months following his return from Ireland is not on record. He was probably at Court, and gaining influence there. When we next have trace of him we find him appointed to an office which, if not of much importance, was at least of considerable dignity.

It was the rule in those days for every young man anxious to make his way in public life to be employed on one of the special missions to foreign sovereigns which were then plentiful, in order both that he might gain experience and that he might prove his fitness for more responsible duties. Occupation of this sort fell to Sidney soon after he had passed his twenty-second birthday, and it is characteristic of his ambitious temper that, young as he was, he somewhat grumbled at it—so his friend Fulke Greville tells us—as " sorting better with his youth than with his spirit," and that he only undertook it on condition that he should be allowed to render the business more serious and comprehensive than had been intended.

The Emperor Maximilian had died on the 12th of October, 1576, at the age of fifty and in the twelfth year of his reign. A wise monarch and an amiable man, he had worthily held the difficult position allotted to him. Closely bound by political and family ties to King Philip of Spain, he had quietly offered steady resistance to Philip's wicked projects. Although a Catholic, he had given open encouragement to Protestants, had allowed them to build churches and conduct worship wherever and however they chose, and had admitted many, like Hubert Languet, to places of trust and influence under him. As far as he could or dared, he had helped the Netherlanders in their brave struggle for religious liberty, and always, by his toleration of free thought and independent action, he had set a rare example of good rule. When his son Rudolph succeeded him all was changed. Trained by a fanatical mother, and for some time educated in Spain and in Spanish policy by Philip, who designed him for his heir, Rudolph had been corrupted by superstition and bigotry. Among his first acts were the persecution of Protestants, the banishment of their leaders, and the forcing of orthodox catechisms upon their schools.

Nor was the accession of Rudolph the Second the only disaster that at this time fell upon Germany. The Elector Palatine, Frederick the Third, had died two days after Maximilian. Frederick had stirred up strife among his people by the violent introduction of Calvinism, and his elder son Lewis was now causing fresh confusion by the violent establishment of Lutheran doctrine and the attempted stamping out of Calvinist tenets, while John Casimir, the other son, was a sturdy champion of the proscribed creed. Bigots of both sects, therefore, each receiving much encouragement, fought desperately for the mastery, and tolerant, charitable men hung down their heads and were heavy-hearted as to the issue of the conflict.

Things were faring ill, too, in the Low Countries. "The pacification of Ghent," as it was called, had been negotiated by Prince William of Orange in the same eventful month, November, 1576, and it gave promise that the Netherlanders, having ostensibly settled the differences among themselves, would be able to make a bold front against the tyranny of King Philip, which had been somewhat languid of late. But straightway Don John of Austria, Philip's half-brother, arrived as a new viceroy in the Low Countries, and made terms with the southern Netherlanders, against the treachery of which William warned them in vain.

In February, 1577, or a little earlier, it was arranged that Philip Sidney should proceed to Prague, taking Heidelberg on his way, to convey messages of condolence, and also of congratulation, to the orphans who had lately become Emperor and Elector Palatine, and to assure them of Queen Elizabeth's good will. Sidney asked and obtained leave to do more

8

than that, to confer both with these princes and with others whom he might visit about the condition of Europe in so far as it affected the welfare of the reformed religion and the progress of civil liberty. At his request, we are told, the instructions were so worded as to leave him free to do anything, so far as talking went, that seemed to him expedient for encouraging union among the various Protestant states and spurring them on to more vigorous effort in the common cause.

The instructions were dated the 7th of February. On the 21st he received £350 from his father, * sent to augment the scanty allowance made by the Queen for his expenses; and a day or two after that he started on his journey. With him went his friend Fulke Greville, released for a time from his duties in Wales; also, among others, Sir Henry Lee, Sir Jerome Bowes, Mr. Basset, Mr. Cressy, and Mr. Brouker.† Of these companions the two knights, at any rate, were considerably his seniors. Sir Henry Lee, now about forty-six, was an indefatigable courtier, famous for his prowess in the tilt-yard and his tact in such ceremonial duties at foreign courts as did not call for much statesmanship. Sir Jerome Bowes, as old, if not older, was also often sent abroad in subordinate capacities; but he was a Puritan, with a political conscience that prevented his rising high or keeping steady place in royal favour. Both men were doubtless useful advisers to Sidney in the work now assigned to him.

---

* Penshurst MSS.
† Belvoir MSS.

Sidney was evidently resolved to make the most of the work. Over the houses at which he lodged during his travels he caused to be fixed a tablet, bearing his arms, and announcing his title in pompous Latin, to the following purport: "The most illustrious and well-born Philip Sidney, son of the Viceroy of Ireland, nephew of the Earls of Warwick and Leicester, ambassador from the most serene Queen of England to the Emperor."

Crossing over to Antwerp, he reached Brussels on or soon after the 1st of March. Thence, on the 5th, he rode out with Dr. Thomas Wilson, the English ambassador in the Netherlands, to pay respects to Don John of Austria, who was then at Louvain. He and Mr. Sidney, Wilson reported, were much pleased with the audience they had on the 6th, when Don John gave a fair and sweet answer to the plain words they addressed to him, and made promises that would be altogether satisfactory if they were in very deed performed.* At the interview, Fulke Greville tells us, Don John began to speak courteously, but with much Spanish haughtiness and show of condescension, to the almost beardless visitor. "Yet after a while, when he had taken his just altitude, he found himself so stricken with this extraordinary planet that the beholders wondered to see what ingenious tribute that brave and high-minded prince paid to his worth, giving more honour and respect to this hopeful young gentleman than to the ambassadors of mighty princes."

---

* State Papers, Foreign, Elizabeth; Wilson to Walsingham, 1, 5, and 10 March, 1577.

It is not likely that Sidney was deceived by the specious talk of Don John, who certainly was brave in his own way, but, as Sidney was well aware, by no means high-minded. Just now, however, Don John was deceiving many who had much wider experience than his visitor. With silver speech and golden coin he was beguiling the Flemings and others, all but those sturdy Hollanders who maintained their faith in William of Orange, into such misreading of the "pacification of Ghent" as would place them at his mercy and prepare for the formal and splendid entry into Brussels which he was to make on the 1st of May, before Sidney had returned from his journey to the south.

Proceeding to Heidelberg, the capital of the Palatinate, which he reached on the 17th or 18th of March, Sidney found that the Elector Lewis was absent; but he spent a few days with Lewis's brother, Count John Casimir, to whom he conveyed a private letter from the Earl of Leicester, as well as more official messages from Queen Elizabeth and her Council. John Casimir, being a Calvinist like his father, was thought better of in England than the Lutheran Lewis. Sidney was commissioned to urge him to waive his scruples so far as to live at peace with his brother, and to do his share towards putting an end to the feud among Protestants which was a scandal to both sects and a source of danger to the cause of religion. In letters that he wrote from Heidelberg to Lord Burghley and Sir Francis Walsingham, Sidney reported that he feared the "jar" would continue, but that there was something to be hoped from John Casimir, who only went to extremes through a mistaken conscientiousness.

The subject-matter of these letters fills so unimportant a place in the history of sectarian quarrelling in the sixteenth century that they are only interesting as showing the nature of Sidney's experiments in diplomacy. His correspondence further indicates that he made careful inquiries as to the way in which the German states were affected by the political movements in France and the Low Countries, and what was the probable policy of the Emperor Rudolph, whom he was about to visit.

One of the topics of his conversation was amusing. It seems that Queen Elizabeth had lent some money to the Elector Palatine lately dead, and Sidney was commissioned to claim repayment. But the Heidelberg exchequer, John Casimir assured him, was all but bankrupt; the French king had failed in his engagement for the paying of certain large sums, and consequently neither Elizabeth nor the knights of the Palatinate, who provided its soldiery, could receive what was due. "I told him," Sidney wrote, "it would be a cause to make her Majesty withdraw from like loans, as the well-paying would give her cause to do it in greater sums. He was grieved with my urging of him, and assured me that if he could get the payment he would rather die than not see her Majesty honourably satisfied. Then I pressed him for certain jewels and hostages I had learned he had in pawn of the French king. He told me they already belonged to the knights; but if her Majesty would buy any of them, she might have a good bargain." The outlook was not bright; but, Sidney added, "Truly, by what I find in the prince, I do hold myself in good belief that her Majesty, within a year or two, shall be honourably answered it."

On the 23d of March Sidney and his suite left Heidelberg and, after looking in vain for the Elector Lewis on their way, passed on to Prague, where the Emperor Rudolph, in his capacity of King of Bohemia, was then staying.

Exactly two years previously Sidney had quitted the city on his return to England. He had come there in company with Hubert Languet, to be present at the Emperor Maximilian's opening of the Bohemian Diet. On that occasion the Emperor had granted to the Bohemians complete freedom in religious matters, and had promised that he and his family would protect them in the same. It was true, he said, that his sons had attached themselves to the Catholic faith; but he had so taught them to love truth and honesty in any form that holders of a different creed had no reason to fear them. The good man neither thought how soon his eldest son would take his place, nor knew how bigoted that son was becoming. Everything looked pleasant then, and the members of the Diet, in return for the favours done to them, elected Prince Rudolph King of Bohemia.

Now Maximilian was dead, Rudolph was Emperor as well as King, and the aspect of affairs was greatly altered. The Bohemians too stoutly held the principles they inherited from Huss and Jerome to admit so much change as Rudolph was effecting elsewhere ; but even they had heavy grounds for alarm. There was no need for Languet, who had gone to Heidelberg to meet Sidney, and who accompanied him to Prague, to inform him of the dark clouds that were hanging over the city and people.

The young ambassador entered Prague on Maundy Thursday, and witnessed the sombre services of Good Friday and the less mournful ceremonies of Easter Sunday, performed by the crowd of priests in attendance on Rudolph and his Court. On Easter Monday he had audience of the Emperor, and, presenting his letters, made suitable discourse.

After assuring Rudolph of the sorrow caused to his mistress and to England by the death of one so worthy as the late Emperor, Sidney went on to say that his Queen desired to be as closely linked in friendship with the son as she had been with the father, and implored him to emulate the private and public virtues of which he had so grand an example. He had been suddenly called to be the foremost potentate in Europe ; on the conduct of his rule largely depended the welfare or the ruin of Christendom ; oh, that he would resolve to follow in the steps of the noble Emperor who was gone ! In Elizabeth's name Sidney urged Rudolph to promote peace both at home and abroad, to give no ear to such violent counsel as some restless courtiers are apt to offer to young princes, and to remember that of idle wars the issues are uncertain, the benefits none, and the harm manifest ; for war, at best, is full of danger, and allowable only in cases of great peril and of great necessity, when public maladies can in no other way be remedied.

In speaking thus far Sidney did little more than repeat and expand the words of his instructions. He added bolder language of his own, prompted by his discernment—doubtless under Languet's guidance—of the evil influences that were gaining ground at Rudolph's Court. He besought the Emperor and his ministers to rouse themselves, and, looking around, to see what dangers were threatening them and growing greater every hour. Whence came these dangers, he asked, save from the fatal conjunction of Rome's undermining superstitions with the commanding forces of Spain?

Thus addressed, as Fulke Greville informs us, the proud Emperor and his frigid courtiers were startled, and their surprise was so great that there was little place for wrath. Sidney saw his advantage, and pursued the theme. This, he declared, was no time for listlessness. Neither its inland situation, its vast population, its natural wealth, nor its valiant soldiery, could protect the great German commonwealth from the dangers threatening it. Such advantages might have sufficed before, but they were not strong enough now; for there was arrayed against it a more baneful league than had ever yet been known. Had not those two powers, Rome and Spain, united in a brotherhood of evil, already shed so much blood that they were become the terror of all other governments? Even now there was but one way of withstanding the great league between them. It could be faced by no other means than the formation of another league, a league of all the nations that cared for their freedom. This, Sidney urged, was the only safeguard ; but here there was real safety. " A bond of conscience for the protection of religion and liberty " would furnish a stronger rampart against the tyrannies of Spain and Rome than " any factious combination in policy, any league of state, or other traffic of civil or martial humours."

The Emperor Rudolph was not converted by the daring discourse of the twenty-two years old ambassador. He tendered his thanks for the assurance of Queen Elizabeth's good-will, and spoke haughtily as to the course he should adopt in the present troublous times. God, he said, was the protector of the empire, and would, he trusted, provide him with fit counsel for its government. Then he wandered off into talk on general affairs, and made no answer to Sidney's appeal.

Judging from this day's experience and from other observations, Sidney concluded, as he reported, that Rudolph was treacherous, Jesuit-bound, and " extremely Spaniolated," a man of few words and sullen disposition, lacking his father's winning manner towards strangers, yet with some skill in controlling those around him.

Next day the ambassador visited Maximilian's widow and widowed daughter. " I delivered her Majesty's letters to the Empress," he wrote, " with the singular signification of her Majesty's good-will unto her, and her Majesty's wishing of her to advise her son to a wise and peaceable government. Of the

Emperor deceased I used but few words, because, in truth, I saw it bred some trouble unto her to hear him mentioned in that kind. She answered me with many courteous speeches and great acknowledging of her own beholdingness to her Majesty; and, for her son, she said she hoped he would do well, but that for her own part she had given herself from the world, and would not greatly stir from thenceforward in it. Then did I deliver to the Queen of France her letter, she standing by the Empress; using such speeches as I thought were fit for her double sorrow and her Majesty's good-will unto her, confirmed by her wise and noble governing of herself in the time of her being in France." This lady, whom Sidney must have known while he was Gentleman of the King's Bedchamber in Paris four and a half years earlier, was Elizabeth, daughter of Maximilian, and widow of the French king, Charles the Ninth, who had died wretchedly in 1574, tormented by delirious recollections of the St. Bartholomew massacre. She had done all she could to promote peace between the opposite parties in France, whereby, if no other benefit resulted, she had won the respect of all right-minded thinkers on both sides. She was now living in retirement with her mother, and preparing to join the sisterhood of St. Anne. "Her answer was full of humbleness," the ambassador reported; "but she spake so low that I could not understand many of her words."

The few remaining days of Sidney's visit to Prague were spent by him in studying the condition of public affairs, and in converse with old friends,

among whom Languet was foremost, as well as with some new acquaintances. One of these acquaintances tells how he and others were entertained by the ambassador's " very memorable discourses," of which he gives two samples. On one occasion Sidney explained to his foreign friends how it was that wolves had been killed off in England, where formerly they had been as plentiful as in Germany, or as they still were in Scotland and Ireland. On another day his learned conversation was, according to the same informant, " touching Ireland, where his father governed, and of St. Patrick's Hole, much esteemed when time was, at this day little set by." *
His talk, it is added, " was very pleasing to the company that sat at table with him, and no man would make any question thereof, especially when he saw it approved by Hubert Languet, a man of most excellent judgment and exceedingly well travelled in the knowledge of things and in the affairs of the world." †

Sidney left Prague near the end of April, after further interviews and farewell speech with the Emperor, of whom he had formed so poor an opinion, albeit just; an opinion which was not altered by the handsome gold chain that Rudolph presented to him at their parting.

---

* " St. Patrick's Hole " was probably St. Patrick's Purgatory, the island in Lough Derg to which pilgrims went to do penance in mediæval times, and which Sidney must have passed on his way from Dublin to Galway, about seven months before.

† " The Living Librarie of Meditations and Observations, Historical, Natural, Moral, Political and Poetical " ; written in Latin by P.Camerarius, and done into English by John Molle (1625), p. 99.

On his homeward journey he performed the second of the two duties primarily assigned to him. To the Elector Lewis, whom he met at Neustadt on the 1st of May, he repeated Queen Elizabeth's messages of condolence on the death of his father, and persuasions to unity between him and his brother. "One thing," said Sidney, "I was bold to add in my speech, to desire him, in her Majesty's name, to have merciful consideration of the Church of the religion so notably established by his father, as in all Germany there is not such a number of excellent men ; and truly any man would rue to see the desolation of them "—that is, of the Calvinists oppressed by the Lutherans. "I laid before him, as well as I could, the dangers of the mightiest princes of Christendom by entering into like violent changes, and the wrong he should do his worthy father by utterly abolishing that he had instituted, and so, as it were, condemning him, besides the example he should give to his posterity to handle him the like. This I emboldened myself to do, seeing, as methought, great cause for it, either to move him at least to have some regard for her Majesty's sake, or, if that followed not, yet to leave with the Church of Germany public testimony that her Majesty was careful of them." The substance of the long answer he received was that the Elector Lewis had no personal misliking of the Calvinists, and that he would gladly do much for the Queen's sake, but that he could not help acting as did other princes in Germany.

From Neustadt, Sidney went to Lauterburg, there to have further conference with John Casimir as to the possibilities of protecting the Calvinists from Lutheran persecution and of bringing about a general Protestant league.* He was thus occupied from the 4th till the 8th of May. Then, preparing to return to England, on his way he paid a visit to the Land-grave William of Hesse, about which we have no details, and he reached Cologne about the middle of the month. The task assigned to him by Queen Elizabeth had been completed, and the larger task he had obtained leave to undertake had been bravely attempted; but he was by no means satis-fied with the result.

It is not easy in this nineteenth century to take much interest in the squabbles of German Calvinists and Lutherans in the latter part of the sixteenth century; but these were grave and momentous then, and, if we wonder somewhat at young Philip Sidney's boldness in aspiring to patch up the squabbles, or rather to remove them and their causes, we must greatly commend the motives that prompted him. His motives and his boldness were notable. Two strong desires possessed him now and to the end of his life. The one was the overthrow of Papal and Spanish tyranny, the double-headed foe to political freedom and to what he regarded as the only true form of religion. The other was the sink-ing of all dissensions among Protestants, in order

---

* State Papers, Foreign, Elizabeth; John Casimir to the Queen's Council, 8 May, 1577. Where no authority is given for the details in this chapter, they are repeated from documents (chiefly among the Cottonian and Harleian MSS. in the British Museum), quoted in my "Memoir of Sir Philip Sidney." I have corrected two or three errors of date therein.

that they might not only live together in peace, but might also be able to withstand the encroachments and to baffle the treacheries of Spain and Rome.

He had found very little to cheer him in his embassage. He had seen with his own eyes how great was the risk of the Emperor Rudolph destroying all the benefits that the Emperor Maximilian had conferred on the princes and people under him or within his influence. He was forced to admit that the Protestant league, which his heart was set on forming, met with favour from none but John Casimir, and one or two others, and that even they were disposed to enter upon it rather out of compliment to Queen Elizabeth than for any stronger reason. The rest of the Protestant leaders, he mournfully declared, thought only of growing rich and amusing themselves, of seeking their own safety—which was no safety—though all the world might be on fire around them. " Every day," he wrote, " my hope grows less and less."

Hubert Languet, to whom Sidney chiefly owed his enthusiasm on this subject, had been with him during several weeks. At Cologne they parted. The noble old Huguenot had to go back to his duties and his griefs in Prague, or Vienna, or other parts of Germany. " I received incredible delight from our intercourse," he wrote a month later ; "but I feel now just as they do who gladly drink too much water when they are hot, and get a fever in consequence. My great pleasure brought about a greater sorrow than I ever before endured ; and it has by no means left me now."

Meanwhile Sidney made a more agreeable ending of his tour as diplomatist than he had expected. The mission assigned to him being over, as he thought, he was anxious to go on a private visit to Prince William of Orange; but from this Languet dissuaded him, on the ground that the Queen might be angry if he exceeded his instructions. He was well pleased when a letter arrived from England, bidding him turn aside in his homeward journey in order to convey to William her Majesty's congratulations on the birth of his son.*

Having reached Antwerp on or before the 27th of May, the ambassador accordingly proceeded on that day to Breda, and thence on the 28th to Geertruiden-berg, where he met the Prince of Orange, and was by him taken to Dort, or Dordrecht, William's residence at that time. The three or four days that followed not only sufficed for the formal delivery of his message by Sidney and for his sharing in the christening ceremony, when he stood godfather to the lately born baby, but also afforded opportunity for the establishment of a firm friendship between the sturdy champion of Dutch liberties, now forty-four years old, and the young Englishman of two-and-twenty, who was dreaming of and sighing for the regeneration of all Europe by means of a Protestant league.

Leaving Dordrecht on the 2d of June, with a letter of thanks from Prince William to Queen Elizabeth in his charge, and a " fair jewel " which

---

* State Papers, Domestic, Elizabeth ; Dr. Thomas Wilson to Lord Burghley, 28 May, 1577, and the Prince of Orange to Queen Elizabeth, 2 June, 1577.

the Princess of Orange had given him as a keepsake,
Sidney made quick passage to London, where he
and all his suite arrived in good health, with the
exception of Fulke Greville, whom sea-sickness
compelled to lie by at Rochester.

Mr. Secretary Walsingham wrote thus on the 9th
of June from Greenwich, where the Queen was holding Court, to the Lord Deputy : " I am to impart
unto you the return of the young gentlemen, Mr.
Sidney, your son, whose message, very sufficiently
performed, and the relating thereof, is no less grate-
fully received and well liked of her Majesty than
the honourable opinion he hath left behind with all
the princes with whom he had to negotiate hath left
a most sweet savour and grateful remembrance of
his name in those parts.   The gentleman hath given
no small arguments of great hope, the fruits whereof
I doubt not but your lordship shall reap, as the
benefit of the good parts that are in him, and whereof
he hath given some taste in this voyage, is to re-
dound to more than your lordship and himself.
There hath not been any gentleman, I am sure,
these many years, that hath gone through so honourable a charge with as great commendations as
he : in consideration whereof I could not but com-
municate this part of my joy with your lordship,
being no less refreshing unto me in these my
troublesome businesses than the soil is to the chafed
stag."

STATE CARRIAGE OF QUEEN ELIZABETH

CHAPTER VIII.

AS SON AND COURTIER.

1577–1578.

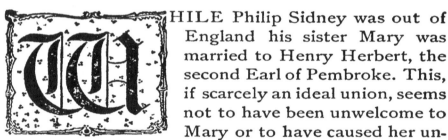

HILE Philip Sidney was out of England his sister Mary was married to Henry Herbert, the second Earl of Pembroke. This, if scarcely an ideal union, seems not to have been unwelcome to Mary or to have caused her unhappiness, and it was helpful to Philip in providing him with another relative at Court who, though less influential, was richer and worthier than his uncle, the Earl of Leicester.

The Earl of Pembroke's father, whose wife was sister to Catherine Parr, the last consort of Henry the Eighth, had been in great favour during that monarch's later years, and had acquired much wealth by the spoliation of Church lands. He had prospered as a zealous Protestant in King Edward's day, as a zealous Catholic under Queen Mary, and as a zealous Protestant again under Queen Elizabeth, until his death in 1570. To please the Duke of Northumberland, he had married his son, then Lord Herbert and a youth of about sixteen, to Catherine, the sister of Lady Jane Grey, on the day of Lady Jane's marriage with Lord Guildford Dudley; but this union was never completed, and the parties were divorced five weeks afterwards with Queen Mary's consent. Lord Herbert's first real wife, Lady Catherine Talbot, daughter of the Earl of Shrewsbury, died in 1575. Mainly, it would seem, by the Earl of Leicester's arrangement, but with Sir Henry Sidney's full concurrence, the widower—now Earl of Pembroke and owner of Baynard's Castle, the sometime royal palace near to Paul's Wharf on the Thames; of Wilton, the stateliest mansion in Wiltshire; and of half a score of other houses and demesnes—was in the spring of 1577 secured as a husband for Mistress Mary Sidney. The lady was not yet sixteen years of age; her husband was forty.

" I find to my exceeding great comfort," Sir Henry wrote to his brother-in-law from Ireland, " the likelihood of a marriage between my lord of Pembroke and my daughter; which great honour to me, my mean lineage and kin, I attribute to my match in your noble house. So joyfully have I at heart that my dear child hath so happy an advancement as this is, as, in troth, I would lie in close prison a year rather than it should break." There was evident exaggeration in Sir Henry Sidney's phrases, but it is clear that he approved the match, and, poor as he was, he undertook to provide his daughter with a dowry of £2,000, which he confessed to be very

much smaller than such a son-in-law might expect.*
"In troth," he said in his letter to Leicester, "I have
it not; but borrow it I must, and so I will. And if
your lordship will get me leave that I may feast my
eyes with that joyful sight of their coupling, I will
give her a cup worth £500. Good my lord, bear
with my poverty; for, if I had it, little would I
regard any sum of money, but willingly would give
it, protesting before Almighty God that if He and
all the powers on earth would give me my choice of
a husband for her, I would choose the Earl of
Pembroke."

Leave was not given to Sir Henry to be present at
the wedding, which took place on the 21st of April.
At the end of May Leicester went down to Wilton
to tender his compliments to the new Countess of
Pembroke, and Philip followed on the same errand
about two months later, as soon as he could be
spared from Court.

This visit to Wilton in July, 1577, was the first of
many. Henceforward, whenever he could absent
himself from Court, Philip seems to have gone
oftener to Wilton than to Penshurst for rest and
refreshment. When in London, also, he appears to
have been as much at home in Baynard's Castle, the
abode of his sister and her husband, as at Leicester
House. He was generally, however, like his mother,
in close attendance on the Queen, and moving about
with her.

---

* In a letter written a year later, Sir Henry Sidney gave the amount
of his daughter's dowry, for which he had made himself responsible,
as £3,000.

He was at Greenwich with Elizabeth and her other chief favourites for some little time after his return to England in June. Thence he followed the Court to Richmond, and at the end of the month he was thinking of going to Ireland on a second visit to his father. His father was just now in need of all the comfort Philip's society could give him; but the project was abandoned, apparently because it was found that Philip might be more useful to Sir Henry in England than in Ireland. .

The Lord Deputy's sturdy performance of his duty had again, as in each of his earlier terms of office in Ireland, brought upon him the opposition of the Earl of Ormond and the other Irish noblemen who professed allegiance to the Queen; and the Queen, as heretofore, took the noblemen's side, partly because she liked flattery, and partly because Sir Henry Sidney, in his efforts to keep order in the country, persisted in spending more money than she approved. "That Henry Sidney," she exclaimed once, and perhaps many times, stamping with her foot the while, "doth always seek to put us to charge." And she objected as much to charge being laid upon Ormond and the others as upon herself.

That was the state of affairs when Philip Sidney returned to his place, and took higher place than he had yet occupied, in Queen Elizabeth's favour. All through the summer of 1577, except during the few weeks he passed at Wilton, he was busy, while himself in the sunshine of the royal smile, considering and scheming with Walsingham and others, especially

with Edward Waterhouse, who was at this time a
sort of agent of Sir Henry in England, how to
remove from his father the shadow of the royal
frown.   At the end of August Waterhouse went to
Wilton, " as well to do my duty to the Countess of
Pembroke "—so he wrote to Sir Henry—" as to have
some speech with Mr. Philip concerning your lordship's affairs, and to understand his advice, what
course he would have me take in your lordship's
defence ; who, because he found such daily alterations in Court, could advise me none otherwise but
to refer me in discretion to do as I saw cause."

There was not much sign of daily alterations, but
rather steady anger on the Queen's part against Sir
Henry, when Mr. Philip hurried up to London after
Waterhouse.   Joining the Court at Oatlands, he
found among other visitors the Earl of Ormond ;
and there was an awkward meeting between Sir
Henry's son and Sir Henry's traducer.   Ormond
stepped up to young Sidney and began to address
him in patronising terms ; whereupon young Sidney
eyed him haughtily and turned his back upon him.
" Mr. Philip," Waterhouse reported, " was in dead
silence of purpose, because he imputeth to the earl
such practices as have been made to alienate her
Majesty's mind from your lordship."   But the bloodshed that the onlookers expected did not follow.
Some one—perhaps Burghley, or it may have been
the Queen herself — intervened, and peace was
patched up.   " The Earl of Ormond," added Waterhouse, " saith he will accept no controversies from a
gentleman that is bound by nature to defend his

father's cause, and who is otherwise furnished with so many virtues as he knows Mr. Philip to be ; and on the other side Mr. Philip hath gone as far and showed as much magnanimity as is convenient."

Philip, indignant at the way in which his father was being treated, not only refused to speak with the Earl of Ormond, but spoke out very forcibly to the Queen. Of a long letter, long enough and closely argued enough to be called a treatise, which he handed to her Majesty on one of the last days in September, only a portion has come down to us, and that not in its finished state, but in his rough draft, with erasures and alterations, careless slips of grammar, and jottings down in the margin of further matters to be touched upon. It was divided into seven sections, the first three of which are missing. Those we have present a masterly defence of Sir Henry Sidney's policy and a trenchant attack on the Earl of Ormond and the other Irish noblemen who claimed the privilege of being exempt from taxation. " And privileged persons, forsooth," he said, " be all the rich men of the Pale, the burden only lying on the poor, who may groan, for their prayer cannot be heard. And, Lord ! to see how shamefully they will speak of their country that be indeed the tyrannous oppressors of their country."

Philip's contention was that his father's plan for the government of Ireland was really the most economical that could be devised in the interests of the Queen, and the most generous and just towards the people. It aimed at nothing more nor less than the levying of equal taxes from all and the spending of those taxes in maintaining such firm discipline as would enable the honest to thrive and would press hardly on wrong-doers alone. The true persecutors and despoilers of the Irish people, he urged, were the nobles of the Pale, robbers and wasters of the country's wealth, and breeders of intolerable mischiefs. If his father was severe either on these nobles or on the common folk, his severity was not a whit more than was needful in dealing with people so turbulent by nature and so easily led astray by their chiefs. For him to have been over-lenient would have been wrong and foolish. "Truly the general nature of all countries not fully conquered is against it. For until they find the sweetness of due subjection, it is impossible that any gentle means should put out the fresh remembrances of their lost liberty. And that the Irishman is that way as obstinate as any nation, with whom no other passion can prevail but fear—besides their history, which plainly points it out,—their manner of life, wherein they choose rather all filthliness than any law, and their own consciences, who best know their own natures, give sufficient proof. For under the sun there is not a nation that live more tyrannously than they do one over the other; and, truly, even in her Majesty's time, the rebellion of O'Neill and all the Earl of Ormond's brethren show well how little force any grateful love doth bear with them."

Philip Sidney's defence of his father proves that he had thoroughly mastered the state of affairs in his day, and could give solid reasons for the policy which Sir Henry deemed to be the only right policy.

Its logic, or the favour with which the writer was regarded by Queen Elizabeth, rendered it for a while successful. Having read it through after it had been handed to her at Windsor, the Queen declared herself satisfied with its arguments. Lord Burghley also took the same view, and backed up his young friend. Moreover, a day or two later there arrived a letter from Sir Henry containing documents supporting Philip's statements. These had weight. "But let no man compare with Mr. Philip's pen," wrote Waterhouse to the Lord Deputy on the 30th of September. "I know he will send it to your lordship, and when you read it you shall have more cause to pray God for him than to impute affection to me in this opinion of him."

Philip's friends had good reason to be proud of his success in curbing Queen Elizabeth's wrath against his father, and that without bringing any disfavour on himself. But it was only for a time that the Queen was pacified. For a few months she sent friendly letters and messages to the Lord Deputy, and then the old grievances were revived. On the 20th of January, 1578, Walsingham gave private warning to Sir Henry that he must expect to be recalled because her Majesty objected as much as ever to the vigour with which he was doing his work and the expenses he was incurring thereby. The letter of recall was actually sent off in March; but Sir Henry was not able to comply with it until September.

All through this trying period his interests were carefully watched, and as far as might be, protected,

by Philip; and not by Philip alone. "In the meantime," Philip wrote on the 25th of April, in a
letter counselling his father to remain at his post,
"your friends may labour here to bring to a better
pass such your reasonable and honourable desires,
which time can better bring forth than speech; and
among which friends, before God, there is none pro-
ceeds either so thoroughly or so wisely as your lady,
my mother. For mine own part, I have had only
light from her."

Except during the three or four weeks he passed
at Wilton in July and August, 1577, and perhaps
some other and shorter holidays at Penshurst, Philip
seems to have been in almost constant attendance
on the Queen for more than two years after his
return from Germany; usually going with her when
she went to keep Court at Richmond, or Windsor,
or any other of her own or her subjects' houses in
the country, and, when she was in London, taking up
his abode, at such times as he could be spared from
the royal presence, either at Baynard's Castle or at
Leicester House. The Queen, as she may have
thought, atoned for her unkindness to the father by
making much of the son, and, if Philip even at
this early stage sometimes found court life irksome,
we may be sure that it yielded him plenty of enjoyment. He had several friends of sterling worth
whose tastes agreed with his own, and in whose
society he could find relief from the excess of
gaieties around him. He had serious public affairs
to interest himself in, moreover, in addition to those
connected with his father's work. His correspond-

ence with Languet shows that he followed closely all the political and religious movements abroad: and he had other foreign correspondents, William of Orange and John Casimir among the number.

In the summer of 1577 Philip du Plessis-Mornay was sent to England to press upon Elizabeth the claims of Henry of Navarre and French Protestant-ism for assistance. He, like Sidney, had been in Paris before and at the time of the St. Bartholomew massacre, and he had there been much in the company of Languet, his devoted friend. But Sidney appears to have then barely made his acquaintance or not to have known him at all. He now brought a letter of introduction to the rising courtier, doubtless from Languet, and they learnt to value one another. " I am delighted to hear that you have become inti-mate with Du Plessis," Languet wrote ; " you cannot possibly have such another friend " ; and the remark was hardly extravagant. Mornay was one of the noblest of the many noble men among the Hugue-nots. All praised him for his gracious manners, his sound learning, his great wisdom, and his thorough goodness of heart. When in June, 1578, he paid another visit to England, bringing his wife with him, Sidney stood as godfather to their infant daughter. Five or six years later Sidney translated a portion of one of Mornay's books, " A Work concerning the Trueness of the Christian Religion."

Sidney soon came to be regarded as the most proper Englishman for foreign Protestants to seek help from when they visited England, more trust-worthy than his uncle, the Earl of Leicester, and

BAYNARD'S CASTLE:

WITH THE TOWER OF OLD SAINT PAUL'S CATHEDRAL IN THE BACKGROUND.

From an engraving by W. Wise.

with more time to give to them than Sir Francis
Walsingham or the other great officers of state. One
such was Baron Henry of Lichtenstein, a kinsman, it
would seem, of Sidney's old friend Count Lewis of
Hanau. Sidney showed him all the courtesy he
could in 1577, but afterwards he sent a message of
apology for any omissions, on the ground that he
was at the time so much occupied with his father's
business. "He is certainly an excellent young
man," he wrote. "Whenever any of his friends come
hither, I shall endeavour to atone for my fault."

At this time, as at others, our handsome young
courtier, liked by nearly all, and, if envied, envied
without grudge, was evidently anxious to be useful,
as well as ornamental, while he was in attendance on
Queen Elizabeth and during such leisure as he could
find.

We have an interesting glimpse of him among the
other courtiers on New Year's Day, 1578, when there
was the usual heaping up of presents to the Queen,
tendered as marks of true respect or as duties it was
not prudent to neglect. The Earl of Leicester was,
of course, prominent in this sort of homage. He
handed to his sovereign a splendid ornament of
wrought gold, loaded with diamonds, rubies, and
opals. Then followed other gifts, some of them
very curious and very characteristic of the givers.
The pompous Earl of Ormond brought a golden
phœnix, whose wings and feet glittered with rubies
and diamonds, and which rested on a branch covered
with other precious stones. Sir Christopher Hatton
tendered a cross of diamonds, bearing a suitable

motto ; also a golden trinket, imaging a dog leading a man over a bridge, which was bordered with
gems.   Lord Cobham handed up a petticoat of yellow satin, laid all over with ornaments of silver and
silk, and lined with tawny sarcenet; and his wife
presented a white petticoat, similarly adorned.   The
Countess of Essex, widow of Philip Sidney's good
friend, offered a dainty little parcel of ruffs.   Yet
daintier was Lady Sidney's gift of a pair of perfumed gloves, together with four and twenty small
buttons of gold, each having a tiny diamond set in
its centre.   Her daughter, the Countess of Pembroke, brought a doublet of lawn, embroidered with
gold and silver and silk of divers colours, and lined
with yellow taffeta.   In odd contrast was her son
Philip's present of a cambric smock, its sleeves and
collar wrought with black work, and edged with
a small bone-lace of gold and silver.   With it was a
pair of ruffs, interlaced with gold and silver, and set
with spangles which alone weighed four ounces.
Sidney and his friend Fulke Greville must have
taken counsel together, for Greville also brought
a cambric smock, very similarly decorated.   His
other great friend, Edward Dyer, with what may
have been better taste, presented a kirtle made
of lawn and embroidered with flowers in gold.

In return for all these presents, and scores of
others, down to the nightcaps and the pocket-
handkerchiefs and the tooth-cloths given by the
servants, the Queen made an almost invariable
allowance of gilt plate, which enabled her to mete
out her thanks by scale.   The Earl of Leicester,

this New Year's Day, received a hundred ounces, while the Earl of Ormond was honoured with a hundred and sixty-one, and Sir Christopher Hatton, just now floating on the high tide of queenly favour, was freighted with as much as four hundred ounces' weight of royal love. These leading courtiers and a few others were, of course, far above the average. It was no slight upon Lady Sidney that she received a present weighing but thirty ounces and three quarters, or upon the Countess of Pembroke that to her only two pounds' weight was given. Queen Elizabeth's affection for Philip Sidney was good for two and twenty ounces, while to Edward Dyer was set down a gift weighing sixteen ounces, and to Fulke Greville another weighing thirteen ounces.

We must not suppose either that Sidney had no pleasure in his almost constant dangling about the Court in the months after as well as before this New Year's Day of 1578, because he often complained about it, or that his complaints were not genuine. There is real pathos in a letter he wrote to Languet from Court on the 1st of March. "The use of the pen," he here said, "has plainly gone from me, and my mind, if ever it was active about anything, is now, by reason of my indolent sloth, beginning imperceptibly to lose its strength, and to lose it without any reluctance. For with what end should our thoughts be directed to various kinds of knowledge, unless the knowledge is put to use for the public good?" And he added: "You see that I am already playing the stoic. Unless you reclaim me, I shall quickly become a cynic too."

There was always a touch of cynicism, along with a fair amount of stoicism, in Sidney's temperament, and both were called out by his experiences just now as enforced attendant on the Queen, and as zealous champion of his father's interests. But there was diversion for him, leading to the formation of new friendships or the strengthening of some that had been already begun, in his participation in the summer holidays of the Court, which in 1578 were livelier than usual, and which were commenced near the end of April.

Going first to Theobalds, in Essex, the residence of Lord Burghley, the Queen lodged there for three or four days, and then proceeded to Wanstead. This place had been purchased a year or so before by the Earl of Leicester, and now, having been fitted up in princely style, it was honoured by a visit from the Queen. No such splendid series of entertainments as those for which Kenilworth is memorable were prepared ; but—and this is a matter more important to us—the pastime included a masque written by Leicester's nephew Philip for her Majesty's amusement.

" Her most excellent Majesty walking in Wanstead garden," we read in the preface to this masque, entitled " The Lady of May," " as she passed into the grove, there came suddenly among the train one apparelled like an honest man's wife, where, crying out for justice, and desiring all the lords and gentlemen to speak a good word for her, she was brought to the presence of her Majesty, to whom upon her knees she offered a supplication."   The supplication was for royal help to the suitor's daughter in the sore trouble that afflicted and imperilled her. "Other women think they may be unhappily cumbered with one master-husband," she said. "My poor daughter is oppressed with two; both loving her, both equally liked of her, both striving to deserve her." Only the Queen's intervention, it was urged, could avert "some bloody controversy" between the furious rivals; and the prose appeal was followed by this verse:

> " To one whose state is raisèd over all,
> > Whose face doth oft the bravest sort enchant,
> Whose mind is such as wisest minds appal,
> > Who in one-self these divers gifts can plant;
> How dare I, wretch, seek there my woes to rest,
> Where ears be burnt, eyes dazzled, hearts oppressed?

> " Your state is great; your greatness is our shield;
> > Your face hurts oft; but still it doth delight.
> Your mind is wise; your wisdom makes you mild:
> > Such planted gifts enrich e'en beggar's sight.
> So dare I, wretch, my bashful fear subdue,
> And feed mine ears, mine eyes, my heart in you."

Philip Sidney was at this time apter as a courtier than as a poet. His compliments doubtless pleased her Majesty as she passed through the grove and came upon a small crowd of shepherds and foresters, who, divided into two parties, were "haling and pulling" in effort to draw the Lady of May to the one side or the other, and from whom Master Rombus, the village schoolmaster, in trying to part them by his "learned wisdom," received only "unlearned blows." At sight of the Queen all stood still and gazed. Thereupon first old Father Lalus, a shepherd, and then Master Rombus, essayed to explain to her the quarrel; but the Lady of May preferred to tell her own tale and to implore " the beautifullest lady these woods have ever received " to choose for her between her two wooers—Therion, the forester, and Espilus, the shepherd. " I like them both, and love neither. Espilus is the richer, but Therion the livelier. Therion doth me many pleasures, as stealing me venison out of these forests, and many other such-like pretty and prettier services; but withal he grows to such rages that sometimes he strikes me, and sometimes he rails at me. This shepherd Espilus is of a mild disposition: as his fortune hath not been to do me great service, so hath he never done me any wrong; but, feeding his sheep, sitting under some sweet bush, sometimes they say he records my name in doleful verses." Next the rivals stated their several claims in song, Espilus's fellow-shepherds, the while, " setting in with the recorders which they bare in their bags like pipes," and Therion's fellow-foresters " with the cornets they wore about their necks, like hunting-horns in baudricks"; and there was further discourse by Dorcas, an old shepherd, and Rixus, a young forester, who exalted each his own calling, and by Rombus, who poured out syllogisms and alliterations in grand style, until the Queen gave judgment in favour of Espilus, and the entertainment ended with a song of triumph by the more fortunate wooer, and with dancing and merrymaking by all.

After spending several days at Wanstead, and

being there provided with many other diversions
besides Sidney's "Lady of May," Queen Elizabeth
turned back with him and the rest of her Court and
went to Greenwich.   There and in other suburbs of
London she remained till July, when she set out on
a progress of unusual splendour.   Visiting other
places on the way, the royal party reached Audley
End on Saturday, the 26th of the month, and thither
on Sunday the Vice-Chancellor of Cambridge and all
the heads of colleges came out, by appointment, to
pay their respects to her Majesty.   On their behalf
was uttered a very laudatory oration, showing how
the universities had been nourished by her, as by a
loving nurse, in piety and learning ; and in token of
gratitude a splendid copy of a new edition of the
Greek Testament issued by Robert Étienne, better
known as Stephens, was presented to her, together
with a pair of gloves, perfumed and embroidered,
worth sixty shillings.   Other gifts of gloves, costing
twenty shillings a pair, were tendered by Lords
Burghley and Leicester, and yet others, of the more
modest value of four shillings and twopence, by the
Earl of Sussex, Lord Hunsdon, Sir Christopher
Hatton, Sir Francis Knollys, and other courtiers.
What Philip Sidney gave is not recorded ; but he
was certainly one of the company, and he listened to
a three hours' philosophical disputation, in which a
prominent part was taken by Master Gabriel Harvey,
of Pembroke Hall, and which lasted till midnight,
when the learned guests were honourably dismissed.
They had to finish their busy Sunday by walking all
the way back to Cambridge, as they were disap-
10

pointed of the night's lodging they looked for at Saffron Walden.

From Audley End Queen Elizabeth passed on, being entertained with feasts and shows at several halting-places in Suffolk and Norfolk, to Norwich, where homage of every sort was paid to her, the masques and pageants being arranged by Thomas Churchyard, who was more skilled than Sidney in that kind of work.

After lingering for some time in the neighbourhood of Norwich, the Queen went home by way of Wanstead. But she had quitted that place before the 20th of September, when the Earl of Leicester was there privately wedded to the Countess of Essex, whose widowhood had lasted two years all but a day. Long before, according to rumour, there had been yet more clandestine espousals, and the report of them having come to the ears of Sir Francis Knollys, the Countess's father, that sturdy old Puritan had insisted on Leicester's clearing her name from all ground of scandal. Even this Wanstead marriage was as secret as possible, only Sir Francis Knollys, and Leicester's brother, the Earl of Warwick, with one or two other witnesses, being present; and for some while longer the Countess of Leicester continued to be known as the Countess of Essex.

Meanwhile Philip Sidney was probably either with the Queen, now at Hampton Court, or with his mother, who was lying ill at Chiswick. His father was lying ill at Chester. Having wound up his necessary business in Dublin, Sir Henry had left Ireland near the beginning of September and had travelled as far as Chester, where he was forced to halt. From the house of Dr. Trevor, in the outskirts of that city, he wrote on the 18th to inform the Queen and her Lord High Treasurer, that he had been detained there by sickness but that he was sending his secretary, Edmund Molyneux, to report upon his affairs, and should proceed on his journey to London as soon as he was able, bringing with him the Earl of Clanricarde, whom he had not dared to leave behind him in Ireland, for fear of his starting a fresh rebellion.*

Molyneux appears to have been at all times a faithful friend and servant to Sir Henry Sidney and the rest of the family; but in the spring Philip had wrongly suspected him of treachery. Writing to his father in April, Philip had said: "I must needs impute it to some men about you that there is little written from you or to you that is not known to your professed enemies." On the 31st of May he wrote very sharply to Molyneux: "Few words are best. My letters to my father have come to the ears of some; neither can I condemn any but you. If it be so, you have played the very knave with me; and so I will make you know, if I have good proof of it. That for so much as is past. For that is to come, I assure you, before God, that if ever I know you do so much as read any letter I write to my father without his commandment or my consent, I will thrust my dagger into you; and trust to it, for I speak in earnest."

---

* State Papers, Ireland, Elizabeth ; Sir Henry Sidney to the Queen, 18 September, 1578 ; the same to Burghley, same date.

Molyneux's reply was a model of dignified reproof, with a touch of scorn. "Sir," he wrote back on the 1st of July, "I have received a letter from you which, as it is the first, so it is the sharpest that I ever received from any; and therefore it amazeth me to receive such a one from you, since I have (the world can judge) deserved better somewhere, howsoever it pleased you to condemn me now. But since it is (I protest to God) without cause, or yet just ground for suspicion, you use me thus, I bear the injury more patiently for a time, and mine innocency I hope in the end shall try my honesty, and then I trust you will confess that you have done me wrong. And since your pleasure so is expressed, that I shall not henceforth read any of your letters (although I must confess I have heretofore taken both great delight and profit in reading some of them), yet, upon so hard a condition as you seem to offer, I will not hereafter adventure so great a peril, but obey you herein. Howbeit, if it had pleased you, you might have commanded me in a far greater matter with a far less penalty. Yours, when it shall please you better to conceive of me, humbly to command."

Let us hope that Philip made prompt and suitable apology. He afterwards asked and obtained many favours from his father's honest secretary, and, when he died, Molyneux was one of the first to applaud in print his virtues.*

Meanwhile Molyneux came to London in September to explain Sir Henry's business to the Queen

---

* The charming little memoirs of Sir Philip Sidney and of both his parents printed in " Holinshed " are attributed to Molyneux.

and her Council, and to him, from her sick-bed at Chiswick, whence she was about to move in order to be with her husband at Hampton Court, Lady Sidney addressed an interesting letter on the 11th of October. "I have thought good," she wrote, "to put you in remembrance to move my Lord Chamberlain, in my lord's name, to have some other room than my chamber for my lord to have his resort unto, as he was wont to have; or else my lord will be greatly troubled when he shall have any matter of dispatch, my lodging, you see, being only little, and myself continually sick and not able to be much out of my bed. For the night-time, one roof, with God's grace, shall serve us. For the day-time, the Queen will look to have my chamber always in readiness for her Majesty's coming thither; and, though my lord himself can be no impediment thereto by his own presence, yet his lordship, trusting to no place else to be provided for him, will be, as I said before, troubled for want of a convenient place to the dispatch of such people as shall have occasion to come to him. Therefore, I pray you, move my Lord of Sussex for a room for that purpose, and I will have it hanged and lined for him with stuff from home." The Earl of Sussex, formerly Lord Deputy of Ireland, was now Lord Chamberlain, and was, it will be remembered, Sir Henry's brother-in-law.

The favour was not a great one to ask, but it was not easily, if at all, obtained. A few days later Lady Sidney wrote again to Molyneux, saying: "You have used the matter very well; but we must do more yet for the good dear lord than let him be thus dealt withal. Hampton Court I never yet knew so full as there were not spare rooms in it when it hath been thrice better filled than at this present it is. But some will be sorry, perhaps, my lord should have so sure footing in the Court. Well, all may be as well when the good God will; the whilst, I pray, let us do what we may for my lord's ease and quiet." She suggested various ways in which Molyneux might seek the loan, during daytime, of a room in which Sir Henry could see his friends on business, without bringing them to her bedside or disturbing the Queen's talk with her there. "But if all these fail," she added, "when the worst is known, old Lord Harry and his old Moll will do as well as they can in parting, like good friends, the small portion allotted our long service in Court."

"When I came to Court," near the middle of October, wrote Sir Henry Sidney, "I was entertained, I confess, well, but not so well as I thought, and in conscience felt, that I deserved." The entertainment he referred to was in respect of the auditing of his accounts and the reception of his reports as retiring Lord Deputy of Ireland, not of the sort of office or parlour provided for him. But he was only at Hampton Court for a week or two before he went down to Ludlow Castle to resume his duties as Lord President of Wales. There he had something like rest. "A happy place of government it is," he said, "for a better people to govern, or better subjects to their sovereign, Europe holdeth not."

Being in Wales, he had the less need of Philip's help in watching and protecting his interests at Court.

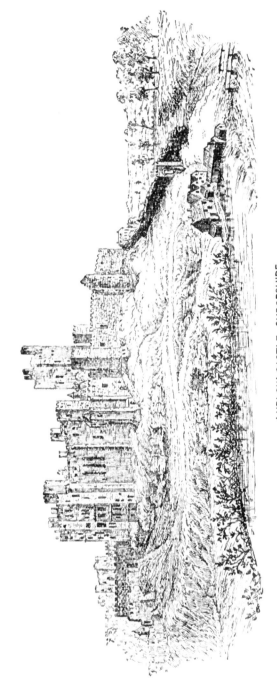

LUDLOW CASTLE, SHROPSHIRE.

FROM AN OLD ENGRAVING.

CHAPTER IX.

META INCOGNITA.

1576–1578.

ERY interesting light is thrown on Philip Sidney's character and temperament by his connections with one of the greatest movements of the Elizabethan age, one in which, blundering and faulty as it was in some respects, the chivalry of the age found almost larger and more memorable exercise than in any other. Accident or necessity rendered his actual share in the enterprise by which England was started on her career of colonial empire and maritime supremacy very much smaller than he desired. He was only able to encourage others, and was debarred from himself joining any of the expeditions he helped to plan. But perhaps his service was none the less important on that account. To follow it in order we must retrace some of the ground traversed in the last few chapters.

His zeal was inherited, and it was fostered by family associations. Richard Chancellor, the brave Englishman who, in May, 1553, eighteen months before Philip was born, accompanied Sir Hugh Willoughby on his famous and disastrous voyage " for the search and discovery of northern parts of the world, to open a way and passage to our men for travel to new and unknown kingdoms," was one of the "servants," as they were called in those days, of Sir Henry Sidney ; and Sir Henry was one of the chief promoters of that voyage.* Sir Henry's interest in the seafaring exploits that did so much to advance the welfare of England was continued, and it was shared by his brothers-in-law, the Earls of Warwick and Leicester. Philip, who had Richard Hakluyt for one of his Oxford companions, must, from his childhood, have heard much of the venturesome and patriotic work. Sir Humphrey Gilbert, his senior by about fifteen years, was one of Sir Henry's principal officers in Ireland, and when Gilbert was not fighting in Ireland, he was scheming methods of reaching Cathay or of founding colonies on the way thither. Another schemer to these ends, but more anxious to be engaged in trade and piracy nearer home, was Martin Frobisher, of the same age as Gilbert, who also, in the intervals of other occupation, served under Sir Henry in Ireland

---

* A remarkable speech by Sir Henry Sidney on the setting out of Willoughby's and Chancellor's expedition is quoted from Eden's " Decades of the New World " (1555) in my " English Seamen under the Tudors," to which I may refer the reader for a fuller account of much that is briefly told in this chapter.

or off the Irish coast. Moreover, Frobisher was a
prime favourite with the Earl of Warwick, and when
Philip came home in June, 1575, from his foreign
schooling, he found nearly all the bold navigators of
the day clustered round his uncle Warwick, busily
discussing ways and means of fitting out a fresh
expedition in search of a north-west passage to the
Indies.

Queen Elizabeth's sanction of this project had
been obtained, probably at the Earl of Warwick's
instigation, in the previous February; but there was
considerable difficulty in collecting the necessary
funds. It was not till the commencement of 1576
that Michael Lock, who acted as treasurer, and who
was a son or nephew of Sir William Lock, the great
merchant, was able to announce a subscription list
amounting to £875. Towards that total Lock contributed £100, and other £100 apiece came from Sir
Thomas Gresham and two other London merchants.
Three of Philip's uncles, the Earls of Warwick,
Leicester, and Sussex, were each set down for £50,
and Lord Burghley was entered for a like amount.
The rest of the fund was made up of £25 shares, of
which one was held by Sir Francis Walsingham and
another by Philip Sidney. As Philip was at this
time only one-and-twenty, and the poor son of a
poor father, forced in the career of courtier on which
he was embarked to run up heavy bills with the
tailors and jewellers and bootmakers, his £25, equal
to £200 or £250 at the present time, was a considerable outlay for him, and marked his keen interest
in the affair. Next year, when Frobisher, having

returned from his first voyage, was preparing for a second, and most of the speculators doubled their subscriptions—Queen Elizabeth risking £500—Philip Sidney also doubled his ; and noteworthy additions to the new list were the names of Philip's sister, Mistress Mary Sidney, and his friend Edward Dyer, each of whom provided £25.*

The first expedition was ready to start on Thursday, the 7th of June, 1576, when the *Gabriel* and *Michael*, two stout little barques of twenty-four tons apiece, with a small pinnace of ten tons attached to each, and a company of thirty-five officers and men, all told, under Frobisher as captain or admiral, weighed anchor and set their sails in the Thames, off old London Bridge. But at Greenwich the adventurers were delayed by Queen Elizabeth, who, as they passed, sent a messenger in a rowing boat to bid them wait till they had taken leave of her, and the voyage was only begun on the 12th of June. Their exploits need not be here recounted at length. Proceeding to the north of Labrador, the two barques were parted by a great storm, and those on board the *Michael*, supposing the other to be wrecked, deemed it prudent to return to England. Frobisher was left to pursue his explorations, with only eighteen gentlemen and mariners on board the *Gabriel* and its pinnace. When the latter, with a crew of five, sent out to inspect the coast, was lost, Frobisher did not venture to go beyond the entrance of the straits that bear his name, and to make some

---

* State Papers, Domestic, Elizabeth, vol. cxi., No. 48 ; vol. cxix., No. 34.

general observations of the land which he had discovered, and to which he gave the title of Meta Incognita.   He had done nothing towards finding the
desired passage to Cathay.   But he had added much
to the map of the Arctic regions, and when he
reached England in October, to disprove the report
brought a month before by the crew of the *Michael*
as to his shipwreck, he and the twelve gallant men
whom he brought home, along with an unlucky
Esquimaux captive, were, according to Michael
Lock, "joyfully received with great admiration of
the people, and their strange man and his boat was
such a wonder to the whole city, and to the rest of
the realm that heard of it, as seemed never to have
happened the like great matter to any man's knowledge."

Sidney sent to Languet an enthusiastic account
of Frobisher's achievements.   His letter, unfortunately, is missing; but its purport, especially as
regards one incident, may be gathered from another
letter that he wrote a year later, after Frobisher had
returned from the second and more important expedition on which he started on the 26th of May,
1577.   "It is a marvellous history," Sidney here
said.   "After having made slow progress in the past
year, Frobisher touched at a certain island in order
to rest both himself and his crew.   And there by
chance a young man, one of the ship's company,
picked up a piece of earth which he saw glittering
on the ground.   He showed it to Frobisher, who,
being busy with other matters, and not believing
that precious metals were produced in a region so

far to the north, considered it of no value. Well, they sailed homewards at the beginning of winter ; and the young man kept the earth by him as a memorial of his labour (for he had no thought of anything else) till his return to London. And there, when one of his friends saw it shining in an extraordinary manner, he tested it, and found that it was the purest gold, unalloyed with any other metal."

The analyst was either much mistaken or anxious to deceive others. But the lump of supposed gold had a wonderful effect in quickening public interest in Frobisher's project. A Cathay Company was started, with privileges equal to those of the Muscovy Company, and Frobisher was appointed its " captain general by sea, and admiral of the ships and navy." Queen Elizabeth not only became the principal shareholder, but she lent a larger vessel, the *Aid*, furnished with sixty-five sailors and twenty-five soldiers, to accompany the little *Gabriel* and *Michael*, which were equipped anew for further search after Cathay. The *Aid*, however, was only to go to Frobisher's Straits and the country thereabout, with a view of planting a colony in this region and of soon returning to England with a cargo of the gold that it was thought would be procured there.

Sidney was sent abroad on his mission to Germany while these preparations were in progress, and the expedition had started before his return. In the letter already cited he gave Languet some account of the work done by the voyagers during a four months' absence from England, in the course of which, braving the perils of storms and icebergs,

Frobisher made further additions to geographical knowledge about Meta Incognita, and loaded the *Aid* with a mineral by no means so valuable as he supposed. " He says," wrote Sidney on the 30th of September, two days after Frobisher's landing at Bristol, " that the island "—now called Hall's Island —" is so productive in metals as far to surpass Peru, at least as it now is. There are also six other islands, near to this, which seem very little inferior. It is, therefore, at this time under debate by what means these hitherto successful labours can be still carried on in safety from the attacks of other nations, especially of the Spaniards and Danes ; the former as claiming all the western parts by sanction of the Pope ; the latter as being more northerly, and therefore nearer and better able, by reason of their possessions in Iceland, and of their skill in that sort of navigation, to undertake the business. Pray send me your opinion on this subject, and at the same time describe the most convenient method of working these ores ; for we know as little about this art as about the cultivation of vines. Remember so to write as that you may justify the great reputation in which you are held here ; for, unless you forbid it, I shall show your letter to the Queen. The thing is really important, and it may probably, at some time or other, be of use to the professors of true religion."

Sidney's association of Frobisher's discovery, and the exaggerated importance attached to it, with the Protestant cause was characteristic ; and his forecasting, to some extent, of the enterprise on which the Pilgrim Fathers were to embark more than forty years later was curious. He evidently was as excited as any one else, too, about the fancied finding of another Peru, of which England might take possession without much fighting, and in which he, as one of the first adventurers, would have a substantial share.

In his next letter to Languet he had to report that, without such guidance in metallurgy as he asked his friend to give them, the assayers had ascertained that the two hundred tons of stuff brought home as gold ore were all dross; but he doubtless thought, as did his partners, that this was only an accident and that there was plenty of wealth to be drawn from Meta Incognita. The ore was declared to be " poor in respect of that brought last year, and of that which we know may be brought next year," and with this assurance the shareholders in the Cathay Company satisfied themselves.

All through the winter they were busy, alike at Hampton Court and Whitehall, on the Exchange, in Mark Lane, and at the docks, preparing for a much larger expedition to be sent out in the spring of 1578. Sidney and his sister, now the Countess of Pembroke, added each of them about a third to their earlier investments, raising the former's to £67 10s., and the latter's to £33 15s.* A fleet of fifteen ships was fitted out, and suitable preparations were made with the intention not only of bringing home at least two thousand tons of ore,—Lord Burghley's

* State Papers, Domestic, Elizabeth, vol. cxxvi., No. 32.

proposal was for five thousand,—but also of settling a hundred colonists in Meta Incognita.

Languet wrote very wisely, but, as it happened, superfluously, in reply to Sidney's letter of the 30th of September, 1577 : " If what you say about Frobisher be true, you have stumbled on that gift of nature which is of all the most fatal and baneful to mankind, yet which most men so madly covet, as it, more than anything else in the world, stirs them to incur every kind of risk. I fear that England, crazed by the love of gold, will now just empty her-self into these islands that Frobisher has been finding. And how much English blood, do you suppose, must be shed for you to keep hold of them ? In old times, when some Carthaginians, on a voyage in the Atlantic, had been carried by a storm to land of some sort, and had come back with wonderful reports of its wealth, the Senate, fearing the people would be tempted to go thither, put to death the men who had brought the report, so that if any wished to emigrate they should have none who could guide them. Do I, therefore, think that you should reject these treasures that God has thrown in your way? Anything but that. Nay ; I thoroughly admire the high spirit, the perseverance, and even the good fortune, of Frobisher. He deserves great rewards. But I am thinking of you, for you seem to rejoice in the circumstance as if it was the best thing possible for your country, especially as I noticed in you last spring a certain longing to undertake this kind of enterprise ; and, if Frobisher's foolish hope of finding a North-West Passage had power then to fascinate you, what will not these golden mountains do, or rather these islands all of gold, as I daresay they shape themselves day and night in your mind? Beware, I do beseech you, and never let 'the cursed hunger after gold,' whereof the poet speaks, creep over that spirit of yours, into which nothing has hitherto been admitted save the love of goodness and the desire of earning the good-will of all men. If these golden islands are fixing themselves too firmly in your thoughts, turn them out before they possess you, and keep yourself safe till you can serve your friends and your country in a better way."

Sidney may have thought now and then of going out with Frobisher in the summer of 1578, as Languet shows us he had been inclined to do a year before; but, if so, Court ties and family duties deterred him. He merely looked on and helped to superintend the preparations. He was with the Queen at Greenwich, having returned from Wanstead, where his " Lady of May " had lately been performed, on the 28th of May, when Frobisher and his fourteen captains kissed her Majesty's hands at parting, and had, according to the record, " good gifts and greater promises " bestowed upon them. He was with the Queen, too, in October, when Frobisher's ships came straggling back, having had many narrow escapes and passed through great difficulties, and when the admiral had to report that, though he had tracked out much coast hitherto unvisited, on both sides of the channel now known as Hudson's Straits, he had seen no place fit for winter habitation, and had left part of his stores behind him, intending to recover them next year. That Frobisher never did ; and the stores were not heard of again until, after a lapse of nearly three centuries, Captain C. F. Hall, the enterprising United States explorer, found traces of them in 1861 and 1862.*

Though Frobisher and his comrades were heartily welcomed home, there was grievous disappointment when the great quantities of mineral they brought back were discovered to be as worthless as their former cargo. Desperate quarrels arose, and mainly on this account, between Frobisher, who claimed the salary due to him, and Michael Lock who, as treasurer of the Cathay Company, defied even the orders of the Privy Council on the subject. Frobisher publicly complained that Lock was "a false accountant to the Company, a cozener to my lord of Oxford, no venturer at all in the voyages, a bankrupt knave" ; and, as Lock urged in a letter to Sir Francis Walsingham, he "entered into great storms and rages with him like a mad beast, and raised on him such shameful reports and false slanders as the whole Court and City were full of."

There was some excuse for poor Frobisher's storms and rages, and Sidney continued his friend, probably helping him and his family in the poverty to which they were reduced ; but so many other friends dropped off that he had no chance of undertaking the fourth voyage he proposed. His Meta Incognita was abandoned until Henry Hudson and others

* Hall, " Life with the Esquimaux " (1864), vol. i., pp. 271, 278, 302, 315 ; vol. ii., pp. 77, 150, 283, 293, etc.

11

made further and more extensive explorations in this barren and ice-bound region. Neither England nor Philip Sidney was corrupted by the gold it had been supposed to contain.

A greater man than Frobisher had set forth on a more famous and eventful expedition on the 15th of November, 1577. This was Francis Drake, who then started in the *Golden Hind* on the voyage which occupied him nearly three years in going round the world. Drake had done much memorable work before that, both in raids on the Spaniards in the West Indies, and in land service under the Earl of Essex in Ireland. In the latter relation, if in no other, Sidney must have seen something of him. It does not appear that Sidney was much concerned in the project of 1577; but at a later date we shall find him closely and curiously associated with Drake, and even now he evidently had some inclination to emulate if not to share Drake's bold enterprise. Writing to Languet in a gloomy strain about the condition of Protestantism in Europe and the failure of his hopes for a Protestant league, he said on the 1st of March, 1578, " Unless God powerfully counteract it, I think I see our cause withering away, and I am even now meditating some Indian project." The Indian project was doubtless akin to Drake's plan for attacking Spain and Catholicism by methods that would nowadays be called piracy.

The overthrow—or, at any rate, the weakening and worrying—of Catholic and Spanish tyranny was at this time, and till the end of his life, the political object that, above all others, Sidney set before him-

self.   He could not break away from the Court
thraldom which was imposed upon him and which,
though he often complained of it, was on the whole
more pleasant than unpleasant to him, and there was
much connected therewith, and with the intellectual
and literary movements incident to it, that afforded
him more than pastime ; but he was always yearning
for occupation in the field of politics, and in that field
he always had the same end in view, however diverse
might be his plans for reaching it.   In so far as he
ever thought seriously of accompanying Frobisher in
his voyages of discovery in northern latitudes, or of
rivalling Drake's achievements in warmer seas, he
was prompted by more than sympathy with such
adventurous work, keen as that was.   His main desire
was to assist in damaging Spain and crippling the
Papacy, both being enterprises deemed by him
necessary for the credit, if not for the safety, of
England, and yet more for the protection of the
Protestant cause in Germany and the Netherlands.
It was because, in the spring of 1578, this cause
appeared to him to be "withering away" that he
then, in desperation, meditated "some Indian project" ; and in the same mood he was oftener,
almost constantly, meditating projects nearer home.

His friend, Count John Casimir,* brother of the
Elector Palatine, was in the autumn of 1577 appointed a sort of agent by Queen Elizabeth to
watch on her behalf the progress of affairs in Germany and the Netherlands, and in the following

* John Casimir, like others in his day, was variously styled count,
and duke, and prince.

summer Elizabeth lent him some money to be spent
in raising a small army with which to go to the
assistance of William of Orange, who was now at open
war with Don John of Austria, King Philip's viceroy. This step was taken in consequence of advice
from Leicester, Walsingham, and others, Sidney
being one of the most zealous, if not one of the
most influential, among them. Sidney not only
urged John Casimir's employment in this way, but
was anxious to take part in the expedition. His
father's business, if nothing else, prevented him.
" By your letters," Sir Henry wrote from Dublin on
the 1st of August, when he was on the point of returning to England to surrender his Lord Deputy-
ship, " you have discovered unto me your intention
to go over into the Low Countries to accompany
Duke Casimir. This disposition of your virtuous
mind I must needs much commend in you. But
when I enter into consideration of mine own estate,
and call to mind what practices, informations, and
wicked accusations are devised against me, and what
an assistance in the defence of those causes your
presence would be unto me, reposing myself so
much both upon your help and judgment, I strive
betwixt honour and necessity what allowance I may
best give that motion for your going. Howbeit, if
you think not my matters of that weight and difficulty, as I hope they be not, but they may well
enough by myself, without your assistance or any
other, be brought to an honourable end, I will not
be against your determination ; yet would wish you,
before your departure, that you come to me at the

water's side, about the latter end of this month, to take your leave of me, and so from thence depart towards your intended journey."

The conflict of feelings shown in this letter, and the fact that Sir Henry Sidney had to excuse himself for not writing it with his own hand, "which I would have done if the indisposition of my body had not been such as I could not," induced Philip to abandon his project of joining John Casimir in the Low Countries. And it was well he did ; for nothing but mischief resulted from the proceedings of John Casimir, who was by no means so capable a man as his friends supposed. Even Languet rejoiced in Philip's absence. " If you had come into Belgium," he wrote, " I should immediately have hurried to meet you. It would have been extremely delightful to me to see you again ; but I should not have been altogether pleased at your coming amongst men whose society you could not have enjoyed. It would have been cheerless work for you, living in a camp where you would have seen no examples of valour, no tokens of good soldiership—only troops disobeying their leaders, and acting with insolence and cowardice."

Languet made some notable remarks in this letter. " If your Queen had been bound by treaty to send troops to the Low Countries, and had ordered you to go with them there, it would have been your duty to regard the enemies of the Netherlanders as your own foes. But from a mere desire for praise and glory, and that you might give public proof of your courage, you determined to treat as your personal enemies those who seem to you to be taking the wrong side in the war. It is not your business, it is not for any private person, to pass judgment on a question of this kind. It belongs to the magistrate (by magistrate I mean the prince), who should decide with the help of counsellors he believes to be wise and just. Young gentlemen like you are apt to consider that nothing brings them more honour than wholesale slaughter. That is quite wrong; for if you kill a man against whom you have no lawful cause of war, you kill one who, so far as you are concerned, is innocent." "Great praise is due," Languet continued, after more discourse on this subject, "to those who bravely defend their country; but they are to be praised, not for the number of men they kill, but for the protection they give to their own land. Those are the wars in which true glory is won ; but in our times they are most admired whose mad ambition causes most bloodshed." Here Languet was evidently thinking of Don John of Austria and others, whom even foes applauded for their wild love of fighting. His reproof was reproof of all the volunteer warfare in which men like Gilbert and Raleigh often engaged.

Yet other sentences must be quoted from this excellent sermon in letter form. "I am much grieved," Languet wrote, "to hear you say that you are weary of the life to which, I doubt not, God has called you, and that you wish to flee from the glitter of your Court and betake yourself to some secluded place, where you may avoid the troubles that hamper and engross all who live within the circle of

government. I know that in the splendour of a
Court there are so many temptations to vice that
it is very hard for a man to hold himself clean
among them, and to stand upright on such slippery
ground. But you must struggle boldly and virtuously against these difficulties, remembering that the
glory of victory is always great in proportion to the
peril undergone. Nature has endowed you with
good gifts of mind and body. Fortune has favoured
you with noble birth and many splendid accomplish-
ments. From your boyhood you have made study
of all the most useful arts. Will you then, furnished
with such weapons, refuse to your country the
service it demands, and bury in the earth the large
talent that God has entrusted to you?"

True and wise words of counsel for the mentor of
sixty to address to the young man who had just
entered on his twenty-fourth year.

CHAPTER X.

IN COURT LIVERY.

1578–1580.

N the summer of 1578 Philip Sidney was appointed to some office under Queen Elizabeth. As there is no record on the subject, the office was probably of a trivial sort, one of the several small sinecures or merely ceremonial posts, such as that of cupbearer, or gentleman-in-waiting, which were bestowed upon him in common with other courtiers whose attendance her Majesty was anxious to ensure by putting them in dignified livery. Whatever it was, Hubert Languet overrated its importance. " Before," he wrote on the 16th of July, " I was fearful lest the ardour of youth should suggest some rash project, and fate snatch you from your country and your friends to bring you to an inglorious end ; for I heard talk about distant voyages and Belgian soldiering. But now that you are no longer your own master,

and that your new honours have so tied you to your country that you must consult its advantage rather than your own pleasure, my anxiety is lessened. Not that I think you less liable to danger than you were before, but that the perils you have to undergo for your country must now bring you fame and praise. I congratulate you, therefore, upon the favour with which your wise soverign has honoured you, only to incite you to further pursuit of virtue."

Though the new duties assigned to Sidney, whatever their nature, cannot have been either as onerous or as perilous as Languet imagined, they probably marked a rise in the courtier's position. Sidney still often thought of breaking away from the thraldom imposed upon him, but during the next year or more he appears to have been in closer attendance on the Queen than heretofore, and, in spite of his complaints and ambitions, perhaps the thraldom was pleasant.

Languet, with amusing persistency, urged other thraldom upon him. "If you marry a wife, and beget children like yourself," he urged, "you will be a better servant of your country than if you were to cut the throats of a thousand Spaniards or Frenchmen"; and he added, "I am not in this recommending to you idleness or ease—at least if we are to believe the poet who advises any man that wishes plenty of trouble to get him a wife."

"I wonder, my dear Hubert," Sidney wrote in answer, not to the letter just quoted from, but to an earlier one containing similar remarks, "what has come into your mind that, when I have not as yet

done anything to deserve it, you would have me
bound in the chains of matrimony ; and this without
pointing out any particular lady, but as though you
extolled the marriage state in itself—which, by the
bye, you have not as yet sanctioned by your own
example.   Respecting one, of whom I readily acknowledge how unworthy I am, I have written you
my reasons long ago—briefly, indeed, but still as
well as I could.   At present, however, I believe you
are entertaining some other notion.   If so, I beg you
to acquaint me with it, whatever it may be."

It is a pity that we have neither the letter in which
Sidney declared his unworthiness of some particular
lady, and apparently his liking for her, nor any other
letters that might clear up the mysteries here indicated.   Allusions in Languet's correspondence render it not impossible that he had a German spouse
in view for Sidney ; perhaps a wealthy widow, or a
daughter of one of the Protestant princes whose
cause both the friends were anxious to advance.   It
is tolerably clear that Sidney liked his liberty too
well to be in any haste about surrendering it, yet had
a mild preference for some one ; and this some one
we may reasonably assume to have been Lady Penelope Devereux, the daughter of his friend, the Earl
of Essex, who on his deathbed in the autumn of
1576, and before, had earnestly desired that there
should be a match between them.

In the summer of 1578 Penelope was in her sixteenth year, Philip in his twenty-fourth.   Penelope
was apparently living with her mother, who was
often at Court, and whose marriage to Philip's uncle,

the Earl of Leicester, was not at present known. It
is difficult to imagine any serious obstacle to their
union, save such as may have come from the inclinations of one or both ; nor is it easy to suppose that
Penelope would have offered much resistance to
Philip's wooing, had he cared to woo in earnest.
Only one thing, however, is clear ; that at this time
Philip felt none of the passion for Penelope which,
as Astrophel, he two or three years afterwards, in his
famous sonnets, professed for her as Stella. As to
the autobiographical value of these poems something
must be said hereafter. He certainly had not begun
to write them, or to entertain the thoughts uttered
in them, in 1578.

About his occupations this year all of importance
that is known has already been recorded. He kept
Christmas, along with his parents, at Hampton
Court. Sir Henry Sidney, having been partly forgiven for his excess of zeal in the Queen's service as
Lord Deputy of Ireland, absented himself for a while
from his post as Lord President of Wales, and came
up to enjoy a holiday with his family as well as to
pay respects to his sovereign. To Queen Elizabeth,
on the first day of 1579, he presented a costly gold
ornament, on which was carved an image of Diana,
richly garnished with diamonds, pearls, and rubies.
Her Majesty's gratitude was marked by a gift of a
hundred and thirty-eight ounces of gold plate. To
Lady Sidney and to Philip, severally, the royal
favour was measured by thirty and by twenty ounces,
in exchange for a smock and two cambric pillow-
cases tendered by the mother, and a white sarcenet

bodice, quilted and embroidered with gold, silver, and silk of divers colours, and with lace of gold and silver round about, which constituted the New Year's gift of the son.

The Christmas festivities were quickly followed by others of special interest to Philip. Prince John Casimir, who had in the previous August gone with twelve thousand soldiers to assist Prince William of Orange, but had caused only trouble thereby, and who had been roundly scolded by Queen Elizabeth for his folly and recklessness, came to England to make his peace with her Majesty. With him came Languet, chiefly, it would seem, for the sake of meeting Philip. The poor old man was afraid he should be deprived of this pleasure. Early in December he had been seized with fever and an affection of the eyes which prevented him from reading or doing any kind of work. " But I shall come if I possibly can," he wrote, " even if it should be at the peril of my life." Fortunately his wish was gratified, and without harm to him.

Sir Henry Sidney was sent as far as Canterbury to meet the visitors and to escort them to the Tower of London, which they reached on Thursday, the 22d of January. They were there received by a number of noblemen and gentlemen, of whom Philip Sidney was one; and they were led by torchlight to Sir Thomas Gresham's house in Bishopsgate Street, where a band of drums and fifes and other musical instruments sounded for them a hearty welcome. By the great merchant they were lodged and feasted during two days, and on Sunday, the 25th, they took boat to Whitehall and waited on the Queen.

As John Casimir entered the palace, her Majesty came out and essayed to kiss him ; but he, we are told, not being trained to the English custom, humbly yet resolutely refused. Nor was this his only resistance to Elizabeth's friendly conduct. She led him with her own hand through the great hall into the presence-chamber, and, as the passages were draughty, she bade him wear his hat. This he would not do, saying he was her Majesty's servant to command. "Then," replied the Queen, "if you are my servant, I command you to put on your hat." The prince's defiance of that order, instead of offending her Majesty, may have made it easier for him to obtain forgiveness for his mismanagement of the business in which he had acted partly on her behalf.

During the eighteen days that followed John Casimir was lodged in Somerset House, where the Queen provided food for him, but he was often feasted elsewhere. On one day he dined in the City with the Lord Mayor and Corporation. On another he visited one of Philip's aunts, the Countess of Sussex, at the Barbican, in Red-Cross Street. On an, other he was entertained at Wanstead by the Earl of Leicester. Some days he spent in hunting at Hampton Court, and he shot one stag in Hyde Park. In all the compliments and amusements contrived for him, with sober Languet looking on, we may imagine the large but unrecorded share taken by Sidney, who, though his name is not mentioned in connection with any particular proceeding, was foremost among the courtiers in their hospitable behaviour.

"I was glad," Languet wrote to Sidney after he had gone back to the Netherlands, "to see you in high favour with your Queen, and so well thought of by your countrymen. But, to tell the truth, the ways of your Court seemed to me less manly than I could have wished. Most of the courtiers sought to win applause rather by an affected courtesy than by those virtues which are healthful to the State, and which are the chief ornaments of generous minds— of high-born men. I was much grieved, and so were your other friends with me, because you seemed to be wasting the flower of your youth upon such things. I fear lest your nature should be warped, lest by habit you should be brought to find satisfaction in pursuits that only weaken the mind." In speaking thus Languet merely gave utterance to thoughts that were often in Sidney's mind, and not seldom expressed by himself in words.

On Thursday, the 12th of February, John Casimir took leave of the Queen, who made him a parting present of two gold cups, valued at £300 apiece. "There hath been somewhat to do," wrote Gilbert Talbot to his father, the Earl of Shrewsbury, "to bring her unto it, and Mr. Secretary Walsingham bore the brunt of it." Besides this, however, the prince had need of gold that he could more easily part with. He borrowed a sum of money from Sidney which six weeks afterwards Languet had considerable difficulty in getting him to pay back.

Sir Henry Sidney accompanied the visitors on their way home as far as the Kentish coast, taking with him his younger son Robert, who was entrusted to Languet's care, and who now started, as Philip had done before him, on two or three years of travel and residence abroad.   A strong friendship had grown up between Sir Henry and Languet.   The sturdy Huguenot also became warmly attached to the Countess of Pembroke and others of the Sidney kindred, as well as to Philip's two dearest friends, Fulke Greville and Edward Dyer.   The former crossed the Channel with him, being sent on a mission to some of the German princes.   Of the latter he said, " His friendship is like a gem added to my treasures."

On his way home, two or three months later, Greville paid a visit to William of Orange, who was then at Delft, and to him William gave a message for Queen Elizabeth.   Greville was to say, on William's behalf, that, in his opinion, " her Majesty had in Mr. Philip Sidney one of the ripest and greatest counsellors of State that lived in Europe," and that, if her Majesty would but make trial of the young man, the Prince staked his own credit on the issue of any business he might be employed upon, either with the friends or with the foes of England. This message seems never to have been delivered. When Sidney heard of it, he bade Greville keep silence on the subject.   If her Majesty did not choose, of her own accord, to trust and advance him, he said with proper dignity, she had better not do it at all, seeing the commendation of another could add nothing to his deserts.

From a letter that Sir Henry wrote to his younger son, Robert, shortly before the lad started on his travels, we may learn something of Philip's demeanour among his associates at Queen Elizabeth's Court, as well as among the foreigners he had made acquaintance with. " One thing I warn you of," said Sir Henry, " arrogate no precedency, neither of your countrymen nor of strangers ; but take your place, promiscuously with others, according to your degree and birth-right, with aliens. Follow your discreet and virtuous brother's rule, who, with great discretion, to his commendation, won love, and could variously ply ceremony with ceremony." In a later letter Sir Henry, after giving Robert some advice about travel, added : " But why do I blunder at these things ? Follow the discretion of your loving brother, who in loving you is comparable with me and exceedeth me. Imitate his virtues, exercises, studies, and actions. He is a rare ornament of this age, the very formula that all well-disposed young gentlemen of our Court do form also their manners and life by. In truth—I speak it without flattery of him or of myself—he hath the most rare virtues that ever I found in any man.'

From Philip himself we have two long and very interesting letters written to Robert while he was abroad. One gives excellent advice as to the way in which he may profit by his experience of the places, people, and institutions he will meet with on his travels. The other treats chiefly of his studies, and especially of the proper way of reading history, which appears to have been Robert's favourite occupation when he turned to his books.*

Of Philip's own movements—apart from his literary exercises which will be referred to hereafter—we have no trace for several months after Robert had started for Germany. We may take it for granted that he was much occupied during the summer of 1579 in superintending, as his father's agent, and himself suggesting and elaborating in many particulars, the enlargement of Penshurst Place which Sir Henry Sidney this year began, giving a new front to the building, and making of it the beautiful mansion that stands to the present day. He was generally in attendance on the Queen; but as the year advanced his position at Court became more and more irksome to him, and early in 1580 his self-respect, if not the Queen's anger, forced him to retire from it for a while.

In the autumn of 1578 the Duke of Alençon—who had in 1576 succeeded to the title of Duke of Anjou, or Monsieur, his elder brother Henry having become King of France—began to be again talked of as a possible husband for Queen Elizabeth. The earlier project had been spoilt by the St. Bartholomew massacre, and since 1572 this contemptible member of the contemptible house of Valois had done nothing to deserve favour. But he had dazzled some people's eyes by his exploits in the Netherlands, where he offered himself as a rival to the Prince of Orange in opposition to Spanish tyranny,

---

* Both these letters have been so often printed that it is unnecessary to say much about them here.

12

and there was in England a faction that urged the political expediency of a match which might induce Elizabeth to place herself at the head of the Protestant movement in Europe. That she should take such a position had long been desired by Sidney; but he was shrewd enough to see that a marriage between the Queen and this ugly, treacherous adventurer, nearly twenty years younger than she was, would in no way promote the wished-for object, and could lead to nothing but mischief. He and Fulke Greville, and all the young patriots who shared their view, stoutly opposed the project, and the leader of the party at Court which condemned it was the Earl of Leicester, at any rate till August, 1579.

In that month Du Simier, the agent of the Duke of Anjou, who for more than six months had been busily pressing his master's suit with the Queen, discovered that Leicester had a year before been married to the Countess of Essex. He lost no time in publishing the secret, and great was Elizabeth's wrath when it reached her ears. Leicester was banished from her presence. According to one authority, he was sent to a fort in Greenwich Park, with orders not to stir thence until leave was given him, and with a threat that, if he disobeyed, he would be committed to the Tower; according to another, which is more credible, he voluntarily shut himself up in one of his country houses, on pretence of being seriously ill. Sidney was not dismissed from Court, but he was regarded with much less favour than heretofore, and those who were not his friends had license to insult him.

THE BARONIAL HALL OF PENSHURST PLACE.

Foremost among his rivals was the Earl of Oxford, the brutal husband of the Anne Cecil to whom ten years earlier it had been proposed to marry Sidney, and, as Oxford was prominent among the Duke of Anjou's partisans, his arrogance knew no bounds.

While Sidney, one day near the end of September, was playing tennis at Whitehall, Oxford entered the court uninvited, and haughtily proposed to join in the game. Sidney at first took no notice of the intrusion. When he did speak he used such dignified words of reproof—" coming," as Fulke Greville tells us, " from an understanding heart that knew what was due to itself and what it owed to others "—that Oxford fell into a violent rage and, after further talk, insolently ordered the whole party to leave the court. Thereto Sidney " temperately answered " that, if his lordship had been pleased to express his wish in courteous terms, he would have been met with courtesy, and " perchance might have led out those that he should now find would not be driven out with any scourge of fury." " Puppy ! " exclaimed my lord, so loudly and angrily that the courtiers who were in the gallery overlooking the tennis-court hurried down to watch the dispute. Among them came Du Simier and the other Frenchmen, before whom Oxford was especially anxious to make a fine show. " They instantly drew all to this tumult," Greville reports ; " every sort of quarrel sorting well with their humours, especially this." Sidney thereupon, " rising with an inward strength by the prospect of a mighty faction against him," asked my lord with a loud voice what it was that he had called him. " A puppy ! " repeated Oxford. " That, said Sidney, " is a lie ! " " and then, after waiting long enough for the retort that he expected, he walked out of the court, saying as he went that this was a business which could be better settled in a more private place. Oxford did not follow him. To the astonishment of all, and with no advantage to his reputation, he blustered out something about having gained his point by being rid of the fellow, and after that proceeded to his game of tennis.

Through a whole day Sidney looked for the message that the code of honour held binding in those times prescribed. None arriving, he sent a friend to ask whether he should hear from the Earl of Oxford, and to say that this was a state of affairs in which his lordship's French companions could teach him, if he did not know, what course he ought to take. Thus provoked, Oxford sent back an acceptance of the challenge. But the time for fighting was over. The matter had in the interval been brought before the lords of the Privy Council, and they, not content with enjoining peace between the young men, besought the Queen herself to effect a conciliation.

Her Majesty accordingly sent for Sidney, and pointing out the difference between peers and commoners, and the respect that inferiors owed to their superiors, bade him apologise. This Sidney refused to do. No peer, he said, had by his rank any privilege to do wrong, and, though the Earl of Oxford might be a great lord by virtue of his birth and the Queen's favours, he was no lord over him. Her

Majesty's father, King Henry the Eighth, he reminded her, had recognised and established the
right of the gentry in England to resist the over-
bearing spirit of the grandees.

There was no duel. The Earl of Oxford took
shelter in the Queen's favour, and in her order that
he was not to fight. Some time afterwards he sent
a messenger, said to have been Walter Raleigh, to
propose to Sidney that their disagreement should
cease; and Sidney appears to have expressed himself satisfied. At any rate, we hear no more of the
quarrel. Two years later several of Sidney's friends
alleged that Oxford had plotted his murder, intending to steal into his bedchamber and stab him ; but
the story needs confirmation, and, if there was any
truth at all in it, it may be assumed that no murder
was actually attempted.

How Sidney regarded the quarrel while it was
hottest may be seen from a letter he wrote to Sir
Christopher Hatton on the 28th of September, 1579.
"As for the matter depending between the Earl of
Oxford and me," he said, "certainly, sir, howsoever
I might have forgiven him, I should never have
forgiven myself, if I had lain under so proud an
injury as he would have laid upon me. Neither can
anything under the sun make me repent it, nor any
misery make me go one half word back from it.
Let him therefore, if he will, digest it. For my
part, I think tying up makes some things seem
fiercer than they would be."

Even the devout Languet considered that Sidney
was right in challenging his insulter to a duel. " I

am aware," he wrote, " that by a habit inveterate in all Christendom a gentleman is disgraced if he does not resent such an insult. I think you were unfortunate to be drawn into this contention ; but I see that no blame can be attached to you for your share in it."

Sidney's conduct was considered at Court to be not so much a bearding of the Earl of Oxford as a defiance of the whole French faction to which Oxford belonged. In that light he himself regarded it ; and from this time we find him taking bolder ground than heretofore with reference to the Queen's projected marriage.

He stayed on at Court till the commencement of 1580, and on New Year's Day he, as usual, made a present to her Majesty. But early in January he addressed to her a very bold and memorable letter.

In this letter he freely stated the objections he had all along felt to the proposed union with the Duke of Anjou. It was really a treatise, skilfully worded, and dealing in a masterly way with some of the chief aspects of the political situation then troubling all English Protestants.

It was the Protestants, Sidney urged, who were the stoutest, if not the only, supporters of the Queen's government. " How their hearts will be galled, if not aliened, when they shall see you take for a husband a Frenchman and a Papist, in whom (howsoever fine wits may find farther dealings or painted excuses) the very common people well know this, that he is the son of a Jezebel of our age—that his brother made oblation of his sister's marriage, the easier to make massacres of our brethren in belief—that he himself, contrary to his promise and to all gratefulness, having his liberty and principal estate by the Huguenots' means, did sack La Charité, and utterly spoil them with fire and sword!" The utter worthlessness and viciousness of the Duke of Anjou, Sidney plainly warned the Queen, "give occasion to all truly religious to abhor such a master and consequently to diminish much of the hopeful love they have long held to you." On the other hand, the Catholics, being always and perforce disaffected, having already and repeatedly plotted rebellions and devised treacheries, "at this present want nothing so much as a head, who in effect needs not to receive their instructions, since they may do mischief only with his countenance."

"Often have I heard you," Sidney wrote in another and especially interesting paragraph, "with protestation, say no private pleasure nor self-affection could lead you to it"—that is, to a married life. "If it be both unprofitable to your kingdom and unpleasant to you, it were a dear purchase of repentance. Nothing can it add unto you but the bliss of children, which I confess were a most unspeakable comfort, but yet no more appertaining to him than to any other to whom the height of all good haps were allotted, to be your husband. And therefore I may assuredly affirm that what good so ever can follow marriage is no more his than anybody's; but the evils and dangers are peculiarly annexed to his person and condition."

Sidney offered much more in the way of argument, entreaty, and expostulation; and in some of his sentences he showed himself a courtier as well as a patriot. After speaking of the scandalous stories that were sometimes floated concerning the Queen, he said: " I durst with my blood answer it that there was never monarch held in more precious reckoning of her people ; and, before God, how can it be otherwise ? For mine own part, when I hear some lost wretch hath defiled such a name with his mouth, I consider the right name of blasphemy, whose unbridled soul doth delight to deprave that which is accounted generally most high and holy. No, no, most excellent lady, do not raze out the impression you have made in such a multitude of hearts, and let not the scum of such vile minds bear any witness against your subjects' devotions ; which, to proceed one point further, if it were otherwise, could little be helped, but rather nourished and in effect begun, by this marriage."

" Since, then," the brave courtier wrote in conclusion—" since, then, it is dangerous for your State— since to your person it can be no way comfortable, you not desiring marriage, and neither to person nor State he is to bring any more good than anybody (but more evil he may)—since the causes that should drive you to this are fears of either that which cannot happen or by this means cannot be prevented— I do with most humble heart say unto your Majesty that, as for your standing alone, you must take it for a singular honour God hath done you, to be indeed the only protector of His Church. As for this man, as long as he is but Monsieur in might and a Papist in profession, he neither can nor will greatly shield

you ; and, if he get once to be king, his defence will
be like Ajax's shield, which rather weighed down
than defended those that bare it. Against contempt,
if there be any, which I will never believe, let your
excellent virtues of piety, justice, and liberality daily
—if it be possible—more and more shine. Let such
particular actions be found out, which be easy as I
think to be done, by which you may gratify all the
hearts of your people. Let those in whom you find
trust, and to whom you have committed trust in
your weighty affairs, be held up in the eyes of your
subjects. Lastly, doing as you do, you shall be as
you be, the example of princes, the ornament of this
age, the most excellent fruit of your progenitors, and
the perfect mirror of your posterity."

The good sense of this long epistle did not per-
suade the Queen, nor did the compliments with
which it ended conciliate her. For at least two
years longer she regarded the Duke of Anjou as her
suitor, and Sidney was punished for his boldness by
several months' exclusion from the royal presence.
But Languet was mistaken in supposing that he was
in danger of imprisonment and might have to flee
the country. "You will hardly find safety in Flanders," Languet wrote on the 30th of January, "and
still less in France ; your religion shuts you out of
Spain and Italy ; so that Germany is the only country left to receive you, should you be forced to quit
your own land."

For some time previous Languet had been anxious
that his friend, whom he had formerly counselled
against taking a personal share in the Protestant

struggle on the continent, should now join in the fight, if only for the sake of shaking off the courtly chains he was wearing. "If the Earl of Oxford's arrogance and insolence have awakened you from your sleep, he will have wronged you less than they who have been so indulgent to you," Languet had written on the 14th of November, 1579, and he had urged Sidney to follow this awakening by enlistment in the service of the Prince of Orange. "If your absence from home is not inconvenient to your noble father and your other kin, I think you ought to come. You will gain experience and information, and will return to them in such high repute that they will be glad of your absence and proud of what you have done."

Instead of crossing the Channel, Sidney went to Wilton and its neighbourhood, to find in the company of his sister relief from the annoyance to which he had been exposed as a wearer of court livery who deemed it his duty to instruct as well as to obey Queen Elizabeth, and to make progress in the literary pursuits that were always pleasant to him.

CORNER OF WILTON HOUSE

CHAPTER XI.

THE AREOPAGUS.

1578–1580.

ENTION has been made of " The Lady of May," the masque written by Philip Sidney for the entertainment of Queen Elizabeth when she visited his uncle at Wanstead on May-day, 1578, and of his presence with the Court at Audley End in the following July, when a leading part in the compliments offered to her Majesty and her attendants was taken by Gabriel Harvey, the Cambridge scholar. Harvey, who was a native of Saffron Walden, wrote and printed in September " Gratulationum Valdinensium Libri Quatuor," in honour of this royal visit to Cambridgeshire and its neighbourhood, and his book included a long poem in praise of Sidney, addressed " *ad nobilissimum humanissimumque juvenem Philippum Sidneium, mihi multis nominibus longe carissimum.*" The poem refers in extravagant terms to Sidney's literary ex-

ploits and other great achievements, and records the admiration in which he was then held by Henri Étienne (generally known in England as Henry Stephens), and many other learned men, besides Hubert Languet. Its absurd panegyric followed the fashion of the day, and needs much curtailment in order to bring it within bounds of sense and reason. But the fact that such a poem was addressed to Sidney in the summer of 1578 is significant and important. It shows us that " The Lady of May " was not a solitary diversion, and that Sidney was already known and highly thought of among men of letters, as well as among courtiers and politicians, promoters of discovery in the New World, and champions of freedom and right government in the Old.

Sidney's birth was contemporary with that of a new period, which was destined to be the greatest, in English literature. Spenser and Raleigh, Lyly and Hooker, were born one or two years earlier; Peel and Chapman two or three years later. Francis Bacon was his junior by six years, Christopher Marlowe by nine, and William Shakespeare by ten. All these, and many others of mark, were children together while early evidence was being given of the literary vigour which, perfected in them, was to make the age of Queen Elizabeth unrivalled in the history of intellectual activity. Sidney was two years old when the poems of Wyatt and Surrey, written long before, but then first published, set the fashion in England both of sonnet-making and of composition in blank verse. He was four when " The Mirror for

Magistrates," chiefly famous for the part supplied by his father's friend, Thomas Sackville, afterwards Lord Buckhurst, and ultimately Earl of Dorset, offered an example of the skilful writing of narrative poetry with which allegory was blended. He was seven when the same lordly poet made the first English experiment in tragedy by the performance before Queen Elizabeth of his and Norton's play of " Ferrex and Porrex," afterwards called " Gorboduc." He was eight or nine when " The Schoolmaster " was written by Roger Ascham, another of his father's friends, and probably his mother's tutor, as well as Lady Jane Grey's and Queen Elizabeth's.

The years before and after the appearance of " The Schoolmaster " are notable for their richness in able works on learned themes, and it is to this class of literature that Sidney seems to have given most heed in his youth. When Sidney was fourteen Ascham died. But Ascham, living in his books and in the memory of his associates, was, together with Hubert Languet, the young man's guide, both in the subjects and in the methods of his study. Zealously applying himself to the study of languages, Sidney valued them, not for their own sakes, but as necessary means to an understanding of philosophy and history. History he read, and enjoined his brother Robert to read, according to the plan indicated by the author of " The Schoolmaster,"—" marking diligently the causes, counsels, acts, and issues in all great attempts ; in causes, what is just or unjust ; in counsels, what is purposed wisely or rashly ; in acts, what is done courageously or faintly; and of every issue noting some general lesson of wisdom and warnings for like matters in time to come." And in pursuing philosophy he followed the same wise teacher, caring little for Duns Scotus and "all the rabble of barbarous questionists," as Ascham had termed them, and mainly fixing his attention upon Plato and Aristotle. Declaring himself anxious to learn Greek, if only for the sake of studying Aristotle's writings in Aristotle's words, he yet felt sympathy for the new Platonism, and the stout arguments against Aristotelian doctrine, urged by Ramus. Ramus was one of the victims of the St. Bartholomew massacre, and it is possible that Sidney met him in Paris. When three years later the then famous Banosius translated his friend's "Commentaries," and prefixed to them a life of the martyr, he promised the first copy of the book to Sidney, at that time only one-and-twenty, because, he said, of the young man's fondness for its theme, and of his ability to make it known among English scholars. With English as well as foreign scholars, including both theologians and anti-theologians, Sidney kept up close acquaintance all through his life. We have seen something of his relations with Philip du Plessis-Mornay. We shall presently find him in the company of Giordano Bruno.

When Sidney began life as a courtier in 1575, the bustle and frivolity of the Court did not favour abstruse study; but, in their own way, they furnished literary suggestion. In such masques and allegorical entertainments as he witnessed at Kenilworth, there was rough preparation for the English drama ; and if they gave hints to Shakespeare— who, it has been guessed, was present as a boy at the Kenilworth pageants, and remembered them when writing " A Midsummer Night's Dream "— they were not without effect on smaller craftsmen like Sidney. At Kenilworth Sidney met Thomas Sackville, and many other courtiers who emulated Sackville's skill in writing. There also he saw, and perhaps began a brief friendship with, George Gascoigne, a man of somewhat humbler birth, but a better poet, with more pungent wit and dramatic vigour, than any of the others. Gascoigne died in 1577, before reaching his fiftieth year, leaving, besides other works, a " Steel Glass," wherein were reflected both his own strength as a satirist and many of the vices and follies of the time.

Gascoigne, who had the Earl of Leicester for one of his patrons, chronicled " The Princely Pleasures of the Court at Kenilworth," which he had had a large share in producing. Another chronicler and part-producer was Robert Langham, a " servant " to Leicester, and a sort of usher to the Privy Council, who has left an amusing account of his experiences and occupations as a hanger-on at Court, a courtier's courtier. " If the Council sit, I am at hand," he reported. " If any make babbling, ' Peace,' say I, ' wot ye where ye are ? ' If I take a listener, or a prier in at the chinks or at the lock-hole, I am by and by in the bones of him. But now they keep good order : they know me well enough." Business being over, Langham went on to say, " for dinner

and supper I have twenty places to go to, and
heartily prayed too.   In afternoons and a nights,
sometimes I am with the right-worshipful Sir George
Howard, as good a gentleman as ever lives; and
sometimes at my good Lady Sidney's chamber, a
noblewoman that I am as much bound unto as any
poor man may be unto so gracious a lady; and
sometimes in some other places; but always among
the gentlewomen, by my good will.   Sometimes I
foot it with dancing; now with my gittern, or else
with my cithern, then at the virginals—ye know
nothing comes amiss to me.   Then carol I up a song
withal; then by and by they come flocking about
me like bees to honey; and ever they cry, 'Another,
good Langham, another!'   And to say truth, what
with mine eyes, as I can amorously gloat it, with my
Spanish *sospires*, my French *heighes*, my Italian
dulcets, my Dutch *hovez*, my double release, my
high reaches, my fine feigning, my deep diapason,
my wanton warbles, my running, my timing, my
tuning, and my twinkling, I can gratify the masters
as well as the proudest of them.   By my troth, it
is sometimes high midnight ere I can get from
them!''

Robert Langham may be taken as a fair specimen
of the tribe of jovial men who helped to amuse the
courtiers of Queen Elizabeth, and the Queen herself
and her ladies too, in days when the drama was in
its infancy, and when all who performed it in rude
or skilful ways only did so by license as " servants "
of one or other nobleman, the Earl of Leicester
being their chief patron.   We may take it for

granted that Philip was often entertained by Langham's buffooning in spare afternoons and evenings at Leicester House, in " my good Lady Sidney's chamber," and elsewhere.	This Robert Langham was doubtless a kinsman, perhaps a brother, of the John Langham for whom, along with James Burbage, John Perkyn, William Johnson, and Robert Wylson, the Earl of Leicester obtained from Queen Elizabeth in May, 1574, a special privilege " to use, exercise, and occupy the art and faculty of playing comedies, tragedies, interludes, stage plays, and such other, like as they have already used and studied, or hereafter shall use and study, as well for the recreation of our loving subjects as for our solace and pleasure when we shall think good to see them." That was the first royal patent for a company of players on record in England.	Beginning his courtier's life just a year afterwards, Sidney was, like his uncle, a great supporter of this movement, siding with the players in their feud with the Common Council of London, and especially with Burbage and the rest of " the Earl of Leicester's men," who obtained leave to build in 1576, the old Blackfriars Theatre, which then had for its only rivals the Theatre —so called by virtue of its claim to priority—and the Curtain in Shoreditch.

Burbage's company included, if not from the commencement, soon afterwards, Richard Tarleton, the most famous of all the clowns of the Elizabethan day, the " fellow of infinite jest, of most excellent fancy," who has been identified with the " poor Yorick " of Hamlet.	Tarleton was of plebeian

13

origin, the son of a swineherd, we are told, whom one of the Earl of Leicester's " servants " found tending his father's swine, and discovered to be a lad of such rare humour that he was brought to Court, where he soon became a prime favourite. " Our Tarleton," says Fuller, " was master of his faculty. When Queen Elizabeth was serious (I dare not say sullen) and out of good humour, he could undumpish her at his pleasure. Her highest favourites would in some cases go to Tarleton before they would go to the Queen, and he was their usher to prepare their advantageous access to her. In a word, he told the Queen more of her faults than most of her chaplains, and cured her melancholy better than all her physicians." Tarleton was one of the twelve players whom the Queen, when she was visiting Sir Francis Walsingham at Barn Elms, appointed " to have wages and livery as grooms of the chamber," one of them being Thomas Wilson, famed for his " quick, delicate, refined, and extemporal wit," while Tarleton, " for a wondrous, plentiful, and extemporal wit, was the wonder of his time, and so beloved that men used his picture for their signs." When not at Court or on the stage, Tarleton lived at the Sheba, a tavern in Gracechurch Street kept by his wife, whose nagging tongue, it was said, was a source of trouble to him.

How well Sidney thought of Tarleton may be inferred from the fact that in 1582 the courtier stood godfather to the player's child, who was christened Philip after him. From his death-bed, two years after Sidney's death, Tarleton wrote to Walsingham

reminding him of this, and imploring him to befriend
the boy who would soon be fatherless and the wife
about to become a widow.*

These things illustrate Sidney's connection with
the English drama before Shakespeare gave it new
life and dignity. Of course he saw more of the plays
and players at performances in private houses than
at places of public entertainment ; but perhaps he
was one of the " lively copemates " of Edmund
Spenser who, according to Gabriel Harvey, were in
the habit of going to " laugh their mouths and
bellies full for pence or twopence apiece," when
" my Lord of Leicester's, or my Lord of Warwick's,
or Vaux's, or my Lord Rich's players " were to be
seen at the Theatre in Shoreditch.†

Sidney had probably made the acquaintance of
Gabriel Harvey some while before they met at
Audley End in July, 1578. Harvey was then one of
the Earl of Leicester's " men." " Who is this ? "
asked the Queen, when the Cambridge teacher of
rhetoric and classical literature came up to pay his
respects to her. " Is it Leicester's man that we
were speaking of ? " On being told that it was, she
added " I will not deny you my hand, Harvey."
There was talk at that time of Harvey's going
abroad, in some unexplained capacity, on Leicester's
behalf. This arrangement apparently fell through,
but one which is far more noteworthy ensued on the

---

* State Papers, Elizabeth, Domestic ; Tarleton to Walsingham,
August (?), 1588.

† " The Letter-Book of Gabriel Harvey " (Camden Society, 1884),
pp. 67, 68.

Audley End meeting. Harvey's favourite pupil, Edmund Spenser, was brought under the Earl's notice, and soon afterwards we find him at Leicester House, as a sort of secretary or confidential agent of its owner, and, what is yet more interesting, as Sidney's friend.*

About two years older than Sidney, Spenser had matriculated at Harvey's college, Pembroke Hall, Cambridge, in 1569, and there he had remained till at any rate 1576, writing poems, and studying older poets, under Harvey's guidance. The guidance is generally supposed to have been, from a literary point of view, more injurious than helpful; but, if Harvey was fond of classical metres and involved diction, his influence certainly had no lasting effect, and there was more jest than earnest in his counsels. Harvey was a genial man of the world as well as a scholar, too much in sympathy with all new movements of thought to seriously approve the pedantries he defended in terms that look more like mockery than praise. Two of his Cambridge friends, who were also Spenser's, were John Still, afterwards

---

* In Spenser's " View of the State of Ireland," Ireneus, who throughout the dialogue speaks the writer's thoughts and relates many of the writer's experiences as his own, says that he was present at the execution of Murrogh O'Brien at Limerick, which occurred in July, 1577, while Sir Henry Sidney was Lord Deputy of Ireland. If we could be sure that Spenser himself saw what Ireneus says was seen by him, we should be able to date back a year or more the poet's acquaintance with Philip Sidney, or at any rate with Philip's father. But there is nothing else to warrant the assumption that Spenser was in Ireland so early as 1577, whereas there are good grounds for supposing that he was in Lancashire at this time.

EDMUND SPENSER.

FROM AN ENGRAVING BY W. B. SCOTT, 1839.

Bishop of Bath and Wells, writer of the old comedy, " Gammer Gurton's Needle," and Thomas Preston, who wrote the old tragedy, " Cambyses, King of Persia." In 1576 Spenser left Cambridge to reside in the north of England, perhaps at Hurstwood in Lancashire, and, if his " Shepherd's Calendar " is to be regarded as history, to fall in love with " the widow's daughter of the glen " whom there and elsewhere he calls Rosalind, styling himself Colin Clout and Harvey Hobbinol. By Harvey's advice and on his introduction, Spenser left the north and became an inmate of Leicester House in the autumn of 1578 or not long afterwards.

This was a memorable incident. If Spenser had a useful patron in the Earl of Leicester, he had a far more useful friend in Sidney; and to Sidney the friendship that sprang up between them was, in literary ways, far more serviceable than to Spenser. To it we must mainly attribute all the seriousness that there was in Sidney's work as an author. He had already, however, begun to find amusement in authorship; and at first—to some extent always—the difference in rank between the two caused Spenser to regard himself, doubtless without being so regarded by them, as inferior to Sidney and the other courtiers who welcomed his company. " The two worthy gentlemen, Mr. Sidney and Mr. Dyer," Spenser said in a letter written to Gabriel Harvey on the 16th of October, 1579, " have me, I thank them, in some use of familiarity; of whom and to whom what speech passeth for your credit and estimation I leave yourself to conceive, having always so well conceived of my unfeigned affection and good will towards you."

The "some use of familiarity" must have been considerable for at least several months before October, 1579. All through this year, while he was finding both pleasure and annoyance in his attendance on the Queen, trying to act with dignity as a courtier and to show himself a statesman as well, taking a prominent part in the opposition to the Queen's talked-of marriage with the Duke of Anjou long before the date of his famous letter to her on the subject in January, 1580, and having to resent or submit to much rudeness from rivals like the Earl of Oxford, it is certain that Sidney, with Dyer, Greville, and other friends, often sought refreshment in the society of Spenser at Leicester House and elsewhere—with perhaps an occasional holiday at Penshurst.

Scarcely any record exists of visits paid by Sidney to Penshurst, and we know of none in which Spenser was his companion there. But there can be no doubt that in the year 1579, while the old house was being enlarged and beautified, he ran down oftener than usual to his father's proper home, though it was rarely tenanted by his father, and that Spenser was frequently there with him before the poet went to Ireland in the autumn of 1580. We see more suggestion of Lancashire than of Kent —from Rosalind's frequent appearance in it down to the dialect it favours—in "The Shepherd's Calendar"; but its many reminiscences of the scenery of Penshurst and the neighbourhood warrant the con-

THE MINSTRELS' GALLERY IN THE BARONIAL HALL OF PENSHURST PLACE.

clusion that it was partly inspired and perhaps in part written there, while other passages could no-where else have been penned so well as at Leicester House or other purlieus of the Court, as the result of the writer's intercourse with Sidney and Sidney's uncle. It was to Sidney that Spenser, calling himself Immerito, dedicated "The Shepherd's Calendar":

> Go, little book, thyself present
> As child whose parent is unkent,
> To him that is the president
> Of nobless and of chivalry ;
> And if that envy bark at thee,
> As sure it will, for succour flee
> Under the shadow of his wing ;
> And, askèd who thee forth did bring,
> A shepherd's swain, say, did thee sing
> All as his straying flock he fed ;
> And, when his honour has thee read,
> Crave pardon for thy hardihead.

The "little book" was not published till the end of 1579, but its editor, E. K.—supposed to be Edward Kirke,—writing to Gabriel Harvey on the 10th of April, said that its author had "already in the beginning, dedicated it to the noble and worthy gentleman, the right worshipful Master Philip Sidney, a special favourer and maintainer of all kinds of learning."

Writing to Harvey on the 16th of October, while "The Shepherd's Calendar" must have been passing through the press, Spenser said of Sidney, Dyer, and their friends: "Now they have proclaimed in their Areopagus a general surceasing and silence of bald rhymers, and also of the very best too ; instead whereof they have, by authority of their whole senate, prescribed certain laws and rules of quantities of English syllables for English verse." This sentence shows us that the Areopagus had been in existence for some time before October, 1579, and that it had then entered on a new pastime.

The Areopagus was a sort of club, composed mainly of courtiers, who aspired to be also men of letters, apparently with Sidney as its president, to which were admitted other men of letters—Spenser in particular—who hardly aspired to rank with the courtiers. It seems to have had Harvey as a corresponding member and counsellor-in-chief. Among its exercises we may reckon Sidney's "Lady of May," produced in 1578, and some other of his compositions which, though undated, bear marks of crudeness. Dyer and Greville were evidently busy members. Though very little of his writing survives, Dyer was accounted a great poet in his time, and the ponderous tragedies by Greville which are extant were, as he tells us, written in his younger days, when Sidney was his associate in literary pursuits. Who were the other members of the club we know not; but its interest to us is in the connection of Spenser and Sidney with it; Sidney as the foremost and worthiest of the Elizabethan courtiers who found refining and exalting occupation for themselves, and relief from Court frivolities and State squabbles, in cultivating the Muses; Spenser, as, apart from Shakespeare who was still in his teens, the greatest of Elizabethan poets. Spenser's fame was of his own winning and his own deserving, but he owed much, and he thankfully acknowledged it, to the high-souled and pure-minded companion who was his patron, in the best sense of the term. And Sidney, only in his twenty-fifth year, was not the helper of Spenser alone. As E. K. testifies, he was " the special favourer and maintainer of all kinds of learning." Of this we shall see more hereafter. At present we must think of him as the president, not only " of nobless and of chivalry," but also of the Areopagus, which in the autumn of 1579 added to its other functions, as Spenser said, " a general sur-ceasing and silence of bald rhymers, and also of the very best too."

This part of the task taken upon itself by the Areopagus has been more ridiculed, and has been made to appear more important, than there is reason for.* There was evidently more frolic than serious-ness in it, and there was a serious purpose in the frolic. We have no account of any contemporary literary club like the Areopagus, but there were other cliques of literary workmen with patrons of their own. One such centred round the Earl of Oxford, and it is noteworthy that the rules for unrhymed versification which Sidney appears to have drawn up with Harvey's assistance were issued only a few weeks after Sidney's open quarrel with Oxford in the Whitehall tennis-court. How much personal feeling or partisanship was mixed up in the adaptation of the classical metres prescribed by the Areopagus may be seen from this example of the rude way in which,

* See especially Haslewood's " Ancient Critical Essays upon English Poets and Poems " (1818), vol. ii.

as Thomas Nash tells us, Harvey "came very short yet sharp upon my lord of Oxford, in a rattling bundle of English hexameters":

Strait to the back like a shirt ; and close to the breech like a diveling ;
A little apish hat, couched fast to the pate, starched to the purpose ;
Delicate in speech ; quaint in array ; conceited in all points ;
In courtly guiles a passing singular odd man.

The poets of the Areopagus were quite as anxious to make fun of their rivals as to establish classical forms in English verse-writing. Gabriel Harvey, however, evidently believed in his hobby ; and Spenser—though he declared with some truth that all such productions stumble "either like a lame gosling that draweth one leg after, or like a lame dog that holdeth one leg up"—rode the hobby with some skill, as appears from this utterance of a lover's woes :

Unhappy verse ! the witness of my unhappy state,
Make thyself fluttering wings of thy fast flying
Thought, and fly forth unto my love, wheresoe'er she be,

Whether lying restless on heavy bed, or else
Sitting so cheerless at the cheerful board, or else
Playing alone, careless, on her heavenly virginals.

If in bed, tell her that my eyes can take no rest ;
If at board, tell her that my mouth can eat no meat ;
If at her virginals, tell her I can bear no mirth.

Tell her that her pleasures were wont to lull me to sleep ;
Tell her that her beauty was wont to feed mine eyes ;
Tell her that her sweet tongue was wont to make me mirth.

Now do I nightly waste, wanting my kindly rest ;
Now do I daily starve, wanting my lively food ;
Now do I always die, wanting my timely mirth.

Sidney played longer than his friend with classic measures. He used them freely in his " Arcadia." Here, for instance, is part of a lover's strain in sapphics :

If mine eyes can speak to do hearty errand,
Or mine eyes' language else do hap to judge of,
So that eyes' message be of her received,
    Hope, we do live yet.

But if eyes fail then when I most do need them,
Or if eyes' language be not unto her known,
So that eyes' message do return rejected,
    Hope, we do both die.

Yet dying and dead do we sing her honour ;
So become our tombs monuments of her praise ;
So becomes our loss the triumph of her gain.
    Hers be the glory,

If the spheres, senseless, do yet hold a music,
If the swan's sweet voice be not heard but at death,
If the mute timber, when it hath the life lost,
    Yieldeth a lute's tune.

But at no time was imitation of classical measures other than a pastime either to Sidney or to Spenser. Sidney was now only commencing the authorship that was never much more than a diversion from what he regarded as the real business of his life. Spenser, in spite of any Areopagus rules to the contrary, was now producing plenty of rhymed verse.

In 1579 and 1580 Spenser wrote several poems, of which all but the titles, and a few vague references to them by E. K. and others, as well as by himself, have been lost, or which may have been re-shaped by him in later works. One of these was called "Stemmata Dudleiana," clearly a poem in praise of the Earl of Leicester and his kindred. "Of my 'Stemmata Dudleiana,'" Spenser wrote to Harvey in April, 1580, "especially of the sundry apostrophes therein, addressed to you know whom"—apparently to Sidney,—"must more advertisement be had than so lightly to send them abroad. Howbeit, trust me, though I do never do very well, yet, in my own fancy, I never did better." Another was a poem called "Slumber," written before October, 1579, when Spenser told Harvey he thought of dedicating it "and the other pamphlets" to Master Dyer—to whom a year later he took upon himself the responsibility of dedicating a work of Harvey's, "Verlayes," as to "the right worshipful gentleman and famous courtier, Master Edward Dyer, in a manner our only English poet." It is worth noting that about this time Harvey, in a letter to Spenser, spoke of Dyer and Sidney as "the two very diamonds of her Majesty's Court for many special and rare qualities."

In Spenser's letter mentioning his "Slumber" there is mention of another and very different work, "The School of Abuse," written by Stephen Gosson in 1579, and dedicated to Sidney. It was according to the title-page, "a pleasant invective against poets, pipers, players, jesters, and such like caterpillars of a commonwealth ; setting up the flag of defiance to their mischievous exercise, and over-throwing their bulwarks, by profane writers, natural reason, and common experience." The book in no way agreed with Sidney's views, and Gosson was, as Spenser informed Harvey in October, " for his labour scorned, if at least it be in the goodness of that nature to scorn : such folly is it not to regard afore-hand the inclination and quality of him to whom we dedicate our books."

Whatever scorn Sidney may have felt he seems to have kindly kept from the knowledge of Gosson, who, in his ignorant boldness, dedicated to him in November another book, " The Ephemerides of Phialo." " I cannot," he here said, " but acknowl-edge my safety in your worship's patronage, and offer you ' Phialo,' my chiefest jewel, as a manifest pledge of my thankful heart."

We may readily imagine that, instead of scorning the poor author, Sidney, poor enough himself, sent him a handsome present for his pains, one of the kind then generally looked for by book-writers from those they complimented with dedications. But Sidney was not converted by " The School of Abuse." On the contrary, he wrote in reply to it " The Defence of Poesy," which is also known as " An Apology for Poetry." *

The polished style and sober judgments on most of the subjects touched upon in this treatise might

---

* It was published under both titles, in separate editions, in 1595. Some critics now prefer to call it " An Apology for Poetry " ; but Sidney himself says, in his opening paragraph : " I have just cause to make a pitiful Defence of poor Poetry."

justify us in assigning it to a later date than "The Arcadia," and "Astrophel and Stella." But there are grounds for thinking that it was written before either of those works. Though in it "The School of Abuse" is not mentioned, and is but vaguely alluded to, it was evidently prompted by Gosson's book, and, as "The Shepherd's Calendar" is here spoken of by Sidney as the latest of the noteworthy poems he had seen, it may be supposed to have been penned soon after the publication of Spenser's work. Two points, at any rate, are clear. The one is, that when Sidney wrote it, he had not broken away from the theories of the Areopagus; the other, that he had already acquired reputation as a poet. "Having," he says in his opening paragraph, "I know not by what mischance, in these my not old years and idlest times, stepped into the title of a poet, I am provoked to say something to you in defence of that my unelected vocation, which if I handle with more good will than good reasons, bear with me." Those are words that might have fallen gracefully from the lips of the president of the Areopagus. Let it be remembered, moreover, that what Sidney regarded as his "idlest times" were the months in 1580 which he passed in enforced absence from the Court, and that, whenever "The Defence of Poesy" was written, the views and criticisms set forth in it were just such as may have been offered by Sidney during the brief period, between the end of 1578 and the autumn of 1580, which covered all his personal intercourse with Spenser.

That intercourse was certainly close while it

lasted, and in it many seeds were sown from which rich fruit resulted for both men. "The Fairy Queen" had been projected, and its earlier portions written or sketched out, before Spenser removed to London and came under Sidney's influence, and by far the larger part of this splendid fragment was not completed till after Sidney's death; and that other splendid fragment, "The Arcadia," was begun and carried on as much under the inspiration of Sidney's sister, the Countess of Pembroke, as of Spenser. But it is not over-fanciful to assume that the schemes of these two works, each an epic in its way, were often discussed by the two friends as they held pleasant converse in Leicester House, or strolled, with opportunities for yet pleasanter converse, through the woods of Penshurst and by the banks of the Medway.

Among the complimentary verses prefixed to the first edition of "The Fairy Queen," in 1590, are some by W. H., which indicate a portion of Spenser's debt to Sidney.

> When Spenser saw the fame was spread so large,
>   Through Fairy-land, of their renownèd Queen,
> Loth that his muse should take so great a charge
>   As in such haughty matter to be seen,
> To seem a shepherd then he made his choice:
> But Sidney heard him sing and knew his voice.
>
> And as Ulysses brought fair Thetis' son
>   From his retirèd life to manage arms,
> So Spenser was by Sidney's speeches won
>   To blaze her fame, not fearing future harms;
> For well he knew his muse would soon be tired
> In her high praise whom all the world admired.

> Yet, as Achilles in those warlike frays
>   Did win the palm from all the Grecian peers,
> So Spenser now, to his immortal praise,
>   Hath won the laurel now from all his feres.
> What though his task exceed a human wit?
> He is excused, since Sidney thought it fit.

And the debt was acknowledged by Spenser himself in the sonnet introducing " The Fairy Queen," which he addressed to Sidney's sister after Sidney had been dead three years:

> ✓   Remembrance of that most heroic spirit—
>   The heaven's pride, the glory of our days,
> Which now triumpheth, through immortal merit
>   Of his brave virtues, crowned with lasting bays
>   Of heavenly bliss and everlasting praise—
> Who first my muse did lift out of the floor
>   To sing his sweet delights in lowly lays,
> Bids me, most noble lady, to adore
> His goodly image, living evermore
>   In the divine resemblance of your face,
> Which with your virtues ye embellish more,
>   And native beauty deck with heavenly grace.
> For his and for your own especial sake,
> Vouchsafe from him this token in good worth to take.

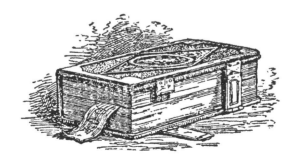

CHAPTER XII.

AT WILTON.

1580.

IDNEY may have paid more than one visit to his sister at Wilton in the course of the two and a half years following the summer of 1577, when he went down to congratulate her on her marriage, and he must certainly have seen much of her during her attendance at Court; but we have no record of his being again, before the early spring of 1580, in the stately mansion, since destroyed by fire, which had been built, according to Holbein's plans, in the loveliest part of Wiltshire. He was now to be there and in the neighbourhood for half a year or more. Withdrawing from the Court in dudgeon and disgrace, he could nowhere obtain so much refreshment as in the company of the Countess of Pembroke, the esteemed lady whom Spenser, and many others, never tired of praising.

> The gentlest shepherdess that lives this day,
> And most resembling, both in shape and sprite,
> Her brother dear,

Spenser calls her in one place; and in another he speaks of her as one

> In whose brave mind, as in a golden coffer,
> All heavenly gifts and riches lockèd are;
> More rich than pearls of Ind or gold of Ophir,
> And in her sex more wonderful and rare.

Sidney was at Wilton on the 25th of March, 1580; and probably his mother was there, too, for a fortnight later his nephew William, afterwards the friend and patron of Shakespeare, was born. He was there, also on the 28th of April, the baby's christening day, when he represented the Earl of Leicester, who was one of the sponsors, the others being the Earl of Warwick and Queen Elizabeth—on whose behalf the Countess of Warwick appeared.

Her Majesty was willing to pay a compliment to the Countess of Pembroke, for whom, from first to last, she had genuine liking, and with whom it was not possible for her to pick a quarrel. But she was angry with the rest of the family. Leicester was still out of favour, and with Sir Henry Sidney she was again displeased.

Ever since his return from Ireland Sir Henry had been busy as Lord President of Wales, and in the early months of 1580 he often resorted to Wilton. Queen Elizabeth sent a message in June to say that she disliked this proceeding, and that, considering

MARY HERBERT, COUNTESS OF PEMBROKE.
FROM ZUCCHERO'S PORTRAIT AT PENSHURST.

the dangerous state of Wales and the need of keeping it in a proper state of defence, Sir Henry ought to be constantly at his post. In August she censured him again ; this time for not being more zealous in hunting down Catholics and thus advancing the reformation of "recusants and other obstinate persons in religion." "Your lordship," Walsingham wrote to him, "had need to walk warily ; for your doings are narrowly observed, and her Majesty is apt to give ear to any that shall ill you."

Philip, holding no important office under the Crown, could not be taken to task. He was free, indeed, to go back to Court much sooner than he thought fit. The Earl of Leicester was restored to favour in July, and it seems that Philip was expected to at once rejoin his uncle. On the 2d of August he wrote to Leicester saying that he had a bad cold which kept him from Court, and that doubtless her Majesty would ask for him. "But," he added, "so long as her Majesty sees a silk doublet upon me, her Highness will think me in good case." *

He was in no hurry to return, and, when he did, it appears to have been by the persuasion of his friends, one of them being Languet, who, as soon as he found his fears that Sidney might be sent to prison were groundless, was anxious he should resume his services to his country and the Protestant cause in Europe. "All who are in these parts," Languet wrote from Antwerp on the 24th of September, "wonder that you should delight in this long re-

---

* MS. in the possession of Mr. Cottrell-Dormer, at Rousham, near Oxford.

tirement of yours. They can readily understand your liking to be with those you especially love; but they think it undignified for you to remain so long concealed. They fear, also, that seclusion will loosen the stern vigour with which you formerly worked so nobly, and that listlessness, which at one time you despised, is gradually possessing your soul."

There was consistency in Languet's alternate counselling of Sidney, when he was at Court, to avoid becoming engrossed in courtly pleasures, and, when he was away from it, to remember that there were duties for him to perform there. " While you were living with me," he said in this letter, " you used to tell me that you hated the noise and glitter of courts, and were resolved to live in honest ease and in the society of a few real friends; but I supposed that your thoughts would change as you grew older, and that your duty to your country would keep you in public life. And I seemed to suppose rightly. No sooner had you returned to England than all men admired you and all good men sought your friendship. Above all, your noble Queen treated you with marked good-will, and admitted you to great familiarity with herself, and honoured you with that famous embassage to the Emperor which, three years ago, you conducted so creditably." One of his reasons for quitting Germany and coming to live in the Netherlands, Languet went on to say, was that he might better watch his friend's advancement. " But when I came hither I found a cloud thrown over your fortunes, which turned my pleasure into sorrow.   Surely this ought not to be.   Ask yourself, I do beseech you, how far it is honourable for you to lurk where you are, while your country is claiming help from all her sons.   If the advice you offered to your Queen, thinking it helpful to the nation, was not taken as it deserved to be, you ought not on that account to be angry with your country or to desist from seeking its safety.   When Themistocles proposed measures beneficial to the State, and Eurybiades threatened to strike him unless he held his peace, he answered, ' Strike, but hear.'   Imitate Themistocles."

In accordance with that advice, Sidney went back to Court in the autumn.   He was at Leicester House on the 10th of October, when he wrote one of the long letters to his brother Robert which has already been mentioned.   It was a very wise letter, full of shrewd and kind remarks, showing his desire that Robert should make good use of his opportunities while studying and travelling abroad ; but its earnestness and forced gaiety betrayed weariness.   " I write this to you," Philip said, " as one that, for myself, have given over the delight in the world."   One of the studies he urged Robert not to neglect was music.   " You will not believe what a want I find it in my melancholy times."

It was by way of shaking off his melancholy, and to please his sister, that Sidney spent much of his time at Wilton in writing " The Countess of Pembroke's Arcadia," of which probably a considerable portion was composed in the course of this summer. " Here now have you, most dear and most worthy to be most dear lady, this idle work of mine," he wrote a year or so later, in dedicating to her so much as he had put together before he set it aside for more serious occupation. " You desired me to do it, and your desire to my heart is an absolute commandment. Now it is done only for you, only to you. If you keep it to yourself, or to such friends who will weigh error in the balance of good-will, I hope for the father's sake it will be pardoned, perchance made much of, though in itself it have deformities. For, indeed, for severer eyes it is not, being but a trifle, and that triflingly handled. Your dear self can best witness the manner, being done in loose sheets of paper, most of it in your presence, the rest by sheets sent unto you as fast as they were done. In sum, a young head—not so well stayed as I would it were, and shall be, when God will—having many, many fancies begotten in it, if it had not been in some way delivered, would have grown a mon-ster; and more sorry might I be that they came in than that they got out."

Those modest, naïve sentences, which must be re-membered in judging the merits of " The Arcadia," show the conditions under which the work, a pastime and rather more, was commenced. Sidney, who a few months before must have seen the first rough sketch of his friend Spenser's " Fairy Queen," had doubtless not only discussed with him the plan and purpose of that poem, but also broached to him the project of a somewhat kindred work of his own, one that, like " The Fairy Queen," should combine alle-gory and satire in a bold presentment, fanciful and fictitious, of an ideal world, typifying vices and follies as well as wisdom and virtue. But perhaps " The Arcadia "—so much as there is of it—would never have been written had not Sidney come down to Wilton for rest and refreshment and, at the bidding of his sister, found both in setting forth the astounding adventures of Musidorus and Pyrocles and the many difficulties and complications that hampered them, and that hampered no less Philoclea and Pamela, before the two brave youths could severally enjoy the love of the two chaste maidens on whom their hearts were set. " My great uncle, Mr. T. Brown," Aubrey, a native of Salisbury, wrote concerning Sidney, " remembered him and said that when he was writing his ' Arcadia ' he was wont to take his table book out of his pocket and write down his notions as they came into his head, as he was hunting on our pleasant plains."

Some of the local colouring in " The Arcadia " is evidently due to the scenery around Wilton, just as in its profusion of jousting and tourneying there are reminiscences of Sidney's own experiences in the Whitehall tilt-yard. For the characters sketched in it, moreover, Sidney may have taken some suggestions from the men and women known to him. But we must not suppose that in any one of them he intended to delineate his kinsfolk, friends, or rivals, or himself. They are all ideals, types of the temperament or deportment, the physical or mental qualities, that he liked or disliked. In Musidorus, for instance, Sidney pictured the man he would gladly be when he assigned to him " a mind of most excellent

composition, a piercing wit quite devoid of ostenta-
tion, high erected thoughts seated in a heart of courtesy, an eloquence as sweet in the uttering as it was
slow to come to the uttering, and a behaviour so
noble as gave a majesty to adversity"; yet Musidorus
is not Sidney. Neither Philoclea nor Pamela, again,
resembles the Countess of Pembroke; but in drawing both portraits Sidney proved that from his
sister Mary, and not from her alone, he had learned
to reverence the finest charms of womanhood.
"When I marked them both," said Musidorus to
Pyrocles, "methought there was (if at least such
perfections may receive the word of more) more
sweetness in Philoclea, but more majesty in Pamela:
methought love played in Philoclea's eyes, and
threatened in Pamela's; methought Philoclea's
beauty only persuaded, but so persuaded as all
hearts must yield; Pamela's beauty used violence,
and such violence as no heart could resist."

"The Arcadia" shows remarkable art, and yet
more remarkable purity, in its portrayal of womankind. As finished studies, endowed with flesh and
blood, and also with mental and moral qualities con-
sistently maintained through a long series of involved
and very trying situations, Philoclea and Pamela are
far more human and far more truly feminine than
most of the conceptions of female character presented by the Elizabethan writers. Nor do these two
heroines stand alone. Some of Sidney's sketches
of women are grotesque; others are extravagant;
but in all, however much mockery or exaggeration
they contain, we see the work of an artist who under-

stands his craft and has a clear vision of the picture he aims at drawing.

In the skill and the delicacy of Sidney's women-portraiture there is welcome indication not only of his talent as an artist, but yet more of his temper as a man. He evidently had such accurate perception of the characteristics and capacities of " the other sex " as few of his own sex possessed or, possessing it, cared to display. It is not strange that, to amuse his sister or himself, he should have chosen to write a long love-story or rather concatenation of love-stories —which " The Arcadia " is, alike in its pastoral and in its heroic passages ; but it is strange that he should either have chosen or have been able to make all his interwoven love-stories serve for so dignified and so discriminating a presentment of womanhood at its best. Or this would be strange if it were not in keeping with all else that is known about his chivalrous disposition, which no adverse conditions could spoil.

No doubt he had special inducements for setting down while he was at Wilton so " many, many fancies " about womankind, " begotten " in his " young head," which, he considered, " if it had not been in some way delivered, would have grown a monster." Pamela was but a vague idealisation of his sister, whose circumstances and experiences were no counterpart to those of the elder daughter of Basilius ; but Lady Pembroke may have suggested Pamela. If so, whence came the suggestion of Philoclea, the sister preferred by Pyrocles, who, more than Musidorus, resembles Sidney himself?

Perhaps we may find a very shadowy suggestion indeed in Lady Penelope Devereux, the Stella to whom Sidney was soon, if he had not already begun, to render homage in verse.

One of his Wilton occupations, during this or a later visit, was in helping the Countess of Pembroke with her rhymed version of " The Psalms of David." But only the first forty-three translations, which are of little merit, are attributed to Sidney. They are chiefly interesting, like his earlier work as a member of the Areopagus, for their evidence of his delight in literary exercises. They may also to some extent indicate his religious mood.

This mood was constant, and was in no way contradictory to the zeal with which he threw himself into the Court gaieties that were part of his daily life as one of Queen Elizabeth's chief favourites, or amused himself with writing love-stories and love-ditties when he was removed from the royal presence. Though in Spenser's pastoral poem, "Astrophel," there is much that must not be taken literally, and though it contains one very suggestive couplet, which speaks of Sidney as

> In one thing only failing of the best
> That he was not so happy as the rest,

we may accept as true this description of his friend :

> His sports were fair, his joyance innocent,
>   Sweet without sour, and honey without gall ;
> And he himself seemed made for merriment,
>   Merrily masquing both in bower and hall.
> There was no pleasure nor delightful play
> When Astrophel soever was away.

> For he could pipe, and dance, and carol sweet
>   Among the shepherds in their shearing feast,
> As summer's lark that with her song doth greet
>   The dawning day forth coming from the east.
> And lays of love he also could compose :
> Thrice happy she whom he to praise did choose !

Sidney, while at Wilton, was not unmindful of the poet-friend whom he had left in London, but whose fortunes must have been to some extent overshadowed by the displeasure that had fallen on the Earl of Leicester and his nephew. Spenser was now busily writing poems, but in want of the more lucrative employment which was soon found for him, apparently at Sidney's instigation. Lord Grey of Wilton, who, in the summer of 1580, was appointed Lord Deputy of Ireland, and who reached Dublin on the 12th of August, was an intimate friend both of Philip Sidney and of his father. He looked to Sir Henry for counsel as to the way in which his troublesome business should be done, and he followed, as far as he could, the example of the experienced administrator of Irish affairs. With him went Spenser, as his secretary, to be in the following March promoted to a well-paid clerkship in the Irish Court of Chancery. The poet may have owed this advancement to his own talents as a man of business, or to Lord Grey's good opinion of him ; but it was probably through the Sidneys' influence that he was started on the career which, distasteful to him in some ways, was on the whole much to his advantage.

Meanwhile other friends were awaiting Sidney in London. Perhaps it was soon after his return to

Court, in the autumn of 1580, that he wrote a pretty pastoral, " upon his meeting with his two worthy friends and fellow-poets, Master Dyer and Master Fulke Greville," which thus begins :

> Join, mates, in mirth to me ;
> Grant pleasure to our meeting :
> Let Pan, our good god, see
> How grateful is our greeting.
> Join hearts and hands, so let it be ;
> Make but one mind in bodies three.

And perhaps it was at about the same time that he wrote another pastoral, " Dispraise of a Courtly Life," in which the same two friends, as well as some others, are alluded to.

> Well was I while under shade,
> Oaten reeds me music made ;
> Striving with my mates in song,
> Mixing mirth our songs among.
> Greater was the shepherd's treasure
> Than this false, fine, courtly pleasure.
>
> Where, how many creatures be,
> So many puffed in mind I see ;
> Like to Juno's birds of pride,
> Scarce each other can abide ;
> Friends like to black swans appearing,
> Sooner these than those in hearing.
>
> Therefore, Pan, if thou may'st be
> Made to listen unto me,
> Grant, I say, if silly man
> May make treaty to god Pan,
> That I without thy denying,
> May be still to thee relying,

FULKE GREVILLE, LORD BROOKE.

FROM AN ENGRAVING IN LODGE'S "PORTRAITS."

Only for my two loves' sake
In whose love I pleasure take.
Only two do me delight
With their ever-pleasing sight ;
Of all men to thee retaining
Grant me with those two remaining.

CHAPTER XIII.

AT COURT AGAIN.

1580–1582.

 "AM glad," Hubert Languet wrote to Sidney from Antwerp, on·the 28th of October, 1580, "that you have abandoned your retirement and returned to the daylight of the Court. But I am afraid that you will soon get weary of it. I see that its honours and dignities are given to age and wealth, rather than to virtue and prudence, so that you, who are yet young and without property of your own, will not easily reap any advantage. It will be dreary work for you, wasting the spring-time of your life amid the formalities and indolence of a Court ; for the occupations of courtiers do not often advance the public good, and are very seldom concerned with the better part of life." "I think there are not many men among you," added the plain-speaking Huguenot, "who would

222

prefer the welfare of the State to their own interests. I foresee many troubles, a future when your noble-men will be separated into factions, and at strife with one another, when the neighbouring nations will throw fuel on the fire which is to be kindled among you. Believe me, there are storms brewing which are not to be dispelled by the fallacies that have well-nigh driven all noble-mindedness and simplicity of thought out of the Christian world."

Languet's forebodings were based especially on the prospect, still desired by some and dreaded by others, of a marriage between Queen Elizabeth and the Duke of Anjou. Sidney's re-instatement in the Queen's favour, like the Earl of Leicester's, appears to have been conditional on his no longer opposing the match. Both he and his uncle henceforward abstained from protests, and left the Queen to amuse herself in her own way with her ungainly and unworthy suitor; perhaps, while quietly aiming at its overthrow, trusting to the chance of the project breaking down through its absurdity.

Leicester was at this time, with Sidney as his associate, if not as his prompter, working secretly for the protection of the Prince of Orange and the few Dutch provinces loyal to the Protestant cause against the encroachments of the Spaniards under the new leadership of the Duke of Parma. There was even some talk of Leicester being nominated to the sovereignty over the Protestant provinces, in the north, which William at length, and much against his wishes, assumed in July, 1581. The Catholic provinces, in the south, had already for some time been under the ostensible headship of Anjou ; all, of course, being still claimed and lorded over by Parma, as King Philip's viceroy. Before William could be persuaded to take up the bold position from which modesty and excess of caution, certainly not cowardice, too long withheld him, he was anxious that it should be assigned to Leicester, whose capacities as a ruler were overestimated, and who was expected to bring into the contest the whole weight of English influence ; and it was now considered by both William and Leicester, and by their friends, that Anjou, contemptible as he was, and partly because of his faults and weaknesses, might serve as a figurehead for such defiance of Spanish authority as the Dutch Protestants did not feel themselves strong enough to maintain without help from their Catholic fellow-countrymen.

There is nothing to show what part Sidney took in these arrangements. From one of the few " Astrophel and Stella " sonnets, in which he touched on public events, it may be inferred that he regarded them with but languid interest and scant approval. In this sonnet he curiously sums up the chief political problems that perplexed and irritated others beside himself in the autumn of 1580 or soon after. He refers not only to the Dutch disasters of this year, which included the Spanish acquisition, by force or guile, of Maestricht, Mechlin, Groeningen, and other towns, but also to the threatened Ottoman crusade against Italy ; to the designs of Stephen Bathori, the newly elected King of Poland, against Russia ; to the religious turmoils in France, where Henry of

Navarre was preparing to seize the crown and change his creed ; to the blundering efforts of Lord Grey of Wilton to carry out Sir Henry Sidney's policy in Ireland ; and to the new broils in Scotland between the partisans and enemies of the imprisoned Queen Mary.

> Whether the Turkish new moon minded be
>> To fill his horns this year on Christian coast ?
>> How Poles' right king means, without leave of host,
> To warm with ill-made fire cold Muscovy ?
> If French can yet three parts in one agree ?
>> What now the Dutch in their full diets boast ?
>> How Holland hearts—now so good towns be lost—
> Trust in the shade of pleasant Orange-tree ?
> How Ulster likes of that same golden bit
>> Wherewith my father once made it half-tame ?
> If in the Scotch Court be no weltering yet ?
>> These questions busy wits to me do frame.
> I, cumbered with good manners, answer do,
> But know not how ; for still I think of you.

Near the end of the long letter that Sidney wrote to his brother Robert from Leicester House on the 18th of October, very soon after his return to Court, he said : "My eyes are almost closed up, overwatched with tedious business." What that business was— over and above the continuing of "The Arcadia," and other literary work, which he can scarcely have found tedious—we do not know. But he was evidently ill at ease.

There must have been grim humour in an earlier letter to Robert, the purport of which appears from the lad's reference to it in writing to his father. "My brother," Robert reported from Prague on the

15

1st of November, " wrote that, if there were any good wars, I should go to them ; but as yet I have heard of none." As a further reason against acting on Philip's advice, Robert pointed out that, even if there were any " good wars " to be gone to, his small allowance would not suffice to procure him safe and dignified equipment for the same. Robert had already been obliged to obtain help from Philip, with which to supplement his father's remittances. " For the money you have received," we read in the letter from Philip already quoted, " assure yourself— for it is true—there is nothing I spend so pleaseth me as that which is for you. If ever I have the ability, you will find it ; if not, yet shall not any brother living be better loved than you of me."

The Sidney family, now as heretofore and hereafter, was short of money. Sir Henry, who through all the years he was in Ireland, had been compelled to spend in the service of the Queen an average of £60 a week, whereas his salary was only about £30, at present found his allowance as Lord President of Wales quite insufficient for the duties he had to perform. " I have only £20 a week to keep an honourable house, and a 100 marks a year to bear foreign charges," we find him complaining from Ludlow Castle, in March, 1583 ; and the complaint was as well founded in the autumn of 1580. " What house I keep, I dare stand to the report of any indifferent man. True books of account shall be shown to you that I spend above £30 a week. Here some may object that upon the same I keep my wife and her followers. True it is, she is now with me, and hath

been this half year; but before not in many years.
And if both she and I had our food and house-room
free, as we have not, in conscience we have deserved
it. For my part, I am not idle, but every day I work in
my function ; and she, for her old service, and marks,
yet remaining in her face, taken in the same "—that
is, the marks of small-pox caught by Lady Sidney
during her attendance on the Queen, which has been
mentioned in its place—" meriteth her meat."

In the same letter Sir Henry rightly took credit to
himself for the real cause of his poverty. It was the
custom of the day for most office-holders, and dis-
pensers of favours and what was called justice, to
eke out their scanty salaries by pocketing bribes;
and Elizabeth expected that all her servants would
do that. Sir Henry Sidney refused to follow the
fashion. " I sell no justice," he proudly averred.
" I trust you do not hear of any order taken by me
ever reversed, nor my name or doings in any court
—as courts there be whereto by appeal I might be
called—ever brought in question. And if my mind
were so base and corruptible as I would take money
of the people whom I command for my labour, yet
could they give me none or very little ; for the causes
that come before me are causes of people mean, base,
and very many beggars." Sir Henry felt the responsibilities attached to his " great and high office "
of Lord President of Wales, and did not choose that
its honour or his own should be sullied by any unworthy action. " Great it is," he said, " in that in
some sort I govern the third part of this realm under
her most excellent Majesty. High it is, for by that

I have precedence of great personages, and far my betters. Happy it is for the people, and most happy for the commodity that I have by the authority of that place to do good every day—if I have grace— to one or other; wherein I confess I feel no small felicity. But, for any profit I gather by it, God and the people, seeing my manner of life, know it is not possible I should gather any." *

Philip Sidney, having as keen and rare a sense of honour as his father, was as poor. He found it no easy matter to maintain a proper dignity at Court, even though Leicester House, his uncle's stately mansion, and Baynard's Castle, the yet statelier residence of his brother-in-law, the Earl of Pembroke, were always open to him, and thus enabled him to dispense with a dwelling-place of his own to which he might resort when he could be spared from the Queen's immediate presence, and had not time to go down to Penshurst or to Wilton. He was constrained to be on the look-out for such sinecures and odd sources of income—like the £60 a year he still drew from his living in Flintshire—as were plentiful in those days; sources of which any one could take advantage without feeling himself disgraced. One such was the stewardship to the bishopric of Winchester, which had been a perquisite of the Earl of Leicester, and which his uncle assigned to him at some time near the end of 1580.† Its money value is not recorded.

---

* The long letter to Sir Francis Walsingham from which several other extracts have been made in earlier pages.

† The document is among the MSS. in the possession of the Earl of Bath at Longleat.

Poor as he was, he contrived on New Year's Day of 1581 to make three characteristic presents to the Queen, as though in token of his entire submission to her Majesty and his complete surrender of himself to the royal keeping.   One was a gold-headed whip, another was a golden chain, and the third was a heart of gold.

We next meet with him in a new capacity.   As knight of the shire, representing Kent, he served in Elizabeth's fourth Parliament during its third session, which lasted from the 16th of January till the 18th of March, 1581.   The previous sessions of this Parliament having been held in 1572 and 1576, when he was too young to sit, he must have been now elected for the first time, the elections in those days being merely nominations by local magnates

This was not an exciting session, and we have but little trace of Sidney's share in it.   On the 27th of January he was appointed on its most important committee, ordered to consider the perils arising to the State from the evil practices of the Papists, to suggest sharper laws for the restraining and bridling of the same, and to fix the amount of subsidy needed for preparing a force sufficient to defend the country both by land and by sea.   One of his colleagues on this committee was Peter Wentworth, the sturdy user and champion of free speech, who in 1576 had been lodged in the Tower for a month because, among other " libels," he had declared that " none is without fault—no, not our noble Queen, but has committed great and dangerous faults to herself " ; and who in 1588 endured like punishment during three weeks because he dared to ask, with other dangerous questions, "whether this council be not a place for any member of the same, freely and without control, by bill or speech, to utter any of the griefs of this commonwealth? whether there be any council that can make, add to, or diminish from the laws of the realm, but only this council of Parliament?"

In the short session of 1581 no such disloyalty to the Queen was shown. The worst offence of Parliament was in venturing to appoint a fast, which was to be optional to the public but compulsory on its own members; and for thus encroaching on the Queen's prerogative, as sole ruler in ecclesiastical and religious affairs, the whole House had to make humble apology. On the other hand, it severely punished one of its number, Arthur Hall, representative of Grantham, who, angry at some proceedings of the previous session, had published a book denouncing the Commons as a drunken body, given up to works of darkness. Hall, vainly offering to apologise, was expelled the House, fined 500 marks, and sent to the Tower for six months.

The committee on the evils of Papistry, of which Sidney was a member, recommended stringent measures, afterwards embodied in an act of Parliament, by which any one who apostatised to the Church of Rome, or encouraged others to do so, was held guilty of treason, any one who said mass was to be subjected to a year's imprisonment and a fine of 200 marks, any one present at such a service was rendered liable to half these punishments, and £20 a month was fixed as the penalty for staying away from church.

Equally fierce legislation followed on the report of another committee of which Sidney was a member. Any one convicted of uttering slanderous words, or like sedition, against the Queen's Majesty was, for a first offence, to be set in the pillory and to lose his ears, and, for a second offence, to be hanged as a felon. Sidney's opinions and actions in Parliament evidently agreed with those of the majority of his colleagues, whose Puritanism had by this time begun to assert itself in plain terms.

A letter which he wrote from Baynard's Castle, on the 10th of April, shows that he was then interesting himself in the affairs of his " cousin Fulke," who in 1577 obtained the reversion of a lucrative office as Clerk of the Signet to the Council in Wales, and who seems at this time, or as soon as he was free from livelier occupations at Court, to have entered upon it.

On the 16th of April there arrived at Dover a splendid embassage from the King of France, sent over to forward the arrangements for Queen Elizabeth's marriage with his brother, the Duke of Anjou. Throughout the next few weeks the visitors were courteously and sumptuously entertained by Queen Elizabeth and all her statesmen and courtiers. Lord Burghley, the Earls of Sussex, Leicester, Bedford, and Lincoln, Sir Francis Walsingham, and Sir Christopher Hatton were commissioned to discuss with them the terms of the proposed wedding contract ; and in the meanwhile all sorts of festivities were

provided. In these Philip Sidney and Fulke Greville took their part.

There was plenty of eating and drinking, with
profusion of other entertainments; but the most
attractive of all was the tournament held in the
Whitehall tilt-yard, at which the new Earl of Arundel, Lord Windsor, Mr. Philip Sidney, and Mr. Fulke
Greville, styling themselves the Four Foster Children
of Desire, essayed to win by force of arms the Fortress of Perfect Beauty, the fancied abode of Queen
Elizabeth, which, by help of wood and canvas and
paint, had been erected on an artificial mound facing
the Queen's window at Whitehall. This performance had been planned to take place on Sunday, the
16th of April; but it had to be postponed for the
arrival of the French visitors, and other delays followed. It was not till Whit-Monday, the 15th of
May, that all was ready for the exploit.

On the morning of that day the Four entered the
tilt-yard. First came the Earl of Arundel, successor
to the nobleman of the same name who had been
suspected of a plot to murder the Earl of Leicester,
and who had died in 1580. He was followed by
Lord Windsor; each of these two, who took precedence by virtue of their rank and wealth, being
gorgeously clad and largely attended. Next arrived
Mr. Philip Sidney, less magnificent, but certainly
splendid enough. Part of his armour was blue, and
the rest of graven gold. Besides his own charger
he had four spare horses, richly caparisoned, ridden
by as many pages. In his train were thirty gentlemen and yeomen, and four trumpeters, all arrayed

THE GATE AT WHITEHALL.

SAID TO HAVE BEEN DESIGNED BY HOLBEIN.

From an engraving by G. Vertue.

in cassock coats, Venetian hose of yellow velvet, adorned with silver lace, yellow caps with silver bands and white feathers, and white buskins. The pages were similarly dressed, but with gold lace and gold bands, instead of silver, and some other special ornaments. On the coat of each attendant was a silver band, passing like a scarf over the shoulder and under the arm, and showing, in both front and rear, Sidney's motto, *Sic nos non nobis.* Last rode Mr. Fulke Greville, wearing gilt armour ; also with four pages on spare horses, four trumpeters, and twenty others, all decked in tawny taffeta, decorated with yellow sarcenet and gold hoops and buttons, in tawny taffeta hats, and in yellow worsted stockings. The whole company formed a little army, numbering in all more than four hundred men.

Speeches were made and alarms were sounded. The Queen was called upon to yield herself and her Fortress of Perfect Beauty to her all-conquering admirers. Then the tournament followed, the Four having challenged any and all who would defend the Fortress against their onslaught. The challengers marched up and down the yard, and at length proceeded to run tilt, each one in his turn, and each running six courses, against any who came to oppose them. Of opponents there were more than twenty, each with his small regiment of mimic warriors. Mr. Henry Grey, Sir Thomas Perrot, Mr. Anthony Cooke, Mr. Thomas Ratcliffe, Mr. Ralph Bowes, four sons of Sir Francis Knollys, and a dozen others presented themselves. It was an idle vanity on the part of the Four to propose resistance to so many, and, as might have been expected, before nightfall they were seriously discomfited.

Next day, being Whit-Tuesday, they entered the yard in a chariot, looking wearied and already half overcome. More speeches were delivered, but in a different tone. " No confidence in themselves," it was now said, " O most unmatched Princess, before whom envy dies, wanting nearness of comparison to entertain it, and admiration is expressed, finding its scope void of conceivable limit,—no confidence in themselves, nor any slight regarding the force of your valiant knights, hath encouraged the Foster Children of Desire to make this day an inheritor of yesterday's action. They are violently borne whither Desire draweth, although they must confess (alas, that yesterday's brave onslaught should come to such a confession!) that they are not greatly companied with Hope, the common supplier of Desire's army ; so as now, from summoning this castle to yield, they are fallen lowly to beseech you to vouchsafe your eyes out of that impregnable Fortress to behold what will fall out between them and your famous knights. Whence, though they be so overpassed with others' valour that already they could scarcely have been able to come hither if the chariot of Desire had not carried them, yet will they make this whole assembly witness so far their will that sooner their souls shall leave their bodies than Desire shall leave their souls."

Then they returned to the tourney, shivering so many swords and dealing so many lusty blows that, says one who stood by, it seemed as though the

Greeks were alive again and the Trojan war renewed. No party was spared, adds our informant, no estate excepted, but each knight strove to be the victor, at any rate in the favouring eye of his mistress—for each had one fair lady looking on, from whom he hoped for guerdon, however the Queen herself might reward him.

Towards evening the martial game ended. A boy, wearing ash-coloured garments in token of sub-mission, and with an olive-branch in his hand, approached her Majesty and humbly tendered an avowal that the Four Foster Children of Desire had been utterly defeated in their essay against the Fortress of Perfect Beauty. But her Majesty gra-ciously declared that thanks and praise were due to all, to the vanquished no less than to the victors, for the pleasant sport they had provided and for the great skill they had shown.

What interest Philip Sidney took in warlike ex-ercises, regarding them as training for real work, appears not only from his numerous descriptions of such affairs in " The Arcadia," but also from one of his letters to his brother Robert. " When you play at weapons," he said, " I would have you get thick caps and brasers and play out your play lustily, for indeed tricks and dalliances are nothing in earnest, for the time of one and the other greatly differs. And use as well the blows as the thrust. It is good in itself, and, besides, exerciseth your breath and strength, and it will make you a strong man at the tourney and barriers. First, in any case, practice the single-sword, and then with the dagger. Let no day pass without an hour or two such exercise."

Worsted, as one of the Four Foster Children of Desire, in the battle for possession of the Fortress of Perfect Beauty on the 15th and 16th of May, Sidney may have triumphed in one or more of the separate encounters that occupied him on the second of the two days. Or it may have been, and probably it was, after some other contest of a like kind, during the weeks given up by the English Court to the entertainment of the French ambassadors, that he wrote the following sonnet:

> Having this day my horse, my hand, my lance
>   Guided so well that I obtained the prize,
>   Both in the judgment of the English eyes
> And of some sent from that sweet enemy France,
> Horsemen my skill in horsemanship advance,
>   Town folks my strength, a daintier judge applies
>   His praise to sleight which from good use doth rise,
> Some lucky wits impute it but to chance,
> Others, because of both sides I do take
>   My blood from them who did excel in this,
> Think Nature me a man of arms did make.
>   How far they shot awry! The true cause is,
> Stella looked on, and from her heavenly face
> Sent forth the beams which made so fair my race.

This sonnet is perhaps more autobiographically accurate than any of the others in "Astrophel and Stella." We may accept as a precise record of fact Sidney's statement that one day while the French ambassadors were in London he took the prize in the tilt-yard and pleased himself by imagining that his success was due, not to his skill or strength, to

training or to chance, but to the ardour roused by
Stella's smile.   By the courtly exaggeration in which
he here indulged we can measure the significance of
other sonnets containing far more extravagance of
phrase and far more affectation of earnestness.   We
may, for instance, discern its affectation, and admire
its grace, without accepting as serious the sonnet
that comes next in the printed order, and looks as
though it was written quickly after the one just
quoted, by way of further poetical tribute to the
potency of Stella's glance.

> O eyes, which do the spheres of beauty move,
>   Whose beams be joys, whose joys all virtues be,
> Who, while they make love conquer, conquer love,
>   The schools where Venus hath learnt chastity !
> O eyes, whose humble looks most glorious prove,
>   Only-loved tyrants, just in cruelty !
> Do not, O do not, from poor me remove ;
>   Keep still my zenith ; ever shine on me !
> For though I never see them but straightways
>   My life forgets to nourish languished sprites,
> Yet still on me, O eyes, dart down your rays !
>   And if from majesty of sacred lights,
> Oppressing mortal sense, my death proceed,
> Wracks triumphs be, which love, high-set, doth breed.

Wherever Lady Penelope Devereux may usually
have been up to the time of her mother's marriage
with the Earl of Leicester, or its discovery, whether
with the Countess of Essex or under other guardian-
ship, she appears afterwards to have been taken care
of by the Earl of Huntingdon, whose wife was a
sister of Lady Sidney, who had been for some time
custodian of Mary Queen of Scots, and who since

1572 had been President of the North and Lord Lieutenant of Northumberland and other counties.

On the 10th of March, 1581, this Earl of Huntingdon wrote from Newcastle to Lord Burghley in terms implying that Lady Penelope Devereux and her sister Dorothy had been for some while under his charge and away from the Court. "Her Majesty," he said, "was pleased the last year to give me leave, at times convenient, to put her in mind of these young ladies." He now desired her Majesty to be put in mind of them, because the son of Lord Chancellor Rich had lately died. The second Lord Rich had been a friend of the first Earl of Essex, one of his colleagues in Ireland, and had accompanied the Earl of Lincoln when the latter went to Paris in 1572, taking young Philip Sidney with him. "Hearing," wrote the Earl of Huntingdon in the letter to Lord Burghley, "that God hath taken to His mercy my Lord Rich, who hath left as his heir a proper gentleman, and one in years very fit for my Lady Penelope Devereux, if with the favour and liking of her Majesty the matter might be brought to pass, and because I know your lordship's good affection to their father gone, and also your favour to his children, I am bold to pray your furtherance in this matter, which may, I think, by your good means, be brought to such a pass as I desire. I have also written to Mr. Secretary Walsingham herein."

This letter makes it plain that in March, 1581, the Earl of Huntingdon was scheming the marriage of Lady Penelope to the "proper gentleman," who had just inherited a title, and wealth to match. The scheme, by whomsoever countenanced and ordered, was successful. When Stella became Lady Rich is not recorded; but it was probably in the summer or autumn of 1581, most likely very soon after the jousting in Whitehall tilt-yard at which "Stella looked on," and by her looking won Sidney's thanks for having helped him to his prize. It was undoubtedly a very unfortunate and unhappy marriage.

Though it carries the story on to a date subsequent to Sidney's death, a curious statement made in 1605 by Lady Rich's second husband, the Earl of Devonshire, must here be quoted. No names are mentioned in it; but they can be easily supplied. "A lady of great birth and virtue, being in the power of her friends," wrote the Earl of Devonshire, "was by them married against her will unto one against whom she did protest at the very solemnity, and ever after; between whom from the first day there ensued continual discord, although the same fear that forced her to marry constrained her to live with him. Instead of a comforter, he did strive in all things to torment her, and by fear and fraud did practise to deceive her of her dowry. And, though he forebare to offer her any open wrong, restrained with the awe of her brother's powerfulness"—the brother being Robert, the second Earl of Essex,—"yet, as he had not in long time before in the chiefest duty of a husband used her as his wife, so presently after his" —that is, her brother's—"death, he did put her to a stipend, and utterly abandoned her, without pre-

tence of any cause but his own desire to live without her."

Much fiercer words than the Earl of Devonshire
used in prose about Lord Rich four and twenty years
after the marriage were used in verse by Sidney
within a short time of the event.   Thus he wrote:

> Rich fools there be, whose base and filthy heart
>   Lies hatching still the goods wherein they flow,
> And, damning their own selves to Tantal's smart,
>   (Wealth breeding want), more blest, more wretched grow.
> Yet to those fools Heaven doth such wit impart
>   As what their hands do hold their heads do know,
> And, knowing, love, and, loving, lay apart
>   As sacred things, far from all dangers' show.
> But that rich fool who, by blind Fortune's lot,
>   The richest gem of love and life enjoys,
> And can with foul abuse such beauties blot—
>   Let him, deprived of sweet but unfelt joys,
> Exiled for aye from those high treasures which
> He knows not, grow in only folly rich.

More poetry and neater punning were in another
of Sidney's sonnets.

> My mouth doth water and my breast doth swell,
>   My tongue doth itch, my thoughts in labour be.
>   Listen then, lordlings, with good care to me,
> For of my life I must a riddle tell.
> Towards Aurora's Court a nymph doth dwell,
>   Rich in all beauties which man's eye can see,
>   Beauties so far from reach in words that we
> Abuse her praise, saying she doth excel ;
> Rich in the treasure of deserved renown ;
>   Rich in the riches of a royal heart ;
> Rich in those gifts which give the eternal crown ;
>   Who, though most rich in these and every part
> Which makes the patents of true worldly bliss,
> Hath no misfortune but that Rich she is.

Many of the sonnets in " Astrophel and Stella " have been supposed to reveal deeper feeling and to express higher admiration than those just quoted. If we are to take them literally, we must believe that, as soon as she was married to another, Sidney was seized with mad passion for the young lady whom he had known and liked in her childhood and afterwards, whom six years earlier it had been expected that he would marry in due course, and of whom—shortly before her marriage, but apparently after her betrothal, though perhaps that was not then known to him—he had gallantly declared that her " heavenly face sent forth the beams " that fired and lighted him to triumph in the tilt-yard. More than that, if we are to interpret verbally some of the other sonnets and some of the songs that accompany them, we must believe, not only that Sidney was filled with rage against Stella's husband and bitter self-reproach for having failed to make her his own bride, but that he straightway laid desperate siege to her heart and only abstained from physical violence in his efforts to injure her.

All this we may well refuse to believe. Such assumptions are wholly inconsistent with everything else that we know about Sidney's character and temperament. And we need not discredit them on that ground alone; ground which, it must be admitted, is too slippery to be trusted to by itself.

Following the sentences we have read from the Earl of Devonshire's report as to Lady Rich's unhappiness in her married life, and the treatment she received from her husband, are these others: " And

16

after he "—that is, Lord Rich—" had not for the space
of twelve years enjoyed her, he did, by persuasions
and threatenings, move her to consent unto a divorce, and to confess a fault with a nameless stranger ;
without the which such a divorce as he desired
could not, by the laws in practice, proceed. Whereupon, to give a form to that separation which was
long before in substance made, she was content to
subscribe to a confession of his and her own counsel's making." That was in 1604 or 1605, and the
" nameless stranger " was the Earl of Devonshire
himself, who was the father of several of her children
before, having been divorced from Lord Rich, she
was able to be legally united to her second husband.
If it is true that Lord Rich had begun to persecute
her immediately after their marriage, although he
then and for some time " constrained her to live
with him," that he separated from her in or about
1592, and that in 1601 he " utterly abandoned her
without pretence of any cause," having still to wait
three years or more before he could find grounds
for a divorce, we may be quite sure that he would
have obtained the divorce at a much earlier date
had evidence been procurable. And such evidence
would not have been far to seek if we are to put a
literal interpretation on "Astrophel and Stella."
The poems, it is true, were not printed until 1591,
nearly five years after Sidney's death ; but they
were freely handed about in manuscript during his
lifetime. Neither he nor his friends made any secret
of them. They furnished his chief title to be honoured as a poet among his contemporaries. As

fanciful poems they were regarded by those contemporaries. Had they been regarded as autobiographical statements, yet more as impeachments
of Lady Rich, they would certainly have provided
the jealous and cruel husband with materials for the
discovery of facts that, if they were facts, are clearly
hinted at in the poems.

Another point should be mentioned. There are
many passages in " Astrophel and Stella " which, in
so far as they refer, even in fun or jest, to the married " nymph " who, rich in all beauties of mind and
heart as well as of body, " hath no misfortune but
that Rich she is," are hardly in good taste when
judged by modern standards. But there was nothing
that could be considered in the least indelicate by
those who first read them, provided they were read
simply as inventions, designed to compliment in fictitious terms the lady whom, both before and after
marriage, Sidney elected to be his patroness in the
tilt-yard, for whom he evidently had honest liking,
and whose sufferings as a wife may well have aroused
in him tender sympathy and respectful homage. On
the other hand, had Lady Rich been to him the
object of a coarse passion, one on whom he desired to
force other miseries besides those which her husband
caused her, it is not credible that he would have gone
out of his way to insult her by name in verses for his
friends to make merry over. We must either acquit
him of any serious intent in his sonnets, or we must
accuse him of wantonly unchivalrous behaviour both
in shamelessly exposing his own weaknesses and in
meanly traducing the lady whom he affected to

honour.　The pleasanter of these alternatives leaves unexplained some passages in "Astrophel and Stella"; but the other raises far greater difficulties.

Sidney's friends evidently took the poems as works of fancy, with no greater basis of fact than served for the building thereon of an imaginative superstructure.　Spenser declared that

> Stella the fair, the fairest star in sky,
> 　As fair as Venus or the fairest fair
> (A fairer star saw never living eye),
> 　Shot her sharp pointed beams through purest air :
> Her he did love, her he alone did honour ;
> His thoughts, his rhymes, his songs, were all upon her.
>
> To her he vowed the service of his days ;
> 　On her he spent the riches of his wit ;
> For her he made hymns of immortal praise ;
> 　Of only her he sang, he thought, he writ ;
> Her, and but her, of love he worthy deemed ;
> For all the rest but little he esteemed.

How much sober history we are to find in that record may be inferred from Spenser's later verse which says that Stella, instead of continuing for nearly twenty years longer to be Lady Rich and ending her days as Countess of Devonshire, tore herself in pieces over the dying body of Astrophel, and only lived long enough to see him die :

> Which when she saw she stayèd not a whit,
> 　But after him did make untimely haste.
> Forthwith her ghost out of her corpse did flit,
> 　And followèd her mate like turtle chaste,
> To prove that death their hearts cannot divide
> Which, living, were in love so firmly tied.

If we would look for autobiographic truth in any
part of "Astrophel and Stella," we must seek it in
sonnets like this, premising that even here it was
only in excess of compliment and with the enthusiasm of a poet that Sidney declared "Stella's eyes
and Stella's heart" to be the all-absorbing subjects of
his thoughts :

> The curious wits, seeing dull pensiveness
>   Bewray itself in my long-settled eyes,
>   Whence those same fumes of melancholy rise,
> With idle pains and missing aim do guess.
> Some, that know how my spring I did address,
>   Deem that my muse some fruit of knowledge plies ;
>   Others, because the prince my service tries,
> Think that I think State errors to redress ;
> But harder judges judge ambition's rage
>   (Scourge of itself, still climbing slippery place)
> Holds my young brain captived in golden cage.
>   O fools, or overwise !   Alas, the race
> Of all my thoughts hath neither stop nor start
> But only Stella's eyes and Stella's heart.

And if we would obtain from Spenser some true
insight into Sidney's bearing at Court, at a time
when Stella was able, in spite of all her woes, to
shine and smile in it, and to lessen for him the irk-
someness of waiting for better work to do than he
could find in setting a brave example to those around
him, we must turn to " Mother Hubbard's Tale."
There, in a sketch clearly intended as a portrait of
his friend, Spenser tells how the ape in man's attire,
seeking his fortune at Court, won favour from many
by his tricks and quips, his scoffings and slanders,
but had only scorn and reproof from "the rightful
courtier."

For, though the vulgar yield an open ear,
And common courtiers love to jibe and flear
At everything which they hear spoken ill,
And the best speeches with ill meaning spill,
Yet the brave courtier, in whose beauteous thought
Regard of honour harbours more than aught,
Doth loathe such base condition, to backbite
Any's good name for envy or despite.
He stands on terms of honourable mind,
Ne will be carried with the common wind
Of Courts' inconstant mutability,
Ne after every tattling fable fly,
But hears and sees the follies of the rest
And thereof gathers for himself the best.
Ne will not creep nor crouch with feignèd face,
But walks upright with comely, steadfast pace,
And unto all doth yield due courtesy—
But not with kissèd hand below the knee,
As that same apish crew is wont to do ;
For he disdains himself to embase thereto.
He hates foul leasings and vile flattery—
Two filthy blots in noble gentery ;
And loathful idleness he doth detest,
The canker-worm of every gentle breast :
The which to banish, with fair exercise
Of knightly feats, he daily doth devise. . . .
For all his mind on honour fixèd is,
To which he levels all his purposes,
And in his prince's service spends his days,
Not so much for to gain, or for to raise
Himself to high degree, as for his grace,
And in his liking to win worthy place.

Though it may be somewhat too flattering, Spenser's sketch vividly sets before us Sidney's ideals and occupations at Court in 1581 and the few years before and after. He was anxious for more important work than fell to him ; but he bore himself as

well as he could among the frivolous surroundings in
which he was constrained to move, and to which his
presence added some dignity and grace. "He was
not only an excellent wit," says Aubrey in the gossip
that tells almost all we know, except from portraits,
about Sidney's personal appearance, "but extremely
beautiful. He much resembled his sister; but his
hair was not red, but a little inclining—namely, a
dark amber colour. If I were to find a fault in it,
methinks 't is not masculine enough; yet he was a
person of great courage."

For diversion we may suppose that in 1581 Sidney
was writing part of "The Arcadia," and many if not
all of the songs and sonnets in "Astrophel and
Stella." From the latter work one other quota-
tion must be made here, as it throws a little light
on one aspect of the writer's deportment at Court,
and strengthens the inference that his worship of
Stella, though there may have been in it some of the
poetic passion that stirred Dante and Petrarch and
scores of humbler sonnet writers, was more playful
than real. Had he "loved indeed," he would, on
his own showing, have "quaked to say he loved,"
sorting rather with the "dumb swans" than with
the "chattering pies."

> Because I breathe not love to every one,
>   Nor do not use set colours for to wear,
>   Nor nourish special locks of vowèd hair,
> Nor give each speech a full point of a groan,
> The courtly nymphs, acquainted with the moan
>   Of them which in their lips Love's standard bear,
>   "What, he!" say they of me; "now I dare swear
> He cannot love; no, no, let him alone."

And think so still, so Stella know my mind !
Profess, indeed, I do not Cupid's art ;
But you, fair maids, at length this truth shall find,
 That his right badge is worn but in the heart.
Dumb swans, not chattering pies, do lovers prove ;
They love indeed who quake to say they love.

There was at least one " special lock of vowèd hair," that Sidney's courtly obligations made him preserve. A tress, soft and bright, and of a light brown colour, approaching to red, wrapped up in paper and thus labelled, is still preserved at Wilton : " This lock of Queen Elizabeth's own hair was presented to Sir Philip Sidney by her Majesty's own fair hands ; on which he made these verses and gave them to the Queen on his bended knee :

" Her inward worth all outward show transcends,
Envy her merit with regret commends ;
Like sparkling gems, her virtue draws the sight,
And in her conduct she is always bright.
When she imparts her thoughts, her words have force,
And sense and wisdom flow in sweet discourse." *

Of more substantial gifts than locks of hair Elizabeth was chary. Sidney had to wait long before any important public duties were assigned to him, and in the meantime he found the expenses of his forced attendance at Court heavier than he could easily meet.

In the autumn of 1581 he was anxious to obtain, if not lucrative employment, a share of the property

---

* The date here given, 1573, is impossible, as Sidney was then a lad of eighteen travelling abroad. The year 1583 would be more likely.

seized from Papists and freely distributed by the Queen among such highly favoured courtiers as the Earl of Leicester. "Yesterday," he wrote to Lord Burghley on the 10th of October, " her Majesty, at my taking leave, said, against that I came up again, she would take some order for care of me. My suit is for £100 a year in impropriations." There is no evidence that Burghley endorsed the suit, but it was supported by Sir Christopher Hatton and the Earl of Leicester. In December Hatton obtained Queen Elizabeth's promise that to Sidney should be assigned a " forfeiture of Papists' goods " ; and it was probably to the same transaction that Sidney referred in a letter written at this time to his uncle, asking his help towards obtaining at least £3,000 from penalties on Papists. Less, he said, in this letter, would not suit him. " Truly I like not their persons, and much worse their religion ; but I think my fortune very hard that my fortune must be built on other men's punishments." * Sidney apparently got what he wanted, as eleven days later he wrote to thank his uncle for his care of him. It may have been about this time, too, that the Queen granted him a sinecure, worth £120 a year, which was conferred on George Herbert, the poet, forty years afterwards.

That Sidney was now on good terms with the Queen, though he spent the Christmas-time of 1581 with his sister at Wilton instead of at Court, may be inferred from a short letter which he addressed to

---

* This letter and the one next cited are among the MSS. in the possession of Mr. Cottrell-Dormer, at Rousham, near Oxford.

her Majesty on the 10th of November, and which also implies that he was just now devising some scheme of secret writing for State use. " Most gracious sovereign," he wrote from Greenwich : " This rude piece of paper shall presume, because of your Majesty's commandment, most humbly to present such a cypher as a little leisure could afford me. If there come any matter to my knowledge, the importance whereof shall deserve to be so marked, I will not fail, since your pleasure is my only boldness, to your own hands to recommend it. In the meantime, I beseech your Majesty will vouchsafe to read my heart in the course of my life ; and, though itself be but of mean worth, yet to esteem it like a poor house well set. I most lowly kiss your hands, and pray to God your enemies may then only have peace when they are weary of knowing your force."

Some of Elizabeth's enemies were now approaching her in the guise of friends. The negotiations for her marriage to the Duke of Anjou were still proceeding, but, happily, sufficient obstacles were raised to prevent it. However willing or unwilling the elderly queen may have been to take to herself a young husband, she was not unmindful of her duty to her country and to the Protestant cause, of which, along with the brave little knot of patriots in the Netherlands, England was the champion. As one of the conditions of her marrying the brother of King Henry of France, she wanted the latter to join her in a league against Spain, and to this intent in July she sent Sir Francis Walsingham to Paris, where three or four months were wasted by the ambassador in useless controversy and efforts to reconcile the contradictory instructions of his mistress. "When her Majesty is pressed to the marriage," Walsingham said in a letter to Burghley, "then she seemeth to affect a league ; and when the league is yielded to, then she liketh better a marriage ; and when thereupon she is moved to assent to marriage, then she hath recourse to the league ; and when the motion for the league or any request for money is made, then her Majesty returneth to the marriage."

Affairs being in this fluctuating condition, the Duke of Anjou thought it well to come and plead his own cause. He reached London on the 1st of November, and was gaily entertained during three months. Sidney appears not to have taken much part in the entertainments. As has been noted, he was at Wilton at Christmas, and there was no interchange of New Year's gifts between him and the Queen. But he was at Whitehall on the 1st of February, 1582, when Anjou quitted London, the Queen herself riding with him as far as Canterbury, and several of her chief courtiers escorting him all the way to Antwerp.

The Earl of Leicester, Lord Hunsdon, and Lord Howard took the lead in this party, and with them were Mr. Philip Sidney, Mr. Walter Raleigh, Mr. Fulke Greville, Mr. Edward Dyer, and a host of others. They were met at Flushing by Prince William of Orange, and deputies from all the neighbouring cities, who came to welcome the bridegroom-elect of the English Queen and the man who was expected to prove himself the saviour of the Netherlands.

Reaching Antwerp on the 19th of February, the son of Catherine de' Medici, the wretch of whom his sister, Queen Margaret of Navarre, had said that, "if fraud and cruelty were banished from the earth, there was in him sufficient stock from which it could be replenished," became the hero in shows of unexampled splendour. Being led to a spacious theatre, and there elected Duke of Brabant, Anjou gave a pledge that he would deliver the Low Country States from the oppression and tyranny of the Spaniards, and would rule them according to their customary laws and privileges. He then took the prescribed oaths, the Prince of Orange putting on him the crimson mantle and crimson bonnet, tokens of the sacredness of his office ; and after that other titles and honours were conferred. These things done, the company passed from the theatre to the open street. There they met a damsel personating the Maid of Antwerp, who placed the keys of the town at his feet. On her right hand walked another maid representing Religion, on her left was one typifying Justice. These were heralded by Concord, with Wisdom on the one side and Force on the other. Then there were some Scriptural shows. Samuel taking the kingdom from Saul and giving it to David symbolised the transference of the States from the wicked rule of Spain to the wise, strong government of the Duke of Anjou and Brabant. In the intimacy of David and Jonathan was found illustration of the alliance between the Duke and Queen Elizabeth. And there were numberless other spectacles, in which metaphorical nymphs and naked men and gorgeously apparelled dames took part.

But it all came to an end. The thunder of applause died out, the glitter of compliment faded away; and presently the Duke of Anjou gave to all the world, even to Queen Elizabeth, overwhelming proof that, if he had more folly than comported with the mock dignity of a proper knave, he was far too knavish to pass for a mere fool.

This happened in Sidney's lifetime, and therefore soon enough for him to hear every one acknowledge the wisdom of his former strictures upon Anjou. But perhaps, even now, in the midst of the splendours he was witnessing he saw abundant confirmation of his view.

Sidney's good friend Hubert Languet had died in Antwerp on the 30th of September, 1581, tenderly nursed by the wife of Philip du Plessis-Mornay, to whom he said, as in less solemn tones he had often said before to Sidney and others, that he had thus far struggled on through life in the hope of seeing, and even helping on, a reformation of which the world had grievous need; but now that he saw how the nations of Europe were steadily growing worse, he was only too glad to leave it.

Sometimes, while in attendance on the Duke of Anjou in Antwerp, Sidney must have turned aside from the false gaiety and have paused sadly by the grave of his old friend, not yet five months dead— the friend whom he praised in " The Arcadia "

> For clerkly rede and hating what is naught,
> For faithful heart, clean hands and mouth as true,

and of whom he testified that

> With his sweet skill my skill-less youth he drew
> To have a feeling taste of Him that sits
> Beyond the heavens, far more beyond our wits.

CHAPTER XIV.

IN THE WORLD OF LETTERS.

1580–1583.

NONE of Sidney's writings were printed until after his death, and we have no precise record of the date at which any, save "The Lady of May," were composed. But, as during the last three years of his life he was busiest in other ways, we may assume that he did not then write much. We may also assume that before 1579 his literary exercises were merely tentative and preliminary; the most notable being "The Lady of May," avowedly prepared for Queen Elizabeth's entertainment early in the summer of 1578. Later in the same summer he was in close intercourse with Gabriel Harvey, and next year he saw much of Harvey's friend, Edmund Spenser, and of others who gathered round him in the Areopagus. It is probable that, with the exception of the translations in which he had a hand and of some stray poems, all

the work that has given him an honourable place in the world of letters was produced within the three years or so that ensued. Before this period he had become honourably known as the associate and helper—the patron, in the best sense of the term—of other men of letters ; and he so continued to the end. But his own literary career, and the three books on which his fame as an author rests, " The Defence of Poesy," " The Countess of Pembroke's Arcadia," and "Astrophel and Stella," may be dated between 1580 and 1583 ; that is, between the twenty-sixth and twenty-ninth years of his short life.

In this interval, feeling himself a full-grown man, fit for greater enterprises in the service of the State than were permitted, and eager for pursuits which he deemed more important and more incumbent on him, Sidney found some vent for his restless energy in the use of the pen. But it must be understood and borne in mind that literature was never more than a pleasant pastime to him. In each of his three books he claimed to be a poet, in the wider meaning of the term then in vogue ; and in each he gave signal and diverse proof of his skill. But in the world of letters he moved only as an amateur.

In these pages there is no room for an adequate and detailed account of Sidney's achievements as an author, or of his relation to other authors in the Elizabethan age. From our present point of view, his writings are chiefly useful in showing him as a courtier and a politician, a representative of the chivalrous thought that in his day struggled, not always successfully, for expression in moods and modes apart

from, though intimately associated with, the intellectual vigour shown by Shakespeare and Spenser
and other giants.   A little must now be said about
them, however, as contributions to English literature.

Whether it was written before or after or concur-
rently with the several portions of " The Arcadia "
and " Astrophel and Stella," both which were evidently produced in scraps and at intervals, " The
Defence of Poesy" may most conveniently be
noticed first.   It was clearly a direct outcome of
Sidney's studies as president of the Areopagus, and
the conclusions set forth in it cannot have much
varied from those formed when he was in frequent
counsel with Spenser in 1579 and soon after.

Of older date than any other English treatise on
poetry, unless we reckon as such George Gascoigne's
"Certain Notes of Instruction concerning the Making
of Verse or Rhyme," a small technical manual published in 1575, Sidney's " Defence" heralded the
revival of an art that had fallen into contempt.   He
looked back with reverence to Chaucer, "of whom,"
he said, "truly I know not whether to marvel more,
either that he, in that misty time, could see so
clearly, or that we, in this clear age, go so stum-
blingly after him."   He acknowledged that " The
Mirror for Magistrates," the first instalment of
which, with his friend Sackville's Induction, appeared in 1559, was " meetly furnished of beautiful
parts."   And in the Earl of Surrey's lyrics, only
printed in 1551, four years after the author's death,
he found " many things tasting of a noble birth and
worthy of a noble mind."   But the " Defence " was

written soon, perhaps no more than a few months,
after the appearance of "The Shepherd's Calendar,"
the prelude to Spenser's greater work and all the
other noble verse for which the Elizabethan genera-
tion is famous; and Sidney had to complain, with
more sorrow than wonder, that poetry, "from almost
the highest estimation of learning, is fallen to be
the laughing-stock of children." His eloquent and
humorous treatise was in reality as much a challenge
to his friends of the Areopagus and others to give
dignity to the poet's calling as a defence of poetry
against such ribald, but not wholly unmerited, attacks as Stephen Gosson had lately made in "The
School of Abuse."

Sidney came forward as the champion not merely
of rhymed verse, but of all imaginative work, and
his definition of poetry covered prose romances like
his own "Arcadia," and much more sober compositions as well. "Poesy," he said, "is an art of imitation; for so Aristotle termeth in his word 'mimesis,'
that is to say, a representing, counterfeiting or figur-
ing forth; to speak metaphorically, a speaking picture—with this end, to teach and delight." "It is
not rhyming and versing," he insisted, "that maketh
poetry. One may be a poet without versifying, and
a versifier without poetry." "Verse is but an ornament and no cause to poetry; since there have been
many excellent poets that never versified, and now
swarm many versifiers that need never answer to the
name of poets." What he undertook to defend,
and in fact glorified, was "that feigning notable
images of virtues, vices, or what else, with that de-

17

lightful teaching which must be the right describing
note to know a poet by; although, indeed, the
senate of poets have chosen verse as their fittest
raiment, meaning, as in matters they passed all in
all, so in manner to go beyond them; not speaking
table-talk fashion, or like men in a dream, words as
they chanceably fall from the mouth, but poising
each syllable of each word by just proportion, according to the dignity of the subject."

There is some pedantry, but much shrewd com-
mon-sense, gracefully and forcibly worded, with
abundant humour, in Sidney's exposition of the
various kinds of poetry and in his strictures alike on
those who ignorantly condemn the art and on those
who bring it into contempt by their ignorant efforts
to practise it.

The last paragraph gives us the measure of Sidney's wit in "The Defence." "Since the ever
praiseworthy poesy," he wrote, "is full of virtue-
breeding delightfulness, and void of no gift that
ought to be in the noble name of learning; since
the blames laid against it are either false or feeble;
since the cause why it is not esteemed in England is
the fault of poet-apes, not poets; since, lastly, our
tongue is most fit to honour poesy and to be honoured by poesy, I conjure you all that have had the
evil luck to read this ink-wasting toy of mine, even
in the name of the nine muses, no more to scorn the
sacred mysteries of poesy, no more to laugh at the
name of poets, as though they were next inheritors
to fools." Believe what Aristotle and Bembus and
Scaliger and others have said about poets and their

art, urged Sidney. "Lastly believe themselves, when they tell you they will make you immortal by their verses. Thus doing, your name shall flourish in the printers' shops ; thus doing, you shall be of kin to many a poetical preface ; thus doing, you shall be most fair, most rich, most wise, most all— you shall dwell upon superlatives. But if (fie of such a but !) you be born so near the dull-making cataract of Nilus that you cannot hear the planet-like music of poetry ; if you have so earth-creeping a mind that it cannot lift itself up to look to the sky of poetry, or rather, by a certain rustical disdain, will become such a Mome as to be a Momus of poetry ; then, though I will not wish unto you the ass's ears of Midas, nor to be driven by a poet's verses, as Bubonax was, to hang himself, nor to be rhymed to death, as is said to be done in Ireland, yet this much curse I must send you, in behalf of all poets—that, while you live, you live in love and never get favour for lacking skill of a sonnet, and, when you die, your memory die from the earth for want of an epitaph."

The mocking tone in which Sidney ended his "Defence of Poesy" often shows itself in his "Arcadia," which was a satire as well as a romance. "His purpose was to limn out such exact pictures of every posture in the mind that any man might see how to set a good countenance upon all the discountenances of adversity," says Fulke Greville ; who also states that "in all the creations of his making his interest and scope was to turn the barren philosophy precepts into pregnant images of life." Though Greville speaks with the authority of a life-long and most intimate friend, there is clearly some exaggeration in this remark. We have Sidney's own assurrance that "The Arcadia" was "but a trifle, and that triflingly handled"; and the evidence of the book itself that it was rather an elaborate web of love-stories than an ethical discourse. Yet it does contain much that was plainly intended to be direct moral teaching, and much wholesome ridicule of the modes of living and thinking in Sidney's day. In no way a rival to Sir Thomas More's "Utopia," which had been written in 1516, it was, with all its difference of style and superiority as a work of fiction, in some respects a competitor of Lyly's "Euphues," of which the first instalment appeared in 1579, and the success of which may have partly induced Sidney to try his hand at another "ink-wasting toy," one that, even in the incomplete form in which we have it, is more than sixteen times as large as "The Defence of Poesy."

In "The Defence" Heliodorus is commended for "his sugared invention of that picture of love in Theagenes and Chariclea." The "Ethiopic History" of the fourth-century romancist, lately translated into English by Thomas Underdown, doubtless inclined Sidney to introduce a heroic element into his "Arcadia"; but its pastoral suggestion was evidently due to the Italian "Arcadia" of Sanazarro, first printed at Milan in 1504, and to the "Diana Enamorada" of Sanazarro's Spanish imitator, Montemayor, which appeared in 1542. From Montemayor's rehearsal, in mingled prose and verse, of his own and his friends' experiences and opinions, under the guise of shepherds and shepherdesses, Sidney translated at least two songs, and his "Diana" served in part as a model for "The Arcadia."

Though cumbrously told, and digressing into other stories of love and war, and speeches as long as sermons, "The Arcadia," in its main thread, makes a nearer approach to the modern novel, with a better-wrought plot and fuller and more varied character-painting, than any English work produced before its day or for some time after.

It has for heroes two cousins, Musidorus, Prince of Thessaly, and Pyrocles, Prince of Macedon, between whom, we are told, there was such notable friendship "as made them more like than the likeness of all other virtues, and made them more near one to the other than the nearness of their blood could aspire to." After passing through many adventures, some of which are recorded in the prelude to the main portion of the romance, the cousins met with other adventures incident to their intruding themselves on Basilius, the eccentric King of Arcadia, who, in jealous care for his beautiful daughters, Pamela and Philoclea, had broken up his court and retired into a forest. There he had built two lodges. In one of these he lived with Philoclea and his wife Gynecia. In the other he placed Pamela, under the charge of one Dametas, a doltish clown, his ugly spouse Miso, and their daughter Mopsa, inheritor of both parents' defects. It was the purpose of Basilius that so long as he lived his daughters should not marry, and that they should be allowed to see no men but a priest and some shepherds skilled in the music that he loved.   His unworthy plot was to be spoiled by Pyrocles and Musidorus.

Pyrocles, having fallen in love with Philoclea on hearing the report of her charms, disguised himself as an Amazon, under the name of Zelmane, and thus gained access to Basilius and his household ; only, however, for a long while to bring trouble on himself and others.   By Philoclea he was taken for the war-like lady whose garb he affected, and therefore she had for him but a sisterly affection.   Basilius, de-ceived as to his sex, regarded him with much warmer liking.   Gynecia, also, her practised eye seeing through the Amazonian dress, cared more for the visitor than sorted with her wifely duty.   That was the state of affairs disclosed to Musidorus when, seeking his truant cousin, he found him in the Arca-dian forest, and, assuming the garb of a shepherd, and calling himself Dorus, obtained admittance to the lodge insufficiently guarded by Dametas, where he was quickly enthralled by the majestic beauty of Pamela.

The perplexities of the lovers, and the perils through which they had to pass before they could achieve their ends, are set forth with great detail in Sidney's romance.   Loving Pamela, but not daring to tell her so, Musidorus was forced to profess affec-tion for her ugly maid Mopsa.   His graceful bear-ing and courteous speech in time bred in Pamela such tenderness that " she could no longer keep love from looking out through her eyes or going forth in her words "; but she, thinking that he favoured Mopsa, and blaming herself for feelings she could not overcome, gave him no opportunity of telling her what were his real thoughts, or of informing her as to his proper rank in life. Yet harder was the case of Pyrocles, who rarely could seek the society of Philoclea without being held back either by the ardent passion of her father, who courted him as a woman, or by the watchful jealousy of her mother, who would win him as a man. " Loathsomely loved and dangerously loving," Pyrocles contrived at length to reveal himself to Philoclea, and to learn from her, as soon as her astonishment was over, that she found it pleasanter to view him as a chaste lover than as a sister. Scarcely had that happened, however, when both Philoclea and Pamela, together with Pyrocles in his Amazonian garb, were stolen by the wicked lady Cecropia, widow of the brother of Basilius, whom she sought to depose with the view of setting up her son Amphialus as King of Arcadia, herself being the actual ruler. Amphialus had long loved Philoclea, and, in hope of now winning her, though he was not base enough to woo with violence, he sanctioned his mother's capture and imprisonment of the sisters. He did little more than look on while the prisoners were being persecuted, and fight bravely against the Arcadians who sought to recover them, and who had Musidorus, in yet another disguise, for their foremost champion.

Sidney revelled in descriptions of successive battles and duels incident to the siege of the castle from which Amphialus and Cecropia defied their assailants ; and the most pathetic passages in his narrative are those which recount the sufferings of the sisters under the wanton cruelties they endured from Cecropia.

There is a break in the story, as it has come down to us, before their sufferings were over ; and the rest of the book—about a fourth of the whole—exists only in fragmentary shape. " All which followeth here of this work," we are told by its old editor, Sir William Alexander, " remained as it was done and sent away in several loose sheets, being never after reviewed nor so much as seen all together by himself, without any certain disposition or perfect order. Yet, for that it was his, howsoever deprived of the just grace it should have had, it was held too good to be lost, and therefore with much labour were the best coherences that could be gathered out of those scattered papers made and afterwards printed, as now it is, only by her noble care to whose dear hand they were first committed, and for whose delight and entertainment only undertaken."

In this continuation, after a gap which Sir William Alexander essayed to fill, we find peace in Arcadia, and Pamela and Philoclea, as well as their disguised lovers, restored to Basilius. The complications consequent on the disguises are not unravelled without difficulty, and some offences against good taste, which Sidney would hardly have retained had he revised his " loose sheets." But all ends happily : Basilius being brought back to his right mind, in respect both of his kingly office and of his duty as a husband ; Gynecia also being purged of her evil inclinations, and acquiring a reputation for wifely excellence, " which, though in that point undeserved, she did, in the remnant of her life, duly purchase with observing all duty and faith, to the example and glory of Greece—so uncertain are mortal judgments the same person most infamous and most famous, and neither justly " ; and Musidorus and Pyrocles being free to return to their own countries, with Pamela and Philoclea as their brides. " The solemnities of their marriages, with the Arcadian pastorals, full of many comical adventures happening to those rural lovers," Sidney or his editor wrote in the final sentence, which makes brief reference to other persons and events in the story, " may awake some other spirit to exercise his pen in that wherewith mine is already dulled."

No wonder Sidney's spirit was dulled. The work was already far too long and straggling, and in it there were many blemishes, by no one else so clearly seen and condemned as by the author. He thought too poorly of it to suffer it to be printed in his lifetime, and on his deathbed he desired that it might be burned. Happily that request was disobeyed. " The Arcadia " was well worth preserving, and it had merits that justified the great favour with which it was regarded all through the seventeenth century and afterwards. But it must be remembered that we cannot fully gauge its merits as it was left by its author. Towards fitting it for presentment to the world, we are told that the Countess of Pembroke did much, and that, " as often, repairing a ruinous house, the mending of some old part occasioneth the making of some new, so here her honourable labour began in correcting the faults, and ended in supplying the defects." Many faults and defects remain, and it is possible that some were the work of the correcting hand.

For all the absurdities in " The Arcadia," Sidney had precedents in the Spanish and Italian romances that he undertook to rival ; and there was no one to complain of them in his day. Shakespeare, who evidently obtained from Sidney many suggestions as to plots, situations, characters, and even phrases and similes, showed in his romantic dramas like contempt of chronology and topography, and as freely violated the probabilities. It is greatly to Sidney's credit that, born nearly ten years before Shakespeare, and having about fifteen years' start of him as an author, he contrived to tell so vigorous, involved, and, in its way, coherent a story as " The Arcadia " ; yet more to draw such living portraits, revealing so much keenness of observation and understanding of human nature, as appear in Pyrocles and Musidorus, Philoclea and Pamela, Basilius and Gynecia, Amphialus and Cecropia, and many others, including with the daintier and more dignified idealisations such comic or farcical studies as Dametas, Mopsa, and Miso. Both as story-teller and as a painter of character, Sidney was vastly superior to Lyly, his chief rival in his own day, and—unless we except Robert Greene, who was his nearest successor—to all who followed him throughout a century.

In literary style, moreover, " The Arcadia," though much inferior to " The Defence of Poesy," is much better than " Euphues," which with it set or encouraged the fashion of strained wit in conversation that prevailed in the Elizabethan age and long after. " She has the most harmonious and musical strain of wit that ever tempted a true ear," it was said of the Lady Saviolina, by her lover, in Ben Jonson's " Every Man out of his Humour," first performed in 1599 ; " Oh ! it flows from her like nectar, and she doth give it that sweet quick grace and exornation in the composure that she does observe as pure a phrase and use as choice figures in her ordinary conference as any be in ' The Arcadia.' " And ten years later, in " The Gull's Horn Book," Thomas Dekker gave this advice to gallants : " Hoard up the finest play-scraps you can get, upon which your lean wit may most savourly feed for want of other stuff, when the Arcadian and Euphuised gentlewomen have their tongues sharpened to set upon you."

Arcadianism, as uttered by its inventor at any rate, was less meretricious than Euphuism. A fair sample of it is in the account of Musidorus's journey from the Laconian shore on which he was wrecked, to Kalander's house, whence he was to start on the adventures set forth in the romance. On the third day of his walk with Strephon and Claius :

" In the time that the morning did strow roses and violets in the heavenly floor against the coming of the sun, the nightingales, striving one with the other which could in most dainty variety recount their wrong-caused sorrow, made them put off their sleep, and rising from under a tree, which that night had been their pavilion, they went on their journey ;

which by and by welcomed Musidorus's eyes, wearied with the wasted soil of Laconia, with delightful
prospects.   There were hills which garnished their
proud heights with stately trees ; humble valleys
whose base estate seemed comforted with the refreshing of silver rivers ; meadows enamelled with
all sorts of eye-pleasing flowers ; thickets which, being lined with most pleasant shade, were witnessed
so to by the cheerful disposition of many well-
tuned birds ; each pasture stored with sheep feeding
with sober security, while the pretty lambs with
bleating oratory craved the dams' comfort ; here a
shepherd's boy piping as though he should never be
old ; there a young shepherdess knitting, and withal
singing, and it seemed that her voice comforted her
hands to work, and her hands kept time to her
voice's music.   As for the houses of the country,
for many houses came under their eye, they were
all scattered, no two being one by the other, and
yet not so far off, as that it barred mutual succour ;
a show, as it were, of an accompaniable solitariness
and of a civil wildness."

And here is Sidney's description of Kalander's
house in Arcadia, which might have stood for his
father's home at Penshurst, or his sister's at Wilton :

" The house itself was built of fair and strong
stone, not affecting so much any extraordinary kind
of fineness as an honourable representing of a
firm stateliness ; the lights, doors and stairs rather
directed to the use of the guests than to the eye of

the artificer, and yet, as the one chiefly heeded, so the other not neglected ; each place handsome without curiosity, and homely without loathsomeness ; not so dainty as not to be trod on, nor yet slubbered up with good fellowship ; all more lasting than beautiful, but that the consideration of the exceeding lastingness made the eye believe that it was exceeding beautiful; the servants not so many in number as cleanly in apparel and serviceable in behaviour, testifying even in their countenances that their master took as well care to served as of them that did serve."

Designed as a poem, according to Sidney's broad interpretation of the term, " The Arcadia " was written throughout in what would now be called poetical prose, except that portions were actually in verse, rhymed or unrhymed. These portions, separated from the context, occupy more space than the whole of " Astrophel and Stella." Some are crude exercises in the classical metres that the Areopagus sought to Anglicise ; others rank among the best specimens of Sidney's poetry. Many are scattered through the narrative, and spoken or written by its leading persons ; but the majority appear in the long eclogues that were appended to all but the last of the five books into which " The Arcadia " was divided. This sonnet, the last of the seven dozen poems it contains, which is put into the mouth of Musidorus, may be an expression of the thoughts that had hold of Sidney's mind when he was reaching the end of his romance :

Since nature's works be good, and death doth serve
    As nature's work, why should we fear to die ?
Since fear is vain but when it may preserve,
    Why should we fear that which we cannot fly ?
Fear is more pain than is the pain it fears,
    Disarming human minds of native might,
While each conceit an ugly figure bears
    Which were not ill, well viewed in reason's light.
Our owly eyes, which dimmed with passion be
    And scarce discern the dawn of coming day—
Let them be cleared, and now begin to see
    Our life is but a step in dusty way.
Then let us hold the bliss of peaceful mind,
Since, this we feel,* great loss we cannot find.

And in this earlier sonnet from " The Arcadia " we see Sidney's poetic fancy and grace of expression, perhaps, at their highest.

My true love hath my heart, and I have his,
    By just exchange one for the other given ;
I hold his dear, and mine he cannot miss ;
    There never was a bargain better driven.
His heart in me keeps me and him in one ;
    My heart in him his thoughts and senses guides ;
He loves my heart, for once it was his own ;
    I cherish his, because in me it bides.
His heart his wound receivèd from my sight ;
    My heart was wounded with his wounded heart ;
For, as from me on him his hurt did light,
    So still, methought, in me his hurt did smart.
Both, equal hurt, in this change wrought our bliss.
My true love hath my heart, and I have his.

In the third of the eclogues, in which various shepherds recount their joys and sorrows, for their own pastime or for the diversion of Basilius and other

---

* That is, " if we feel this."

onlookers, Philisides is introduced as a stranger, sitting among the shepherds, "resolving in his mind all the tempests of evil fortune he had passed "; and among the matters that, on the last page of " The Arcadia," Sidney said he must leave for some other spirit to exercise his pen with, were " the poor hopes of poor Philisides in the pursuit of his affections." Philisides was a pseudonym for Philip Sidney, the word itself being made up of the first halves of his Christian name and surname, and it is in one of his lays that the grateful mention of Languet, which has already been quoted, occurs.

Another song of Philisides, in " The Arcadia," recounts his griefs as an ill-used lover.

> Each thing both sweet and sad
>   Did draw his boiling brain
>   To think, and think with pain,
> Of Mira's beams, eclipsed by absence bad.

To the ground on which he gazed tearfully, to the stream that trickled past, to the flowers blooming around him, to his oaten pipe, to the lambs he was tending, to the widowed turtle-dove that " on a barèd root sat wailing without boot," Philisides vainly appealed for comfort.

> Earth, brook, flowers, pipe, lamb, dove,
>   Say all—and I with them—
> Absence is death, or worse, to them that love.
>   So I, unlucky lad,
>   Whom hills from her do hem,
>   What fits me now but tears and sighings sad !
>   O, fortune too, too bad !

With some important exceptions, all Sidney's best poetry is in " Astrophel and Stella," where Philisides, under another name, tells how, when it is too late for him to claim and to enjoy her love, another Mira has enthralled him by her charms, and how at length he learns by hard experience that his quest is vain.

> When sorrow, using mine own fire's might,
>   Melts down his lead into my boiling breast,
>   To that dark furnace to my heart oppressed,
> There shines a joy from thee, my only light :
> But soon as thought of thee breeds my delight
>   And my young soul flutters to thee, his nest,
>   Most rude despair, my daily unbidden guest,
> Clips straight my wings, straight wraps me in his night.

In " Astrophel and Stella," besides eleven songs, there are a hundred and eight sonnets ; with which may be grouped about a dozen others allied to them in theme, but not included in the series, either because no convenient place could there be found for them, or because in them Stella was not named or clearly alluded to.

Reasons have already been given for declining to believe that in the series itself Sidney intended to lay bare the secrets of his heart and to make either confession or pretence of an unworthy passion for Lady Rich. But it is certain that Lady Rich was their heroine, and that Sidney would not have taken such pains to compliment her had he not found pleasure or relief in writing love-poems concerning her. The blending of seriousness and affectation in his work is shown by the opening sonnet.

Loving in truth, and fain in verse my love to show,
  That she, dear she, might take some pleasure of my pain,
Pleasure might cause her read, reading might make her know,
  Knowledge might pity win, and pity grace obtain,
I sought fit words to paint the blackest face of woe ;
  Studying inventions fine her wits to entertain,
Oft turning others' leaves to see if thence would flow
  Some fresh and fruitful showers upon my sunburnt brain.
But words came halting forth, wanting invention's stay ;
  Invention, Nature's child, fled step-dame Study's blows ;
And others' feet still seem but strangers' in my way.
  Thus, great with child to speak, and helpless in my throes,
Biting my truant pen, beating myself for spite,
" Fool," said my muse to me, " look in thy heart and write."

Sidney did much more than look into his heart
before writing. Even those who see tragic meaning
in his sonnets must admit that there was frequent
turning of " others' leaves," and much studying of
" inventions fine," in his efforts to paint for Stella's
entertainment " the blackest face of woe." He followed and improved upon the artifice of Wyatt and
Surrey, who, at times translating from Petrarch and
his school, at times closely imitating them, set the
fashion of sonnet-making in England. The great
Italian bard sang sweetly to his Laura, and many,
both in and out of Italy, sought to rival him in his
vows and protestations. During Sidney's youth,
Surrey's conceits in honour of the fair Geraldine
were emulated by every courtier who knew how
to string rhymes together, and the pretty trick was
carried on by the greatest poets of his day and after
it, by Spenser and Shakespeare among the rest.
Sidney, like his friends Edward Dyer and Fulke
Greville, and like the Earl of Oxford and other foes,

18

but, so far as we can judge from their extant productions, with much more grace and skill than they could command, learned to write sonnets in a school that not only tolerated but prescribed extravagance of phrase and as much fantastic thought as might be compressed into fourteen lines of verse.

With how much grace and skill Sidney paid his sonnet-tribute to Stella may be seen from passages already quoted. The different mood in which he sometimes wrote appears in this, from his miscellaneous poems ; and let it be noted that even here he could not abstain from punning on Lady Rich's name :

> Leave me, O love, which reachest but to dust ;
>   And thou, my mind, aspire to higher things ;
> Grow rich in that which never taketh rust :
>   Whatever fades but fading pleasure brings.
> Draw in thy beams, and humble all thy might
>   To that sweet yoke where lasting freedoms be,
> Which breaks the clouds, and opens forth the light
>   That doth both shine and give us sight to see.
> O take fast hold ; let that light be thy guide
>   In this small course which birth draws out to death,
> And think how ill becometh him to slide
>   Who seeketh heaven, and comes of heavenly breath.
> Then farewell, world ; thy uttermost I see :
> Eternal love, maintain thy life in me !

A few of Sidney's miscellaneous poems, as well as the grouping together in some sort of sequence of those collected in " Astrophel and Stella," and the editing of three fourths of " The Arcadia," may have occupied his leisure in or after 1583.

A short " Discourse in Defence of the Earl of

Leicester," which he penned in 1584 or 1585, can scarcely be included among his literary achievements. Angry at an attack made upon his uncle in a scurrilous "Dialogue between a Scholar, a Gentleman, and a Lawyer," better known as "Leicester's Commonwealth," which had been written by a Jesuit slanderer, he replied to it very indignantly, and in terms too furious to have much weight. It is probable that he soon repented of his essay, and that his friends thought poorly of it. It was not published until some generations had elapsed.

About contemporary with that pamphlet was another and a more important undertaking. Pleased with a treatise, "De Veritate Christiana," lately written by his friend Philip du Plessis-Mornay, and anxious that its wise teachings should be within reach of unlearned Englishmen, Sidney began a translation of it. Before many chapters had been prepared, public matters claimed his attention, and he had to devote all his time to politics; but the work was, in his opinion, too important to be neglected. He therefore intrusted it to Arthur Golding, an industrious scribe, with a request that he would complete the translation as soon and as well as he could, and dedicate it, when done, to the Earl of Leicester. The order was complied with, and, as the result, "A Work concerning the Trueness of the Christian Religion," was published in 1587.

It is instructive to note how Sidney, following authorship only as a pastime, left his mark in so many fields of literary work, from sonnets and love-stories to criticism and theology. And in estimating his place in the world of letters, we must remember how short, as well as how early, was his day. Spenser died young; but Spenser, born a year before Sidney, outlived him by thirteen years, and in those thirteen years wrote most of the works on which his fame rests. Shakespeare, born ten years later, died in the very prime of manhood; but his lifetime exceeds Sidney's by twenty years, and, had it been as brief, neither " Hamlet " nor " Othello " nor " Macbeth " nor " King Lear " would have been written. Neither Francis Bacon nor Ben Jonson could be called old men when they died; but Jonson's years lacked only one of being twice as many as Sidney's, and Bacon's were one more than twice as many.

And in his own age Sidney was more highly thought of as a friend of authors than as an author. " Gentle Sir Philip Sidney ! " exclaimed Thomas Nash, in his " Pierce Penniless "; " thou knewest what belonged to a scholar; thou knewest what pains, what toils, what travail, conduct to perfection. Well couldst thou give every virtue his encouragement, every wit his due, every writer his desert, 'cause none more virtuous, witty, or learned than thyself. But thou art dead in thy grave, and hast left too few successors of thy glory; too few to cherish the sons of the muses, or water with their plenty those budding hopes which thy bounty erst planted ! "

Budding hopes without number Sidney's generous friendship quickened during his gracious life. Not only did his genius influence the minds of many.

SIR PHILIP SIDNEY.
FROM THE MINIATURE BY ISAAC OLIVER, AT WINDSOR CASTLE.

Poor as he was, he was able to give them material
encouragement. " He was a very munificent spirit,"
Aubrey wrote of him, " and liberal to all lovers of
learning, and to those that pretended any acquaintance with Parnassus." All the hardworking and
scantily recompensed book-writers of the day—
writers on theology and politics, history and geogra-
phy, what then passed for science and the arts then
necessary to a gentleman's career, as well as poets
and romancers—looked to Sidney for help and
encouragement. Among these were his friends
Camden and Hakluyt. It was under his patronage that Nicholas Litchfield, in 1581, issued his
translation of a treatise, " De Re Militari," on the
plea that no one was more forward to further or
favour military knowledge than he, being of all men
ever the most ready and adventurous in every exercise of war and chivalry. But his most illustrious
debtor was Edmund Spenser, who, dedicating " The
Ruins of Time " to the Countess of Pembroke in
1591, lamented that " God had disdained the world
of that most noble spirit which was the hope of all
learned men and the patron of my young muses."

CHAPTER XV.

NEW OCCUPATIONS.

1582–1585.

ARLY in March, 1582, Sidney returned to London from his short visit to the Netherlands, and for the next two-and-forty months he remained in England, chiefly at Court, but with an ever-growing desire to be employed in more useful work than he could obtain. Work gradually came, but during these three and a half years it was not such as he was satisfied with, and even in the offices to which he was appointed he appears to have been hindered by courtly thraldom from making full and proper use of his opportunities. He was too great a favourite with the Queen to be often or for long allowed out of her presence, either for his own enjoyment or in the service of his country.

For this reason, if for no other, nothing came of a project for his going to Ireland. His own and his father's friend, Lord Grey of Wilton, who had been made Lord Deputy in 1580, and who appears to have been really anxious to carry out Sir Henry's views as to the government of the turbulent country, was not equal to the task; and he was recalled in August, 1582. " Sir Henry Sidney is the only man that is wished for here by the country people," Sir Nicholas Malby, the Governor of Connaught, had written in the previous May to the Earl of Leicester; and that wish was repeatedly expressed and communicated to the Queen's Council by others. There was some thought of complying with it, and overtures were made to Sir Henry with a view to his resuming the post he had already thrice filled.

Sir Henry's answer to the suggestion is interesting. As a prime condition of his undertaking the irksome but serviceable business, he stipulated that his son Philip should share it with him. " The principal and chief cause that moveth him to fancy or have any liking to take the charge of the government of Ireland, if the same be offered to him," we read, " is the respect he beareth him "—that is, Philip. " So that, if he " —Philip—" will assuredly promise to go with him thither, and withal will put on a determinate mind to remain and continue there after him, and succeed him in the government, if it may so like her Majesty to allow him, he will then yield his consent to go. Otherwise he will not leave his quiet and contented life at home, considering his years, and the defects of nature that accompany age, to enter into so toilsome a place, both of body and mind." Sir Henry made three other stipulations. In the first place, the

Queen must publicly acknowledge that, during his three previous terms of office in Ireland, he had done as good service as any other rulers before or since ; in other words, he required from her an apology for her unreasonable misconstruing of his motives and disparaging of his achievements. In the second place, he asked for a peerage, with a grant of land or a fee-farm sufficient to maintain it with dignity ; " so that it may be known and better apparent to the world that her Majesty hath had gracious consideration of his service past." In the third place, he considered that, if he returned to Ireland, it should be with the more impressive title of Lord Lieutenant, instead of Lord Deputy.

Either Queen Elizabeth was of opinion that Sir Henry asked too much for himself, or she objected to part with Philip, or Philip could not " put on a determinate mind " to become assistant Lord Lieutenant of Ireland, or some other obstacle arose. Neither father nor son crossed over to Dublin to repair the blunders of Lord Grey of Wilton's administration.

Yet Philip was absent from Court during parts of the summer and autumn of 1582. He was in Wales in July, busy about his father's affairs ; and in November and December he was at Wilton, seeking in his sister's company relief from some unexplained troubles of his own. From Wilton, on the 16th of December, he wrote to the Earl of Leicester, who, though not now so influential as he had been before the discovery of his marriage with Stella's mother, again stood high in the Queen's favour. " I am bold to trouble your lordship," Sidney said, " that I may not offend in my want of service, to let me understand whether I may remain absent from the Court this Christmastime. Some occasions, both of health and otherwise, do make me much desire it." But the holiday asked for was not granted. He was in attendance upon the Queen on the 1st of January, 1583, when, poor as he was, he contrived to hand to her, as a New Year's present, a beautiful golden flower-pot, shaped like a castle, and daintily adorned on one side with small diamonds.

His prospects brightened with the new year. More than one cheap compliment was shown to him in 1583. The first, however, appears to have been bestowed under conditions that robbed it of grace. As far back as 1579, when Prince John Casimir was in England, the Queen had made him a Knight of the Garter, with her own hands fastening the badge of the order on his leg ; but he had been unable to wait for the formal installation at St. George's Chapel, Windsor, and he had therefore selected his " very dear friend," Mr. Philip Sidney, to act as his proxy. For some reason the ceremony was delayed nearly four years. It took place on the 13th of January, 1583, the anniversary of Elizabeth's coronation, and as, according to the rule of the order, no one below the rank of knight was competent to serve as proxy on such an occasion, it was necessary that Philip should first be qualified. This was done on the 8th of January, and henceforth, no longer plain Philip Sidney, esquire, he was known as Sir Philip Sidney, knight, of Penshurst.

A more substantial favour soon followed, or at any rate was promised. "The Queen," Sir Philip wrote from Court to Lord Burghley on the 27th of January, "at my Lord of Warwick's request, hath been moved to join me in his office of Ordnance, and, as I hear her Majesty yields gracious hearing unto it, my suit is your lordship will favour and further it, which, I truly affirm unto your lordship, I much more desire for the being busied about some serviceable experience than for any other commodity, which I think is but small, that can arise out of it." "I have from my childhood been much bound unto your lordship," we read in the same letter, "which, as the meanness of my fortune keeps me from ability to requite, so it gives me daily cause to make the bond greater by seeking and using your favour towards me."

We have seen so little of the Earl of Warwick— who, indeed, lived too quietly, and apparently with too much unobtrusive dignity, to obtain any considerable notice in the annals of his time—that it is necessary to remind the reader that he was Philip Sidney's uncle, Ambrose, older than the Earl of Leicester by four or five years. Spenser wrote of him, in "The Ruins of Time," as one

> That whilst he livèd was of none envied,
> And, dead, is now, as living, counted dear,
> Dear unto all that true affection bear.

Warwick had been appointed Master of the Ordnance in the second year of Queen Elizabeth's reign, and had held the office a quarter of a century before he "moved" the Queen to allow his nephew to share

AMBROSE DUDLEY, EARL OF WARWICK.

FROM AN ENGRAVING IN "HEROOLOGIA ANGLICA."

it with him. Though the request seems to have been informally assented to, the appointment was not made for some time. Letters patent were issued on the 21st of July, 1585, cancelling the Earl of Warwick's former warrant of office and assigning the post to him and Sir Philip Sidney, to be held by them jointly during life, and, on the death of either, to be retained by the survivor. But these letters patent appear to have been prepared long before, under somewhat mysterious conditions.

On the 13th of February, 1583, Sir Francis Walsingham wrote from the Court at Richmond to Mr. Egerton, the Solicitor-General, officially requesting him to prepare a fresh patent for the Mastership of the Ordnance in the joint names of the Earl of Warwick and Sir Philip Sidney : but, as he added, "praying you withal that for some considerations you will keep the matter secret, and give especial charge unto your clerk that shall engross the book to use the same in like sort." * The motives for secrecy are not evident. Perhaps Queen Elizabeth had not made up her mind, and, until she could be persuaded to sign the document, Sidney's friends deemed it better that nothing should be publicly known about it. From this time, or soon afterwards, records show that Sidney was frequently acting as his uncle's assistant, probably without even the "small commodity" in the way of salary that he looked for; and he was not quite satisfied with this arrangement. On the 22d of July he wrote thus to Lord Burghley from Ramsbury in Wiltshire : "Without carrying with

* " Egerton Papers " (Camden Society), p. 92.

me any further reason of this boldness than your
well-known goodness unto me, I humbly crave of
your lordship your good word to her Majesty, con-
firming that grant she once made unto me of joining
me in patent with my lord of Warwick, whose desire
is that it should be so."

Sidney was a candidate for another post. Sir
Edward de Horsey, Captain of the Isle of Wight,
died on the 23d of March, 1583. Four days later
Edward Dyer wrote to Walsingham, saying it was
"generally reported" that Sir Philip was to be the
new Captain, and urging that "certain imperfec-
tions" in Sir Edward's patent should be amended
in "any new patent for Sir Philip Sidney." * The
post, however, was assigned to Sir George Carey, son
of the first Lord Hunsdon.

But Sidney held at least one dignified office in
and after the early part of 1583. In a list of "principal officers of the army," under that date, his name
is entered as General of the Horse ; his three more
important associates being Lord Grey as General-in-
Chief, Sir William Peckham as Lieutenant-General,
and Sir Robert Constable as Marshal.†

Yet another document shows that, if Sir Philip
obtained no direct salary for the work he was now
permitted to do in the service of his Queen, indirect
recompense was found for him. Of sundry amounts
to be levied on recusant clergymen in 1583 a portion
was assigned to him, other portions going to his

---

* State Papers, Elizabeth, Domestic, vol. cxli., No 47.
† *Ibid.*, vol. cxli., No. 46.

uncle the Earl of Leicester, and to his friend Sir Thomas Cecil, Lord Burghley's son.*

Thus it is clear that early in 1583, he being then in his twenty-ninth year and having already waited long enough for important service under the Crown and on behalf of the State, Sidney's merits as something more than a courtier were at length beginning to be recognised, and his wishes to be somewhat gratified. This advancement he doubtless owed in part to the efforts of his influential friends in Elizabeth's Council, one of whom in particular had a special reason for helping him.

In a short letter that he wrote from Wilton to Sir Francis Walsingham as far back as the 17th of December, 1581, Sidney said: "The country affords no other stuff for letters but humble salutations, which humbly and heartily I send to yourself, my good lady, and my exceeding like to be good friend." The "exceeding like to be good friend," it is reasonable to assume, was Frances Walsingham, the Secretary's daughter, whom Philip must have known from her early childhood, and who was at that time about fourteen years of age, old enough to be thought of as a future wife for some one.† But we have no certain knowledge that she was thought of as a wife for Sidney before the commencement of 1583.

A letter from Sir Henry Sidney to Walsingham,

---

* State Papers, Elizabeth, Domestic, vol. cxli., No. 52.

† There is no record of her birth, but this was probably in 1567, as Sir Francis Walsingham married Ursula, the widow of Sir Robert Worsley, in or near July, 1566.

written on the 1st of March in this year, which has been already quoted from, shows that the project had then been long enough mooted for further delay to seem undesirable. " I have understood of late," wrote Sir Henry, " that coldness is thought in me in proceeding to the matter of the marriage of our children. In truth, sir, it is not so, nor shall it ever be found. I most willingly agree, and protest I joy in the alliance with all my heart." It was only his embarrassments and his inability to furnish his son with an income suitable to his needs as a husband, Sir Henry urged, that had made him backward in acceding to it ; and then followed a curious sentence. " As I know," he said, " that it is for the virtue which is, or which you suppose is, in my son, that you made choice of him for your daughter, refusing haply far greater and far richer matches than he, so was my confidence great that by your good means I might have obtained some reasonable suit of her Majesty, and therefore I nothing regarded any present gain, for, if I had, I might have received a great sum of money for my good will of my son's marriage, greatly to the relief of my present biting necessity."

Let us hope that Sir Henry never had any serious thought of selling his son, as some people sell their daughters, for a marriage portion to be applied to his own use. But, if we are to credit an old writer, Sir Philip had more than one damsel, besides Frances Walsingham, to choose from. Many noble ladies, we are told, " ventured as far as modesty would permit to signify their affections unto him," and the tokens that their modesty permitted were " obvious to every eye." It is worth noting that Spenser says pretty much the same, but in fanciful verse which makes Stella the sole cause of Astrophel's coldness towards others.

> Full many maidens often did him woo
>   Them to vouchsafe amongst his rhymes to name,
> Or make for them as he was wont to do
>   For her that did his heart with love enflame ;
> For which they promisèd to dight for him
> Gay chapelets of flowers and garlands trim.

Another statement by the gossip just cited, and one which we can more readily believe, especially as Sir Francis Walsingham, if influential enough to help his future son-in-law to some employment under the Crown, was too poor to provide his daughter with a large dowry, is that the marriage was of the sort likeliest to lead to happiness on both sides. " Though Sir Philip received no considerable accrument of means by his match," we are told, " yet, accounting virtue a portion to itself, he so affectionately loved her that herein he was exemplary to all gentlemen not to carry their love in their purses, or so to consult profit as to prefer it before merit in marriage." Sir Henry too, in his letter of the 1st of March, speaks of " the joyful love and great liking between our most dear and sweet children, whom God bless." "Commend me," he adds, "most heartily to my good lady cousin and sister, your wife, and bless and buss our sweet daughter."

We have much less information than we could wish concerning the circumstances of Sir Philip

Sidney's marriage with Mistress Frances Walsingham.*   On the 10th of February, 1583, Lord Burghley wrote to congratulate Sir Francis on the "comfortable purpose" regarding his daughter.   "God
bless it," the Lord Treasurer said. †   But the
wedding did not take place until the 20th of September, 1583, ‡ having been delayed at least two or
three months by the Queen's objection to it.   On
the 10th of March Walsingham wrote from Barn
Elms, his house near Putney, to thank Sir Christopher
Hatton for his "honourable and friendly defence of
the intended match."   "I find it strange that her
Majesty should be offended withal," he said, it being
only "a private marriage between a free gentleman
of equal calling with my daughter."   "I hope," he
added, "when her Majesty shall weigh the due
circumstances of place, person, and quality, there

---

* There is reason to suppose that Frances Walsingham, young as
she was, had clandestinely engaged herself to an earlier lover.   Early
in 1583 one John Wickerson wrote from the Marshalsea, pointing
out that he had been two years in prison for his "rash contract of
matrimony with Mistress Frances, which to relinquish would be a
perpetual scruple and worm in conscience, and hazard of body and
soul," and imploring Sir Francis "to weigh and have remorse unto
his perilous state, and vouchsafe the word at the length to grant your
consent and goodwill for performance of their said contract in the
holy state of matrimony."   The petition is endorsed by Walsingham :
"Desires to be enlarged after his long imprisonment, and that I
would not any longer continue my dislike of his contract with
Mistress Frances."—State Papers, Elizabeth, Domestic, vol. clviii.,
No. 84.

† *Ibid.*, vol. clviii., No. 62.

‡ Friday, the 21st of September, is the date given in Sir Henry
Sidney's Psalter ; but as in 1583 the 21st of September fell on a
Saturday, the wedding was probably on Friday, the 20th.

can grow no just cause of offence. I pray you, sir, if she enter into any further speech of the matter, let her understand that you learn the match is held for concluded, and withal let her know how just cause I shall have to find myself aggrieved if her Majesty still show her mislike thereof." Her Majesty's "mislike" was not easily overcome. Next month, on the 20th of April, Roger Manners wrote to his nephew, the young Earl of Rutland, saying: "I have been with Mr. Secretary, who is somewhat troubled that her Majesty conceives no better of the marriage of his daughter with Sir Philip Sidney; but I hope shortly all will be well." So it proved; and apparently her Majesty's wrath was not very great, no greater than she felt whenever a favourite showed by marrying that he acknowledged allegiance to any besides herself. A fortnight later the same correspondent reported that the Queen had "passed over the offence." * Two and a half years afterwards, one day in November, 1585, her Majesty rode up from Richmond to London on purpose to be godmother at the christening of Sir Philip's daughter, who was named Elizabeth after her, and on this occasion she made a present of a hundred shillings to the nurse and midwife.

During these two and a half years, when not absent on official duties, or in attendance at Court, Sidney seems generally to have resided at Walsingham House or at Barn Elms, with his wife's parents, it being the custom of young wives in those days to

---

* Belvoir MSS.; Roger Manners to the Earl of Rutland, 20 April and 7 May, 1583.

remain with their parents until their husbands had homes of their own to take them to. In Sidney's case, Penshurst, which would come to him on his father's death, was available for his and his wife's use, and they were doubtless sometimes there on visits; but he could not often be long absent from London and the Queen's presence, and neither at Leicester House nor in the sumptuous residences of his sister, the Countess of Pembroke, is it likely that he was entertained as frequently as in his bachelor days.

For some time after his marriage, however, we meet with but few records of Sir Philip's movements and employments, and these, with important exceptions, are rather trivial. Thus in December, 1583, we find him writing from Walsingham House a pleasant complimentary letter to his kinsman, the Earl of Rutland ; and we hear nothing more of him till the following February when it was reported to the same Earl of Rutland by his secretary or agent that Sir Philip Sidney and the Earl of Warwick seemed jealous at his having lent a horse of special value to the Earl of Cumberland.* A month later Sir Philip, being away from Court, bespoke Sir Francis's favour for one Captain Gore, the bearer of the letter ; and added that Lady Cheke blamed him for not pushing her interests with the Queen, but that the fault must lie between her Majesty and Sir Francis.†

---

* Belvoir MSS. ; Sir Philip Sidney to the Earl of Rutland, 20 December, 1583 ; Thomas Scriven to the same, 6 February, 1584.

† State Papers, Elizabeth, Domestic, vol. clxix., No. 13 ; Sir Philip Sidney to Walsingham, 6 March, 1584.

Other documents show that Sidney was now expected to perform work as a Master of the Ordnance, though he had not yet been duly installed in the office.   In June a request was made that he should go down to Dover and take counsel with Sir Thomas Scott and other commissioners respecting plans for improving the defences of the harbour, making fresh jetties, and other necessary business ; and to this request Walsingham replied that Sidney would not be able to take part in the deliberations.*

He was probably in Glamorganshire on the 23d of September, 1584, when his brother Robert was married to Barbara Gamage—in later days the Countess of Leicester, who was Ben Jonson's friend and patroness ; and he was at Wilton next month, when he and Robert stood as godfathers, their mother being the other sponsor, to Philip, the second son of Lord and Lady Pembroke, who was born on the 16th of October.†

Of Sidney's occupations about this time in another way we have welcome but inadequate evidence. Giordano Bruno, the famous Italian philosopher and bold speculator in science and theology, who was six years older than Sidney, visited England in 1583, under the protection of M. Castelnau de Mauvissière, the French ambassador in London, who was a very enlightened thinker and patron of free thought, albeit the official representative of a political organi-

---

* State Papers, Elizabeth, Domestic, vol. clxxxi., No. 13, and vol. clxxii., No. 12 ; Thomas Digges to (?) Walsingham, 8 June, 1584 ; note by Walsingham, 4 July, 1584.

† Sir Henry Sidney's Psalter.

sation under Henry the Third not less vicious and more contemptible than that controlled by Philip the Second of Spain. In June Bruno went down to Oxford, and there took part in a public disputation before the Chancellor, still the Earl of Leicester, besides delivering a course of lectures on the immortality of the soul and other subjects. He was not well received by the professors and students, whom he afterwards denounced for their pedantry, bigotry, and bad manners. Returning to London, he lived there and thereabouts for some two years. He tells how, on the evening of Ash Wednesday, the 13th of February, 1584, he was invited by Fulke Greville to meet Sidney and others in order that they might hear "the reasons of his belief that the earth moves"; and this seems to have been only one of numerous gatherings—a revival or a continuation, in another form and for graver purposes, of the Areopagus of 1579. "We met," Bruno says, "in a chamber in the house of Mr. Fulke Greville, to discuss moral, metaphysical, mathematical, and natural speculations." What would we not give for a detailed report of those discussions!

Bruno had heard of Sidney as a great student and a good friend of students, he informs us, as far back as 1579, when he was in Milan. While in London, he evidently saw much of the large-minded courtier, and received many kindnesses from him. To "the most illustrious and excellent knight, Sir Philip Sidney," he dedicated his "Spaccio de la Bestia Trionfante," which was published early in 1584. To Sidney he also, in 1585, dedicated another work in poetic guise, "Degli Heroici Furori." "There is none more proper to receive the dedications of these discourses, excellent sir," he here said. "To you they are presented in order that the Italian may reason with one who has understanding, that verse may be under the countenance and judgment of a poet, that philosophy may show itself in its present nakedness to your fair discernment, that heroic things may be directed to a heroic and generous soul, that honour may be offered to one possessing such worth as is ever made manifest in you." *

The heresy-hunters of Sidney's day and afterwards found fault with him for his sympathy with the valiant, if somewhat whimsical, freethinker who in 1600 was burnt for his boldness; but, befriending and agreeing in many ways with Giordano Bruno, perhaps Sidney was in closer agreement with his friend Philip du Plessis-Mornay, whose "Work concerning the Trueness of the Christian Religion" he was now translating, or having translated. Of the contempt in which he and his friends held the traditions and superstitions of the Church of Rome we have a small instance in a letter that Sir John Perrott, his friend and his father's great disciple as Lord Deputy of Ireland, wrote to Sir Francis Walsingham from Dublin on the 20th of October, 1584. "For a token," said Sir John, "I have sent you a holy Columkill's Cross—a god of great veneration with Sorleyboy and all Ulster; for so great was his grace as happy he thought himself that could get a

---

* Bruno, "Opera" (Leipsig, 1830), vol. ii., pp. 117, 137, 150, 311. See also Mr. Frith's "Life of Giordano Bruno" (1887).

kiss of the said cross. I send him unto you that when you have made some sacrifice to him, according to the disposition you bear to idolatry, you may, if you please, bestow him upon my good Lady Walsingham or my Lady Sidney, to wear as a jewel of weight and bigness, and not of price and goodness, upon some solemn feast or triumph day of the Court." *

Sidney and his friends had some excuse for scoffing at what they regarded as idolatrous perversions of the Christian religion. He and they were sturdy Protestants and they saw so much danger to the political as well as the social well-being of England in the efforts of Catholics, not only to strengthen and enlarge a failing tyranny in the continent of Europe, but also to harass and undermine Queen Elizabeth's authority and influence by plotting in Scotland and Ireland, and even in the English provinces and in London itself, that they could not be in tolerant mood as regards any teaching that came from Rome or any ignorant and extravagant outcome of that teaching.

Events were now moving rapidly towards the great crisis in European affairs for which Sidney had long been hoping, and, so far as he could, had long been working ; but they were not moving fast enough to satisfy him. Restless desires and fitful efforts to hasten the crisis, chagrin at what he regarded as waste of opportunities, and endeavour to make use of such opportunities as he considered to be within his reach, marked the brief remainder of his life.

* " Ulster Journal of Archæology," vol. ii., p. 125.

His temper and his leanings in one direction are shown in a letter he wrote on the 21st of July, 1583, to his friend Sir Edward Stafford, at that time ambassador at the French Court : " We are here all *solito*," he said. " Her Majesty seems affected to deal in the Low Country matters ; but I think nothing will come of it. We are half persuaded to enter into the journey of Sir Humphrey Gilbert very eagerly ; whereunto your Mr. Hakluyt hath served for a very good trumpeter." Richard Hakluyt was as much Sir Philip Sidney's as Sir Edward Stafford's, and part of his trumpeting had been done in the first small edition of his " Voyages," which he dedicated to his old college friend in 1582.

Sir Humphrey Gilbert, who had spent much time in valiant service under Sir Henry Sidney in Ireland, was one of the pioneers of American colonisation in which Philip had been interested from the time of his participation in Martin Frobisher's abortive expeditions to Meta Incognita between 1574 and 1576. Others specially concerned in these and like enterprises were Sir Richard Grenville, Sir George Peckham, Christopher Carleill, who married a daughter of Sir Francis Walsingham, and was thus closely related to Sir Philip Sidney, and Gilbert's half-brother, Sir Walter Raleigh, the friend of Edmund Spenser, with whom he was associated in Ireland under Lord Grey of Wilton. The journey into which Sidney was half persuaded to enter very eagerly was the famous expedition to Newfoundland, on which Gilbert started in the summer of 1583, and in which he was wrecked on the 9th of

September, uttering with his last breath the memorable words, " Courage, my friends, we are as near to heaven by sea as on the land ! "

Meanwhile Sir Philip Sidney was paying at any rate some attention to other parts of the stupendous plan for the conquest and colonisation of America by Englishmen. Early in 1583, or at some previous time, letters patent were issued by which he was " licensed and authorised to discover, search, find out, view, and inhabit certain parts of America not yet discovered, and out of those countries, by him, his heirs, factors or assigns, to have and enjoy, to him, his heirs and assigns for ever, such and so much quantity of ground as should amount to the number of thirty hundred thousand acres of ground and wood, with all commodities, jurisdictions and royalties, both by sea and land, with full power and authority that it should and might be lawful for the said Sir Philip Sidney, his heirs and assigns, at all times thereafter to have, take and lead in the said voyage, to travel thitherwards or to inhabit there with him or them, and every or any of them, such and so many of her Majesty's subjects as should willingly accompany him and them, and any or every of them, with sufficient shipping and munition for their transportations."

Philip Sidney did not seriously contemplate going out himself to plant and manage a colony in America. The Queen would not have allowed him to do that ; and as he was about to take to himself a wife, there were special reasons against the project in the spring of 1583. But it is significant that he should

have sought and obtained the charter, and thus constituted himself a pioneer in the great enterprise
about which so many other far-seeing Englishmen
were henceforward to be busied. Probably he
thought rather of encouraging others in the work
than of personally engaging in it, and of course,
poor as he was, he had an eye to the chances of
profit from the possession and development of his
three million acres of as yet undiscovered land.

Accordingly we find that in July, 1583, as soon as
was convenient after his letters patent had been
secured, he assigned to Sir George Peckham a small
part of his American rights. " For the more speedy
execution of her Majesty's grant and the enlargement of her Majesty's dominions and governments,
for the better encouragement of Sir George Peckham and his associates in so worthy and commendable an enterprise, as also for divers other causes
specially moving him," according to the document,
he authorised Peckham, or any persons, guild or
company Peckham might depute the license to, to
discover and in his name take possession of thirty
thousand out of the three million acres granted to
him, and to have absolute holding of " all royalties,
titles, pre-eminences, privileges, liberties and digni-
ties thereunto belonging." Sidney may have
thought that, if Peckham and the adventurers allied
with him made a start, he would gain by the improved value of the property remaining to him. But
in 1583 Peckham had done as much as he was prepared to do in helping to fit out Gilbert's luckless
expedition, and next year whatever action he pro-

jected or Sidney was concerned in appears to have been limited to co-operation in the larger scheme pushed forward by Raleigh.

Gilbert being dead, Raleigh had acquired a title to leadership in carrying on his kinsman's work. In March, 1584, he obtained from Queen Elizabeth a charter similar to that granted to his half-brother, and the two small vessels that he sent out before the end of April, under Captain Amadas and Captain Barlow, had good fortune. Roanoke was discovered and the colony of Virginia was founded. In this expedition Sidney apparently had no direct share, Raleigh prudently keeping it in such small proportions that the whole management could be in his own hands. When it was deemed necessary, however, that the Queen's charter to Raleigh should be confirmed, and the limits of the new colony defined by Parliament, the matter was on the 14th of December referred to a committee of which Sidney was one of the members, Sir Francis Drake being another. The bill approved by this committee of the House of Commons was passed on the 18th of December.

The next year steps were taken to render the colony prosperous, and in these Sidney evidently had a considerable share, though we can only guess that it was his intention, by assisting Raleigh's work, to prepare for exercising his own rights as a colony-maker. Of the seven vessels that set sail for Virginia on the 9th of April, 1585, Sir Richard Grenville was appointed admiral, and with them went Ralph Lane to take office as governor on land. Lane, now about fifty-five years old, had done his share of fighting under Sir Henry Sidney and others, and had been one of " Leicester's band " of equerries to the Queen. " Having served her Majesty these twenty years, spent my patrimony, bruised my limbs, and yet nevertheless at this day not worth one groat by her Majesty's gift towards a living," as he stated in a petition to Lord Burghley in July, 1583, he was in February, 1585, appointed to the Virginian post at the instigation of Sir Francis Walsingham and Sir Philip Sidney, from both of whom he acknowledged having received favours. It was chiefly to Walsingham, but also to Sidney, that he sent home the letters that fill out the first chapter in the history of Virginia. Lane was not strong enough or wise enough for his work. His governorship was a failure, and the blunders committed by him, or by others whom he was not able to control, had to be corrected as far as might be, and atoned for.

While the experiment was being made, Sidney was too busy with other matters to pay much or steady attention to it.

NOBLEMENS DRESS

NETHERLANDS XVITH. CENTURY

CHAPTER XVI.

IN THE WORLD OF POLITICS.

1584–1585.

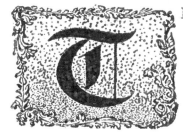

HE Duke of Anjou, who a year before had abandoned his crazy claim to partnership with William of Orange in rule over the Netherlands, but had continued to be talked of as a possible husband for Queen Elizabeth, died on the 13th of June, 1584. A month later, on the 12th of July, William was murdered. The second event, occasioning special grief to Sir Philip Sidney when the news reached him, as thereby he lost one of his worthiest friends and the one from whom he rightly hoped most for the advancement of Protestantism and political liberty in Europe, was far more momentous than the first in bringing about a crisis from which Sidney was anxious that public advantage should result.

Henceforward, until his own untimely death, he applied himself to political work with much greater zeal than he appears to have lately shown, although the views he now held and sought to enforce were in effect no different from those we have seen him advocating in earlier days. The lessons he had begun to learn when, as a youth of seventeen, he was an eye-witness of the St. Bartholomew Massacre in 1572, the influence exerted on him after that by Hubert Languet and other sturdy Huguenots, the bold schemes for a general Protestant league that he had put forward during his short embassage to Germany in 1577, were at no time forgotten. But the busy idleness of Court life which was imposed upon him and against which he vainly rebelled, the pleasure he found in literary and other pursuits, and, above all, perhaps, the fickleness and perversity of Queen Elizabeth, which vexed the souls and crippled the hands of her ablest statesmen, had stood in the way of such service as he desired to do to his country and the world. Now that he was in his thirtieth year, not deeming that so short a time remained in which he could live and work, but deeming that he had already wasted time enough, he was eager to take advantage of the better opportunities for patriotic effort that he saw to be within reach and to be more than ever incumbent on all honest Englishmen.

One task proposed for him can scarcely have been to his taste. On hearing of the Duke of Anjou's death, Queen Elizabeth resolved to send a special message to Anjou's brother, King Henry the Third of France, and their mother, Catherine de' Medici,

assuring them of her extreme grief at the loss of so
rare and noble a friend, and of her unfeigned love
and esteem for the survivors; and for messenger she
chose Sir Philip Sidney. While the embassage was
being arranged the report of William of Orange's
assassination reached England, and on this account,
perhaps, weightier words, which read as though he
had drafted them himself, were added to Sir Philip's
instructions. He was to ask whether King Henry
felt disposed to do anything for the relief of "those
poor afflicted people of the Low Countries," and to
urge that, should they be overcome by Spain—as,
unless some prompt assistance was rendered to
them, was likely — all Christendom would suffer.
The world had long wondered, Sidney was commissioned to say, why King Henry had so overslipped
the means proper to keeping Spain in check. King
Philip lacked only the quiet possession of the Low
Countries to make him the most powerful monarch
that had ever been in Europe, and, if he were allowed
thus further to aggrandise himself, the consequences
would be most perilous to everyone of his neighbours, and especially to the King of France.

Sir Philip never delivered the message. After he
had, at great trouble and expense, made the necessary preparations, and had even, near the end of
July, proceeded some way on his journey, it was announced that King Henry had gone to Lyons and
could not receive the message unless it was kept till
his return to Paris a couple of months later. Therefore the project came to nothing; and this was just
as well. The formalities of condolence on the Duke

of Anjou's death were quite uncalled-for, and no good could have been effected by the most eloquent language it would have been possible to offer to the French king respecting the Netherlands. Sidney shared the opinion of his friend Sir Edward Stafford, the regular English ambassador in Paris, who, writing about this time to Walsingham, described Henry as " a king who seeketh nothing but to impoverish his poor people and to enrich a couple, who careth not what cometh after his death so that he may rove about while he liveth."

Being persuaded that France would render no assistance to the Low Countries, and that Germany would be equally apathetic, Sidney watched with growing alarm the disasters consequent to the Netherlanders on the loss of their head, and on the quickened energy with which Alexander Farnese, the Duke of Parma, Philip's new viceroy, was corrupting many of them with bribes and overcoming others by the sword. The Spanish occupation of Dendermonde on the 17th of August, of Ghent on the 17th of September, and of other towns of more or less importance during the ensuing weeks, convinced Sidney that, unless strong measures were quickly taken for thwarting the designs of King Philip and his agents, the cause of the Netherlands and all that went with it would be ruined.

But the measures he now chiefly favoured were not, as heretofore, the sending of English soldiers to aid in the defence of the Dutch towns. He was anxious for a more direct attack to be made upon Spain. Flanders, he insisted, as we learn from his friend, Fulke Greville, was the best fortified part of the Spanish dominions and the worst battle-ground that Queen Elizabeth could choose, if, as seemed more and more certain, the task of helping the Netherlanders was to be shirked by France, Germany, and all the other nations of the continent, and to be undertaken, single-handed, by England. For England to send an army into the Netherlands, " without any curious examination as to what power the adverse party hath prepared to encounter, by defence, invasion, or division, must probably make us losers both in men, money, and reputation." Some better mode of weakening King Philip must be found, and, in Sidney's opinion, " there were but two ways left to frustrate this ambitious monarch's designs ; the one, that which diverted Hannibal, and, by setting fire to his own house, made him draw in his spirits to comfort his heart ; the other, that of Jason, by fetching away his golden fleece, and not suffering any man to enjoy that which every man so much affected." *

In taking this view Sidney was at one with Gilbert, Raleigh, Drake, Frobisher, and the other bold seamen who, with a keen eye to their own profit as well as to their country's good, purposed, not only to plant colonies in regions claimed by King Philip as his property, but also to hamper and despoil the trade of Spain with its possessions in both the Indies, and even to make raids on Cadiz, Seville, and the thriving

---

* A very full account of Sidney's and of his own views on the political situation at this time is given by Fulke Greville in his life of his friend.

marts and ports of Spain itself. He had lately, it will be remembered, obtained from Queen Elizabeth a charter to establish a colony of his own in America, and had made over a fraction of his rights to Sir George Peckham. His share in the work of a committee of the House of Commons on Raleigh's new colony in Virginia has also been mentioned.

The session of the House of Commons in which the business was considered sat from the 23d of November till the 21st of December, 1584, and, after six weeks' Christmas holidays, from the 4th of February to the 29th of March, 1585. In it, as in the previous Parliament, which had its last session in 1581, Sir Philip Sidney sat as a member for his native county of Kent. Its occupations were, with a few exceptions, unimportant. In December, besides his service on the Virginian bill, Sidney was placed on a committee that considered a measure for the preservation of timber in Sussex. In February and March he was on committees concerned with the maintenance of Rochester Bridge, the preservation of woods in Kent, and the privileges of curriers.

The weightiest performance of the session was its legislation against Jesuits. On the 18th of February Sidney was deputed, with Fulke Greville and others, to confer with the Lords respecting a severe project approved by the Commons, but objected to by the Upper House on the score of its excessive Puritanism. The compromise arrived at was sufficiently tyrannical, and only to be excused by the fact that many treacherous schemes were now working in the minds of rebellious Catholics and showing themselves

20

in conspiracies like the one presently to be led by Babington. The new law required all Jesuits, seminary priests, and other priests to quit the kingdom within forty days, on pain of being dealt with as traitors if they remained ; it declared any who harboured or relieved these recusants to be felons, worthy of fine and imprisonment; and it outlawed every clergyman residing in a foreign seminary who did not within six months return to England and make humble submission.

Sidney's well-grounded hatred of the political designs of the foreign Catholics, suborned by many in England, which caused him to urge on the Queen the duty of taking up her rightful position as Defendress of the Faith and, as Fulke Greville said, to effect "a safe unvizarding of this masked triplicity between Spain, Rome and the Jesuitical faction of France," explains, if it does not justify, his participation in the Puritan bigotry of the day. But it is not pleasant to reflect that he was personally a gainer by some of the fines and forfeitures prescribed for recusant Catholics.

An important part of the political problem with which Sidney and his friends were confronted, and which they aimed at solving, had to do with Scotland. He appears to have been less interested in the affairs of Queen Mary and King James, and their rival partisans and betrayers, than in Low Country concerns ; yet he could not but be mixed up in these also, and he was one of the many dupes of an archplotter among the Scotsmen of the day.

Queen Mary, who had been a prisoner in England

for eighteen years, was now, in desperation, giving more heed than heretofore to the revolutionary efforts of her supporters. Her disagreeable son, too, who all through this time had borne the title of king, was now more than ever being played with by rival sections of his followers, and was growing restive under their control. The Earls of Arran and Lennox having been King James's chief favourites since 1580, the Earl of Gowrie and others had in 1582 captured him at Ruthven and imprisoned or banished their rivals. After a year's feigned liking of his position, King James had broken loose from his guardians and reinstated the Arran faction. Thereupon, in September, 1583, Sir Francis Walsingham had been sent to inquire into the state of matters. His report was to the effect that Queen Elizabeth had formed a true estimate of her kinsman's character; King James was ready at any moment to requite kindness with ingratitude; everywhere he was misliked for his dissimulation and treachery; and now the captive Queen his mother, ever the chief author of trouble, had half persuaded him to change his religion, promising him the support of a large party in England and the willing aid of Spain. Walsingham considered that he had done something to lessen the threatened dangers by extracting pledges from James and weakening Arran's influence over him.

Thus matters stood in 1584, when we first get trace of Sidney's connection with Scottish politics. About Queen Mary's or her friends' conspiracies, and King James's plots for succession to the rule of

England on Queen Elizabeth's demise, Sir Philip does not appear to have much troubled himself until there was a revival of the old fear that the Scottish plotters would obtain substantial help from Spain. Then he was stirred to action. Through his old friend Edward Wotton, who had been his fellow-student at Vienna ten years before, and was now ambassador in Scotland, he obtained information from the northern capital ; and he was in close inter-course with Patrick, sixth Lord Gray, better known as the Master of Gray, who in 1584 paid a long visit to London with the ostensible object of arranging an alliance between King James and Queen Eliza-beth from which Queen Mary was to be excluded.

This Master of Gray was accounted one of the handsomest men of the time, skilled in all the arts and graces of courtiership. Though few then knew it, he was as unscrupulous as he was clever, a man who shrank from no trickery and meanness, betray-ing every one who trusted him, and cared for nothing but his own advancement. For some time a creature of the Earl of Arran, he cheated Arran as readily as he cheated Gowrie and all the rest of King James's advisers. Professing himself a hater of Papists, he was a Catholic in so far as he had any religion. Unfortunately, though thence came no great harm to the State or to Sidney himself, he deceived Sidney along with men of longer and wider experience in statesmanship.

In nearly every letter that the Master of Gray, after his return to Scotland, wrote to his other friends in London, as well as to Sidney, he sent some affectionate message to Sir Philip. "I commend me heartily unto you," we read in one, "and will you do the same to all my friends in my name, but chiefly to Sir Philip Sidney. Pray him do according to the postscript in my letter; for in that stands my weal, and otherwise my overthrow." The postscript is missing. It probably referred to the efforts to prevent King James from joining the Spanish league, about which Sidney was more eager than any one else, and in which the Master of Gray pretended to be his ally.

It was doubtless at the Master of Gray's instigation that Sidney took the lead in procuring from Queen Elizabeth an offer of a pension to King James if he would hold aloof from King Philip's schemes. On the 23d of May, 1585, Walsingham wrote by his son-in-law's advice to impress upon Wotton the importance of thus working upon the Scotch king's greed; "but," said the prudent Secretary, "you must be cautious how you broach the subject, lest the smallness of the sum allowed by her Majesty do more harm than good." The sum was so small that Wotton deemed it best not even to broach the subject at all. There were other ways of propitiating the monarch's little mind. In June the Queen sent him a present of horses, most beautiful in shape and bearing, and we are told that he mounted and managed them to the great contentment both of himself and of his courtiers.*

---

* Much fuller information than I have thought it necessary to repeat about Sidney's relations with the Scottish Court, the subject being of small importance, will be found in the "Scottish Correspondence" in the Record Office.

Sidney now held as influential a position among Queen Elizabeth's advisers as was possible to one moving, with no dignified office, among officials whose high rank and great responsibility were over-ruled by their mistress's whims. " Sorry I am," wrote Walsingham to William Davison, the ambas-sador to the Netherlands, concerning the question that to both of them was of supreme importance, " sorry I am to see the course that is taken in this weighty cause ; for we will neither help these poor countries ourselves nor yet suffer others to do it." Then he went on to deplore the underhand policy of those in chief authority, and the great discredit that must ensue, not only to the State, but also to her Majesty, " as never a wise man that seeth it and loveth her, but lamenteth it from the bottom of his heart."

Though Sidney was not formally installed as the Earl of Warwick's colleague in the Mastership of the Ordnance until the 21st of July, 1585, the duties had more and more devolved upon him, and he found much embarrassment in having responsibility without authority assigned to him. On the 13th of May he received a letter from Lord Burghley, in which he was blamed for having spoken too plainly to the Queen about the destitute condition of the stores, and thus brought a scolding on the great Lord Treasurer himself. " I will not fail on Monday morning," he wrote back on the same day, " to wait at the Tower for the performance of her Majesty's commandments therein. Your lordship, in the post-script, writes of her Majesty's being informed of great wants and faults in the office, wherewith her Majesty seemeth to charge your lordship for lack of reformation more than your lordship doth deserve. For my part, I have ever so conceived. But, because your lordship writes it particularly to me, who of that office am driven to have speech of her Majesty, I desire, for truth's sake, especially to satisfy your lordship, if perhaps your lordship conceive any doubt of me therein. Indeed, having in my speech not once gone beyond these limits, to acknowledge, as I could not deny, the present poverty of her Majesty's store, and therein to excuse my lord of Warwick, as in conscience I might and in duty I ought to do, without further aggravating anything against any man living; for I cannot, not having been acquainted with the proceedings." The grammatical faultiness of that sentence only brings out more clearly the thoughts that Sir Philip was too courteous to put in words. A postscript followed : " Her Majesty did not once name your lordship nor any belonging to the office, but Sir William Pelham, who, her Majesty said, did lay all the fault on my lord of Warwick's deputy "—Sidney himself ; " whereupon I only answered that the money neither my lord nor any of his had ever dealt with."

It was quite necessary for Sidney to keep the Queen informed as to the lack of fighting material and even of what little money she permitted to be spent in improving it. The time had at length come when the assistance so often asked for by the Netherlanders from England could not further be delayed.

In the spring of 1585 deputies from the Low Countries presented themselves in Paris and besought King Henry and the Queen-Mother to protect them from utter overthrow by Spain. Antwerp had been undergoing a siege by the Duke of Parma since the previous June, and there seemed small prospect of its holding out much longer without help from France or some other nation. From the French sovereigns the Dutch delegates received rough treatment, and they soon saw, as it was intended they should see, that no help was to be looked for in that quarter. Therefore they turned to Elizabeth, and reached London on the 26th of June.

On Tuesday, the 29th, they had audience of her Majesty at Greenwich. In an eloquent address their spokesman implored her to rescue them from the tyranny and servitude aimed at by Philip of Spain, and to preserve for them those liberties, rights, and privileges they had been so painfully defending; and they humbly tendered to her the sovereignty of the United Provinces, if she would aid them by doing a work right royal and most magnificent, acceptable to God, profitable to all Christendom, and worthy of immortal fame. The proffered sovereignty was at once declined; but in gracious terms Elizabeth promised to assist the Netherlanders with men and money. Six weeks were occupied in settling details, and on the 16th of August a treaty was concluded by which the Queen undertook to send over an army of five thousand foot and a thousand horse, equipped and paid out of the English Exchequer, and to carry on the war against Spain until both allies agreed to peace-making. It was stipulated that the English general to be selected and two others should take rank and have voice in the Council of the States, that at the close of the war all the expenses disbursed by England should be recouped by the Netherlanders, and that the towns of Flushing and Brielle, with the castle of Rammekins, should be held by the Queen meanwhile as security for liquidation of the debt.

From the first the Earl of Leicester was talked of as certain to be leader of the expedition, and it was expected that Sir Philip Sidney would have high rank under him as Governor of Flushing. But Sidney appears to have held aloof, partly because he doubted whether the post would be offered to him, partly because he was planning work in another direction. As has been noted, his opinions as to the right method of attacking Spain had altered. He no longer considered the Netherlands the best battleground for maintaining even the Netherlanders' cause, and he had a reasonable mistrust as to the sort of warfare that would be allowed or possible under constant interference from home. According to a noteworthy statement by Fulke Greville, "he found greatness of worth and place counterpoised by the arts of power and favour; the stirring spirits sent abroad as fuel to keep the flame far off, and the effeminate made judges of danger which they feared, and honour which they understood not." He knew that Queen Elizabeth and Lord Burghley were honest in their wish to help the cause of European liberty;

"yet," says the same trustworthy informant, "he perceived her governors to sit at home in their soft chairs, playing fast and loose with those that ventured their lives abroad." He was anxious to embark on an enterprise by which, as he wisely judged, and as events proved, a more effective blow might be struck at Spain than could come from any fighting in the Low Countries, and one in which he would be too well out of reach for any arm-chair governors to play fast and loose with him.

This was no hasty notion. The part he took in the sending out of Raleigh's second Virginian expedition has already been mentioned. That expedition left England in April, 1585 ; and with Ralph Lane, who went out as governor of the young colony, it is clear that Sidney had fully discussed further projects. Lane had not been long in Virginia before he wrote thus, on the 12th of August, to his friend : "We have, by our dwelling upon the islands of St. John and Hispaniola for the space of five weeks, so discovered the forces thereof, with the infinite riches of the same, as that I find it an attempt most honourable, feasible and profitable, and only fit for yourself to be chief commander in. This entry would so gall the King of Spain as it would direct his forces, that he troubleth your part of Christendom with, into these parts, where he cannot greatly annoy us with them. And how greatly a small force would garboil him here, when two of his most richest and strongest islands took alarms at us, not only landing, but dwelling upon them with only a hundred and twenty men ! I refer it to your judgment. Finding, by my own view, his force at hand to be so mean, and his terror made so great amongst those in England, considering that the reputation thereof doth altogether grow from the mines of his treasure, and the same in places which we see here are so easy both to be taken and kept by any small force sent by her Majesty, I could not but write these ill-fashioned lines unto you, and to exhort you, my noble general, by occasion not to refuse the good opportunity of such service to the Church of Christ of great relief from many calamities that this treasure in the Spaniards' hands doth inflict unto the members thereof—very honourable and fit for yourself to be the enterpriser of."

This letter, if it was seen by Sidney at all, could not have reached him before he had abandoned for a time, and as it proved for ever, his intention of taking personal share in the conquest of the Spanish settlements in the West Indies; but it helps us to see what the project was with which he was busy during the spring and summer months of 1585, before and after Queen Elizabeth's treaty of the 16th of August with the Netherlanders. In those months, besides giving much thought and all the money he could spare out of his own scanty resources, he induced thirty gentlemen of his acquaintance to subscribe £100 apiece towards fitting out a fleet powerful enough to act vigorously against Spain. " To martial men," we are told by Fulke Greville, " he opened wide the door of sea and land for fame and conquest ; to the nobly ambitious, the far stage of America to win honour in ; to the religious divines, besides a new apostolical calling of the lost heathen to the Christian faith, a large field of reducing poor Christians, misled by the idolatry of Rome, to their primitive Mother Church ; to the ingeniously industrious, variety of natural riches for new mysteries and manufactures to work upon ; to the merchants, with a simple people, a fertile and unexhausted earth ; to the fortune-bound, liberty ; to the curious, a fruitful womb of invention."

In that bold and brilliant project Sidney obtained the co-operation of Sir Francis Drake, who had returned in 1580 from his famous voyage round the world in the *Golden Hind.* Not with one little ship alone, but with five and twenty, and with a party of more than two thousand officers, soldiers, and seamen, the new enterprise was to be started. It is probable that Drake contributed at least half the labour by which the scheme was developed, and, as Sidney had good reason for expecting that the Queen, if she knew of it beforehand, would forbid his sailing with the fleet, the expedition was announced to be under Drake's sole leadership. But it was privately arranged that, as soon as they had left Plymouth behind them, Sidney and Drake should have equal authority, an important post being assigned to Fulke Greville, whose participation in the plot was also to be kept secret until the last moment.

Thus matters were proceeding when the Dutch delegates arrived in England, and while the treaty with them was being negotiated. It is doubtful whether, on there being a prospect that he would be sent to Flushing, Sidney thought of leaving Drake to sail alone. If so, the Flushing appointment not being at once or for some while given to him, he reverted to his original plan. Drake may have at first intended loyally to share with Sidney the management of the business which they had planned together; but he no sooner saw a chance of the sole command devolving upon him than he resolved to play a treacherous game.

The fleet was all but ready to leave Plymouth by the end of August, and Drake then sent word to Sidney that they were waiting for him to join them. Sidney and Greville hurried down, finding excuse for the journey in the fact that Don Antonio, a feeble claimant for the crown of Portugal which Philip of Spain had usurped, and an old acquaintance of Sidney's, was expected at Plymouth. Their avowed intention was to meet Don Antonio and to escort him back to London. When they reached Plymouth, however, Drake, while making great show of friendship, was in no hurry to set sail. Day after day the departure was postponed on frivolous excuses, and, at length Sidney, although "not apt to discredit others," as Greville says, seeing "some sparks of false fire breaking out from his yoke-fellow daily," was induced to share Greville's earlier formed suspicion as to Drake's honesty. It was afterwards placed beyond doubt that Drake, after waiting a few days in the hope that Sidney would be recalled without his intervention, caused a message to be conveyed stealthily to the Court at Nonsuch, informing the Queen of her courtier's intention to run away.

On the receipt of this news the Queen instantly

had three letters written; one to Sidney, commanding his immediate return; one to Drake, threatening him with her eternal displeasure if he allowed Sidney to accompany him; the third to the mayor of Plymouth, bidding him see that her orders were obeyed. But Sidney was prepared for the emergency. A friend at Court warned him of the despatch of these letters, and the messenger bearing them was met four miles from Plymouth by a couple of Sidney's henchmen, disguised as sailors, who purloined the letters. " The bruit runneth on stilts in London, and amongst many courtiers," wrote a gossip from Nonsuch on the 12th of September, " that Sir Francis is gone and Sir Philip too." * Even Sidney's father-in-law was misled and in the dark. " Sir Philip," Walsingham wrote on the 13th of September, " hath taken a very hard resolution to accompany Sir Francis Drake on his voyages, moved thereto for that he saw that her Majesty was disposed to commit the charge of Flushing unto some other; which he reputeth would fall out greatly to his disgrace, to see another preferred before him, both for birth and judgment inferior unto him. The despair thereof and the disgrace, that he doubted he should receive, have carried him into a different course."

Drake left Plymouth on the 14th of September, having for one of his chief officers Captain Christopher Carleill, a young veteran in naval enterprise, who had lately married Mary Walsingham, Sir

---

* Belvoir MSS.; John Stanhope to the Earl of Rutland. This letter and others confirm the strange narrative given in great detail by Fulke Greville.

Philip Sidney's sister-in-law. Sidney, however, did not go with the party. Intelligence as to the trick played on her first messenger having reached the Queen in time, she despatched another and more imperious mandate, and care was taken that it should be properly conveyed. It was delivered into Sir Philip's own hands by a peer of the realm, as Fulke Greville tells us, and it carried with it "in the one hand grace, in the other thunder." The thunder was a threat that, if Sidney quitted the Court in this way, he should never again be admitted to the Queen's presence. The grace was that he should have employment under his uncle in the Low Countries. Thereat, we are told, he was in no way pleased; but " the confluence of reason, the transcendency of power, and the fear of staying the whole fleet," made him immediately give way.

This episode is not creditable to Sir Philip Sidney. The trickery to which he resorted, and in which he was foiled, was by no one in those days considered undignified or dishonest. But in the fact that he should have been driven to such straits and such expedients in his anxiety to do good work for his country, instead of longer dangling about the Court, we have an illustration of the unhealthy conditions by which the chivalry of the Elizabethan age was hampered.

Sailing without his partner, Drake spent nine and a half months in his memorable sea-crusade against the Spanish power in the West Indies and nearer home, thereby so far arousing King Philip's wrath that King Philip straightway planned the great Armada which was wrecked in 1588, and the ruin of which weakened Spain for ever.

Sir Philip Sidney made his peace with Queen Elizabeth at Nonsuch on the 21st of September. On the 7th of November she signed at Westminster a patent appointing him Governor of Flushing and of Rammekins; Sir Thomas Cecil, eldest son of Lord Burghley and Sidney's senior by a dozen years, being nominated to the humbler post of Governor of Brielle, and the Earl of Leicester being commissioned as Lord Lieutenant for the Queen of England and Commander-in-chief of her forces in the Low Countries.

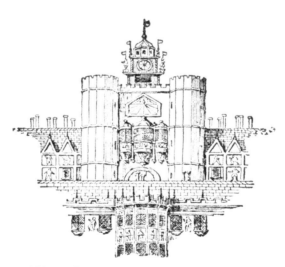

CENTRAL TOWERS, NONSUCH HOUSE.

ENTRANCE TO THE PORT OF FLUSHING

CHAPTER XVII.

IN THE LOW COUNTRIES.

1585–1586.

N Tuesday, the 16th of Novem-
ber, 1585, Sir Philip Sidney, ac-
companied by young William
Temple as his private secretary,
left Gravesend to enter on his
duties as Governor of Flushing
and Rammekins.

If he still regretted not having been allowed to
take part with Sir Francis Drake in a more daring
and more deadly attack on Spanish power than
seemed to him possible in the Netherlands, there
was in his present employment much to hope for and
to aim at. Not yet quite one and thirty years of age,
he now had an opportunity of fighting in defence,
not only of the hardly treated Dutchmen, but also
of the whole cause of political and religious liberty
which it was the dream of his life to aid. It was
his first opportunity of putting to serious test, and

devoting to grave issues, the prowess and skill that hitherto he had shown merely in mimic warfare at joust and tournament; and a prospect of chivalrous work in other ways as well as in mere fighting opened before him as he crossed the Narrow Seas and approached the Scheldt, the entrance of which was guarded to the north by Flushing, on the island of Walcheren, and by the neighbouring castle of Rammekins.

The prospect was quickly darkened, and soon altogether destroyed. All was not bright even on landing. " Upon Thursday," he wrote from Flushing to his uncle, who was to follow three weeks later with most of the troops, Sidney taking with him only a small escort and a parcel of gold,—" upon Thursday we came into this town, driven to land at Rammekins because the wind began to rise in such sort as our mariners durst not anchor before the town, and from thence came with as dirty a walk as ever poor governor entered his charge withal." But that was a small matter. " I find the people very glad of our coming and promise myself as much surety in keeping this town as popular good will, gotten by light hope and as light conceits, may breed; for, indeed, the garrison is far too weak to command by authority; which is pity. For how great a jewel this place is to the Crown of England, and the Queen's safety, I need not write to your lordship who knows it so well. Yet I must needs say, the better I know it, the more I find the preciousness of it."

That letter was written on Monday, the 22d, after Sidney had been but four days in Flushing;

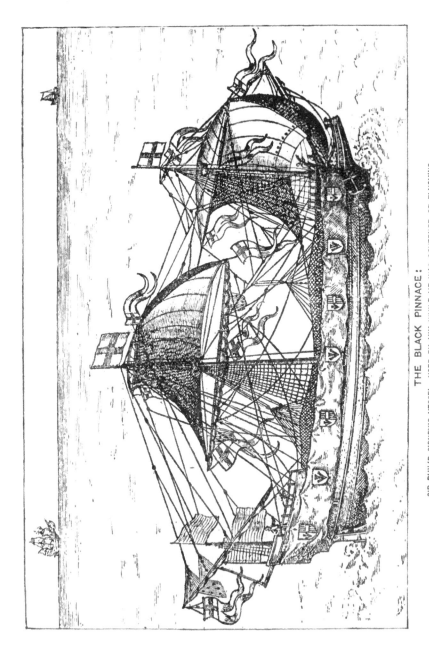

THE BLACK PINNACE:

SIR PHILIP SIDNEY'S VESSEL, USED BY HIM WHILE HE WAS GOVERNOR OF FLUSHING.

(From Thomas Lant's "Procession at the Obsequies of Sir Philip Sidney," 1587.)

yet already he had made plans for strengthening the defences, and for gradually correcting abuses in ways calculated to avoid " breeding jealousies in this people, which is carried more by shows than substance." " I am more and more persuaded," he added, " that, with the proportion which her Majesty alloweth, the country is fully able to maintain the wars, if what they do be well ordered, and not abused, as it is by the States ; it being strange that the people show themselves far more careful than the governors in all things touching the public welfare." Yet the citizens were down-hearted. " I think truly, if my coming had been longer delayed, some alteration would have followed ; for the truth is, the people is weary of war, and if they do not see such a course taken as may be likely to defend them, they will on a sudden give over the cause."

Having on Sunday taken formal possession of his office and exchanged the requisite oaths with the magistrates of the town—the States or Estates, as they were called,—Sir Philip, continuing his arrangements and preparations the while, awaited his uncle's coming. The Earl of Leicester reached Flushing on the 10th of December, with the bulk of his little English army, and a throng of gay and gallant followers; among them Sidney's old rival, the Earl of Oxford, and Stella's brother, the young Earl of Essex, now just twenty, and Sidney's youngest brother, Thomas. The other brother, Robert, had been of Philip's party, and had been placed by him as his deputy in charge of Rammekins Castle. Count Maurice of Nassau, son and successor to the

murdered William, and many of the leading Dutchmen welcomed the English Lord Lieutenant.   They
escorted him to the Hague, and there were splendid
entertainments on the way as the company passed
through Middelburg, and Dordrecht, and Rotterdam,
and Delft.

At the Hague and elsewhere Leicester maintained
almost royal state, wasting in idle shows both the
impoverished exchequer of the Netherlanders and
the money brought from England, while there was
the utmost need of prompt action against the Duke
of Parma and his Spanish garrisons.*   The climax
was reached when, on New Year's Day, 1586, a
deputation waited upon him and proposed that, in
addition to his humbler office of Lord Lieutenant
under the Queen of England, he should accept title
and rank as Governor-General of the United Provinces, with supreme authority in all military and
civil affairs, and almost greater power than had ever
been accorded to William of Orange.   That offer
his vanity led him to accept, in contempt of Elizabeth's instructions, and the news of his having done
so only reached England some weeks later and by a
roundabout course.   Thereupon ensued one of the
quarrels that were frequent between the Queen and
her unruly favourite.   After prevaricating and for a

---

* One of the letters that Sidney wrote to his father-in-law was for-
warded, as he said, by " Will, my lord of Leicester's jesting player."
It has been rashly suggested that " Will" was Shakespeare.   He
may have been William Kemp, a noted comedian in " the Earl of
Leicester's company."   Whoever he was, it is significant that
Leicester, going over ostensibly to fight the Spaniards, should have
found it necessary to have players to amuse him in the Netherlands.

time defying his mistress, Leicester wrote humbly to surrender everything and to beg for his recall to Court. "Here," he said, "I can do your Majesty no service. There I can do you some, at least rub your horse's heels, a service which shall be more welcome to me than this, with all that these men can give me." More than one such appeal had to be made before her Majesty was appeased, and returned to her old-womanish dalliance. Leicester might be her "Sweet Robin" again, she at length sent word; and, hard as she found it to be so long without him, she would suffer him, for the good of the Netherlands and of Europe, to retain his post as her Lord Lieutenant until he had won glory for himself and her by crushing the Spanish foe.

While this farce was being played out and succeeded by other follies on the part of his uncle, Sidney vainly endeavoured to forward the work that had to be done, and was being made harder by each day's delay. Antwerp had fallen into the Duke of Parma's hands on the 17th of August, 1585, and the Spaniards had since been making other encroachments on the Netherlanders. If the speedy recovery of Antwerp was not to be hoped for, it was the duty of the English expedition to keep the enemy at bay and drive them back as far and as fast as possible. Flushing being the key to the Scheldt, so long as it was held no Spanish reinforcements could reach Antwerp by sea, and Sidney's primary task was, as its governor, to retain firm possession of it. He wanted to do that and much else; but his efforts were frustrated at every turn, not only by the apathy and meanness of many of his Dutch associates, but yet more by his uncle's recklessness and frivolity, and by the neglect and niggardliness of the home authorities. Each letter that he wrote during more than eight months was laden with just complaints, and showed alike the straits to which he was reduced, and the wise and generous views that he was not suffered to carry out. Let a few instances be given.

" We want supplies exceedingly," Sir Philip wrote to his father-in-law, on the 14th of December, when he had been three weeks at his post. " I am in a garrison which is as much able to command Flushing as the Tower is to answer for London ; and, for aught I can learn, it is hardly to be redressed. I mean truly, if I cannot have it helped here, to write a protestation thereof to her Majesty, and to the Lords of the Council, as a thing that I can no way take upon me to answer, if I be not increased at the least by four hundred men more than yet I have." In the same letter he pleaded for the soldiers who were being defrauded. " The treasurer "—who was Lord Norris—" here pays our Zeeland soldiers in Zeeland money, which is five per cent. loss to the poor soldiers, who, God knows, want no such hindrances, being scarce able to keep life with their entire pay. If the commodity thereof be truly answered the Queen, yet truly is it but a poor increase to her Majesty, considering what loss it is to the miserable soldier. But if private lucre be made, it hath too hurtful a proportion of other such abuses here."

"It grieves me very much," he wrote six weeks later, on the 2d of February, 1586, "the soldiers are so hardly dealt with in your first beginning of government. When soldiers grow to despair, and give up towns, then it is late to buy that with hundred thousands which might have been saved with a trifle." More reproachful was another letter sent to Leicester, on the 12th of February, from Rotterdam. "Here are no news," he wrote, with proper sarcasm, "but that your band is of very handsome men, but unarmed, and merely spending money and time to no purpose."

Yet another and a more urgent letter was written a week afterwards, while Leicester was fretting over his quarrel with the Queen. "The enemy stirs on every side, and your side must not be idle; for, if it be, it quickly loseth reputation. I beseech your Excellency, be not discouraged by the Queen's discontentments; for, the event being good, your glory will shine through those mists. Only, if it please you, have daily counsel taken of your means, how to increase them and how to husband them; and when all is said, if they can serve, we shall make a noble war."

In doing his share towards making a "noble war," Sidney went more than once to the Hague, there to appeal in person to his uncle. He was often in other Dutch towns, putting pressure on the local authorities. He even, in March, made an excursion into Germany, where he induced some of his friends to help the Netherlanders with recruits. He also addressed earnest petitions to Lord Burghley. "I beseech your lordship," he wrote on the 18th of March, "give your hand to sending over the moneys, or there will be some terrible incident follow to the caution towns,"—that is, to Flushing, and to Brielle, the key to Rotterdam on the Maas, just as Flushing was to Antwerp on the Scheldt—which towns were to be held in pawn until the cost of English assistance was repaid.

One especially characteristic letter was addressed to Sir Francis Walsingham on the 24th of March. Sidney excused himself for distressing his father-in-law by his complaints and entreaties to the Queen and her ministers. "I think," he wrote, "such is the good will it pleaseth you to bear me that my part of the trouble is something that troubles you. But, I beseech you, let it not. I had before cast my count of danger, want and disgrace ; and, before God, sir, it is true in my heart, the love of the cause doth so far overbalance them all, that, with God's grace, they shall never make me weary of my resolution. If her Majesty were the fountain, I would fear, considering what I daily find, that we should wax dry. But she is but a means whom God useth ; and, I know not whether I am deceived, but I am faithfully persuaded that, if she should withdraw herself, other springs would rise to help the action ; for methinks I see the great work indeed in hand against the abusers of the world, wherein it is no greater fault to have confidence in man's power than it is too hastily to despair of God's work. I think a wise and constant man ought never to grieve while he doth play, as a man may say, his own part truly,

though others be out ; but if he himself leave his
hold because other mariners will be idle, he will
hardly forgive himself his own fault. For me, I
cannot promise of my own course, because I know
there is a higher power must uphold me, or else I
shall fall ; but certainly I trust I shall not by other
men's wants be drawn from myself. Therefore, good
sir, to whom, for my particular, I am more bound
than to all men besides, be not troubled with my
troubles, for I have seen the worst, in my judgment,
beforehand, and worse than that cannot be. If the
Queen pay not her soldiers, she must lose her garrisons. There is no doubt thereof. But no man
living shall be able to say the fault is in me. What
relief I can do them, I will. I will spare no danger,
if occasion serves. I am sure no creature shall be
able to lay injustice to my charge ; and for further
doubts, truly I stand not upon them."

"I understand I am called very ambitious and
proud at home, but certainly if they knew my heart
they would not altogether so judge me," Sidney
wrote in this letter. Ambition and pride he had,
but both of the right sort. He had tenderness, too,
and humour. "We shall have a sore war upon us
in the summer," he added. "I know not what to
say to my wife's coming till you resolve better ; for,
if you "—that is, the English authorities—"run a
strange course, I may take such an one here as may
not be fit for any one of the feminine gender." Very
soon after the receipt of this letter Lady Sidney
did go to the Netherlands, and she lived at Flushing
while her husband was away in battle or other occu-

pation not " fit for any one of the feminine gender."
Two months later Sidney wrote from Utrecht to tell
Walsingham that he was presently returning to
Flushing, " where I hear that your daughter is very
well and merry."

Sidney was not able to take part in any important
fighting until July.

He had vainly besought Leicester on the 2d of
February to support him in a project for besieging
Steenbergen, near the western extremity of North
Brabant, which was then held by a Spanish force,
and of thus diverting from Grave, on the eastern
side of the province, the fierce attack that was being
made by the Duke of Parma upon its garrison of
Netherlanders. " With two thousand of your footmen, besides them that these quarters may spare,
and three hundred of your horse, with them here-
about," he wrote, " I will undertake, upon my life,
either to win Steenbergen, or to make the enemy
raise his siege from Grave, or, which I most hope,
both. If God will, I will do you honour in it." The
supplies he asked for were not granted, and he proceeded against Steenbergen with such troops as
he could collect ; but a sudden thaw delayed his
movements, and he was not allowed to persevere in
them. Although on the 6th of April Count Hohenlo
and Sir John Norris, Lord Norris's elder son, drove
off the besiegers of Grave and gave temporary relief
to that " strongest town in all the Low Countries,
though but a little one," as the strategists of the
day considered, it was won by Parma on the 7th of
June.

Count Hohenlo, generally called Hollock by the English, was a dashing warrior, able to do good work when he was sober; but his drunken habits rendered him untrustworthy. On that account, if on no other, there was good reason for not assigning to him any place of permanent responsibility. But he was jealous of Sir Philip Sidney, and when in February Sidney was appointed colonel of the Zeeland regiment of horse, and thus placed in an office that would give him increased opportunities for adding fighting work to his government of Flushing, Count Hohenlo, who wanted the post for himself, protested on the ground that "no stranger might have any regiment." Queen Elizabeth, strange to say, took Hohenlo's part. Walsingham wrote to tell Leicester how angry she was at Sidney's preferment. "She layeth the blame on Sir Philip, as a thing by him ambitiously sought. I see her Majesty very apt upon every light occasion to find fault with him." It would appear that now, as on former occasions, Sir Philip was made the whipping-boy for his uncle's offences against her Majesty. After Elizabeth had forgiven Leicester for wanting to be Governor-General of the United Provinces, she was still angry with Sidney, whom she unjustly suspected of being one of "the chief actors and persuaders in the matter," and she was all the more angry because Sidney sent home troublesome appeals for money and stores, and bold complaints when these were not supplied. Leicester, being restored to the Queen's favour, humoured her. Therefore Sidney was kept in the background.

His first chance of distinguishing himself was in the capture of Axel on the 7th of July, and that was only sanctioned by the Earl of Leicester on Count Maurice insisting that the task of leading it should be assigned to none but his friend Sir Philip.

Axel, about twenty miles from Flushing, on the southern side of the Scheldt, was a strongly fortified town in the hands of the Spaniards. After Grave had been lost, and while other Dutch positions were being surrendered, Sidney and Maurice agreed between them that a blow must, at all hazards, be struck at the enemy, if only to revive the flagging spirits of the Netherlanders; and they resolved that this could in no way be done so effectively, should it prove successful, as by a dash at Axel.

On the moonless night of Tuesday, the 6th of July, a thousand soldiers, in boats, met in front of Flushing, five hundred being of Sir Philip's Zeeland regiment, under his immediate command, and five hundred being Englishmen under his friend Lord Willoughby.* They rowed up and across the Scheldt as far as Terneusen, where they landed

---

* After his appointment to command of the Zeeland regiment Sidney had for a time established himself at Bergen-op-Zoom. " I am delighted in it, I confess, because it was near the enemy," he wrote to Walsingham on the 24th of March ; " but especially, having a very fair house in it, and an excellent air, I destined it for my wife. But finding how you deal there "—in England,—" and that ill-payment in my absence thence might bring some mischief, and considering how apt the Queen is to interpret everything to my disadvantage, I have resigned it to my Lord Willoughby, my very friend, and indeed a valiant and frank gentleman, and fit for that place. Therefore I pray you know that so much of my regality is fallen."

and joined company with two thousand other soldiers, brought hither by Count Maurice and his captains, of whom one was the son of Sir Christopher Hatton. Their destination was known to none but Count Maurice and Sir Philip. They marched stealthily up to Axel, encouraged on the way by a speech from Sir Philip which, according to the testimony of one who was present, " did so link their minds that they did desire rather to die in that service than to live in the contrary."

Not one of them had to die. At two o'clock after midnight, Axel being reached, some thirty or forty men, headed by Sir Philip, jumped into the moat, swam warily across, scaled the wall, and opened the gate for the rest. The sleepy garrison only aroused itself and offered brave resistance when resistance was too late. By placing a band of picked soldiers in the market-place, to assist any of the straggling companies that might be too fiercely opposed by the enemy, Sir Philip ensured strength to every section of his party, and accomplished all the terrible work that he and his colleagues deemed necessary. About half of the twelve hundred men garrisoning the city, besides very many burghers, were slain by the sword or pushed into the water. Five ensigns and a large quantity of rich spoil were taken, and property worth two million florins was destroyed. Four citadels in the neighbourhood were forced to surrender, and the dykes were cut, so that a vast tract of the country round about was flooded.

Sir Philip spent ten or twelve days in seeing that everything was safe, and then, rewarding out of his own purse those who had best acquitted themselves under him, and leaving a strong garrison in Axel, he joined his uncle, who was with the main body of the army at Arnhem. Thence Leicester wrote proudly and graciously to inform the Queen how " my nephew Sidney," and Walsingham how " your son Philip," was to be thanked for the bravest deed yet done by the English in the Low Countries.

Philip had no other father to rejoice over the valour and shrewdness he had shown in this his first great military exploit. On the 5th of May, Sir Henry had died at Worcester after seven days' illness. He wanted six weeks of being fifty-seven years old, and might have expected to add many years to the six and twenty during which, with interruptions in Ireland and elsewhere, he had served as Lord President of Wales. His heart was interred at Ludlow, the seat of his long and worthy rule. The rest of his body was taken to Penshurst for burial. " For his death," wrote Edmund Molyneux, his sometime secretary, " there was great moan and lamentation, especially by those under his government, as having lost that special nobleman whom for courtesy they loved, for justice amongst them they highly honoured, and for many other and rare gifts and singular virtues they in his lifetime greatly esteemed, and at his death marvellously bemoaned."

Though we have many letters written by Sir Philip in the summer of 1586, there is none extant in which reference is made either to the great loss that must have been reported to him seven or eight weeks before his taking of Axel, or to another loss, as great or greater, of which he must have heard five or six weeks after the exploit. His mother died at Penshurst on the 9th of August, tenderly cared for by the friends, " not few, who loved and honoured her," and who were at hand to comfort her in her brief widowhood, and to admire the beautiful ending of her life. " Though before," says the same informant, concerning these friends, " they knew her to exceed many of her sex in singularity of virtue and quality—as good speech, apt and ready conceit, excellence of wit, and notable eloquent delivery (for none could match her, and few or none come near her, either in the good conceit and frame of orderly writing, inditing and speedy despatching, or facility of gallant, sweet, delectable and courtly speaking)—yet in this last action she so far surpassed herself in discreet, wise, effectual, sound and grounded reasons, all tending to zeal and piety, as the same almost astonished the hearers to hear such plenty of goodly and pithy matters to come from such a creature."

Meanwhile the worthy son of these worthy parents was busy with the work remaining to be done in his own short life.

HEARTH IN THE OLD HALL AT PENSHURST

SIDNEY AT THE BATTLE OF ZUTPHEN

CHAPTER XVIII.

THE LAST WEEKS.

1586.

THE ten weeks following the capture of Axel were for the most part spent by Sir Philip Sidney at Flushing. But he was often with his uncle at or near Arnhem, the handsome town built on the site of the old Roman Arecenum, on the northern bank of the Rhine, near the channel by which the Romans had connected that river with the Yssel. The Earl of Leicester had made Arnhem his headquarters, and Sidney was anxious that the success at Axel should be promptly followed by other attacks on the Spanish garrisons, with the special object of hampering the Duke of Parma's operations against Rheinberg and other places thereabout. A few desultory movements were made, in some of which Sidney took part. But nothing important was done: partly because the Earl of Leicester lacked all the qualities of a good general and successful strategist, and relied chiefly on men as incapable as himself ; partly because the money Queen Elizabeth had promised to supply for carrying on the war was greatly in arrear.

On this score Sidney continued to make frequent and bitter complaints, especially in respect to his own direct responsibilities as Governor of Flushing. His views were forcibly expressed in three letters that he wrote on the 14th of August, 1586. One was addressed to the Queen's Privy Council, calling its attention to " the weak store of all sort of necessary munition that both this town and the castle of Rammekins have." " The States," he said, " I have tried to the uttermost ; but, partly with the opinion it more toucheth her Majesty because it is her pawn, but principally because they have ever present occasion to employ both all they have and indeed much more upon the places nearest to the enemy, we in this town, and as I think, Brielle, shall still demand and still go without. By the grace of God, my trust is in Him, that my life shall discharge of blame ; but not I nor all that be here can perform the services that we owe to her Majesty without such merely necessary things." The second letter was addressed to Walsingham. " I beseech you, sir, labour for me, or rather for her Majesty, in it," he wrote touching the need of supplies. " We do still make camps and straight again mar them for want of means, and so lose our money to no purpose." The third letter, also to Walsingham, and sent by another messenger, was intended by Sidney for his father-in-law's private reading and guidance. In it he spoke more

22

plainly, both of the difficulties he was in and of his uncle's share of the blame, than he could do in a public communication. "I assure you, sir, this night we are at a fair plunge to have lost all for want of money. We are now four months behind, a thing insupportable in this place. To complain to my lord of Leicester you know I may not ; but this is the case. If once the soldiers fall to a thorough mutiny, this town is lost in all likelihood."

Though he did not feel himself at liberty to complain openly to others about his uncle, Sidney did not shrink from complaining to him. This appears from the Earl of Leicester's own half confession. "He told me, after Sir Philip's and not long before his own death," says Fulke Greville, "that when he undertook the government of the Low Countries, he carried his nephew over with him, as one among the rest, not only despising his youth for a counsellor, but withal bearing a hand over him as a forward young man. Notwithstanding, in short time he saw this sun so risen above his horizon that both he and all his stars were glad to fetch light from him." But the light, if really sought at all, was only sought when it was too late. Sidney's share in the minor incidents of the mismanaged campaign need not be detailed ; but one episode must be mentioned as evidence that the want of money, the consequent risk of mutiny among the common soldiers, and the Earl of Leicester's arrogant incapacity, were not the only difficulties to be contended with.

Count Hohenlo, with Sir William Pelham and some other friends, had planned a military excursion into the Spanish portion of North Brabant, to be made on the 6th of August, and Sidney had been invited to be of the party. He hurried from Flushing to Geertruidenberg with Edward Norris, the younger son of Lord Norris, but was too late to share in the sport. Perhaps it was well, since nothing was done beyond the wanton burning of a village and the killing of some boors. Sir Philip was waiting in Hohenlo's quarters when the marauders returned, and the Count, though glad to see him, was much displeased at the presence of his friend, the Pelhams and the Norrises being old enemies. He invited them both to supper, however, and soon drank himself into a quarrelling mood. Norris, also, knowing himself to be an unwelcome guest, was prepared for a dispute. Therefore one quickly arose. High words passed between the angry men, and Hohenlo, maddened by his potations, was not satisfied with merely swearing. With the gilt lid of a goblet he cut open Norris's forehead, and he was rushing at him with a drawn dagger when Sidney intervened, and, with help from members of the company who like himself had kept sober, pushed the Count out of the room. A few days afterwards Sidney was the bearer of a challenge from Norris to Hohenlo; but the duel was not fought. While the Earl of Leicester was trying to patch up the quarrel the sharers in it had to be comrades on the field of Zutphen.

On the 28th of August Sidney took part in a review of the troops at Arnhem, and he then persuaded his uncle to agree to the bold movement against the enemy which had been delayed too long. Doesburg, a weak fortress about fifteen miles beyond Arnhem, and on the east side of the Yssel, was invested on the 30th. On the 2d of September it was taken by assault, in which, besides Sir Philip, his brother Robert and the young Earl of Essex distinguished themselves. The next business to be attempted, and a more difficult one, was the capture of Zutphen or South-Fen, the strongest city in Gelderland, fifteen miles north of Doesburg, and well placed on the same side of the Yssel. Zutphen was a day's march from Deventer, also on the Yssel, which Sidney's Zeeland regiment was helping to protect from Spanish attack, although he was himself, with nearly all the English officers, in attendance on the Earl of Leicester.

On the 13th of September Leicester encamped his army outside Zutphen. Crossing the Yssel with the main body of his infantry, he proceeded to throw up entrenchments and to threaten the city and its approach from the opposite side of the river. Most of the cavalry were left on some rising ground, known as Gilbert Hill, less than a mile from the east gate of Zutphen and close to the pretty village of Warnsfeld ; and the custody of this commanding situation was entrusted to Count Lewis William of Nassau, Sir John Norris, and Sir Philip Sidney. Thus matters continued for a week, preparations being vigorously made for an attack, when on the 21st news arrived that a great quantity of provisions was on its way from the south, to be smuggled into Zutphen before daybreak next morning.

ROBERT DEVEREUX, SECOND EARL OF ESSEX.

The spies who brought this information to Leicester were not aware, or did not tell him, that with the convoy of provisions between two and three thousand fighting men, the flower of Parma's army, were marching up to the beleaguered city ; and Leicester considered he had done all that was necessary in ordering Sir John Norris with two hundred horsemen, and Sir William Stanley with three hundred pikemen, to hold the ground between the east gate of Zutphen and Warnsfeld, and to intercept the approaching convoy.

Sir Philip Sidney was not included in the commission, nor were his brothers Robert and Thomas, nor the Earl of Essex, Lord Willoughby, Sir William Pelham, Sir William Perrott, Sir William Russell, and the other cavaliers, some fifty in all, who, as soon as they heard that there was fighting on hand, hurried up, of their own accord, to take part in it. Sir Philip had fully equipped himself, but, when he was joined by Sir William Pelham, who had not time to find his leg-armour, he rashly threw off his own cuisses that they might run equal risk.

The morning of Thursday, the 22d of September, was so misty that nothing could be seen ten paces off when the small English force heard the rumble of waggons and the tramp of horses in the distance. Suddenly the fog cleared, and the five or six hundred Englishmen found themselves confronted by five times as many Spaniards, Italians, and Albanians, and saw that they were within range both of the great guns which played from the ramparts, and of the still more effective muskets handled

by the soldiers in the trenches.   Intending to surprise
the enemy, they had been themselves entrapped.

An hour and a half of desperate fighting ensued.
The Englishmen might have honourably withdrawn,
covering their retreat as best they could.   But that
was not thought of.   " For the honour of England,
good fellows, follow me ! " shouted the young Earl
of Essex, and dashed up to the thousand Spanish
horsemen facing him.   With him went others, and,
soon dropping their lances, they used their curtle-
axes with such effect that the enemy fell back for a
time.   There were notable feats of individual
prowess.   Lord Willoughby, for one—

> The brave Lord Willoughby,
> Of courage fierce and fell,
> Who would not give one inch of way,
> For all the devils of hell,

as the old ballad describes him—spurred on till he
was completely surrounded, and his trappings were
being torn from him when Sidney and a few others
broke through the ring and brought their comrade
out.

There were three onsets, in the course of which
the Englishmen, losing about a fourth of their own
number, killed thrice as many of their foes.   The
gaps in their ranks were filled by new-comers who,
so soon as they heard and saw what was going on,
rode up to vie with their friends in a struggle that,
however foolhardy at the commencement—and in
the case of Sidney, who had not been appointed
to it, however blameworthy—had, when begun, to be
continued.   Sidney forgot or scorned the prudent

words addressed to him eight years before by Hubert Languet. " Do not," Languet wrote, " give the glorious name of courage to a fault resembling it. It is the folly of our age that most men of noble birth think it more honourable to do the work of soldiers than that of leaders, and would rather be praised for boldness than for judgment."

At the close of the second charge Sidney's horse was killed under him. He straightway mounted another and forced his way right through the enemy's ranks, to see bare entrenchments before him. As he was turning back a ball from one of the concealed muskets entered his left leg, at some distance above the knee, where the cuisse should have been, and, cleaving the bone, glanced upward far into the thigh. He would still have fought on ; but his new charger, not well trained to battle, took fright and galloped off the field. The brave rider, though bleeding and faint, retained his seat till he reached the camp, a mile and a half distant, where Leicester was in safety with the main body of the army.

Then it was that, overcome with thirst, Sidney called for something to drink. A bottle of water was brought, and he hastily put it to his lips. But at that moment a foot-soldier was being carried past, and the dying man set greedy, ghastly eyes upon the flask. Sidney handed it to him, saying, as he did so, " Thy necessity is yet greater than mine."

" Oh, Philip ! " exclaimed his uncle, " I am truly grieved to see thy hurt ! " " Oh, my lord," answered Philip, " this have I done to do you honour, and her Majesty some service."

" Oh, noble Sir Philip, never did man attain hurt so honourably, or serve so valiantly, as you ! " cried Sir William Russell, himself bleeding from wounds he had just bravely received. But Sidney declared that he had only performed his duty to God and England, and that his life could not be better spent than in such an exploit as that day's. " For you have now such success as may encourage us all," he said ; " and this my hurt is the ordinance of God by the hap of war."

In that temper, the wounded soldier was conveyed in his uncle's barge, along the Yssel and the Rhine, to Arnhem, quitting for ever the battle-field in which he had hoped to achieve so much. The war was waged without him, and, after a time, without the Earl of Leicester, whose management had done nothing but harm to the cause he essayed to help.

Throughout five and twenty days Sir Philip Sidney lay at Arnhem, in the house of a lady named Gruithuissens. His wife, as soon as she heard of his condition, though she was far advanced in pregnancy, hastened from Flushing to attend upon him. Nor were there wanting other anxious watchers by his bedside, or expressions of sympathy from those who were absent. His brothers, Robert and Thomas, both winning fame in the Netherlands, were with him as often as they could be spared from their military duties. The Earl of Leicester, moreover, went to Arnhem whenever he was able, to show real grief at his nephew's trouble, and to offer such words of kindly meant but hollow comfort as none so well as he knew how to use. The Queen, when she heard of the fight at Zutphen, and its main incident, with her own hand wrote Sidney a comforting letter, and sent it by a special messenger, who was ordered to return immediately with full information as to the sufferer's health and the chances of his recovery.

The surgeons in charge of Sidney seem to have erred through over-tenderness or ignorance. When they came to him, he bade them freely cut and probe to the bottom of the wound. They were content to deal with it on the surface. "With love and care well mixed," says Fulke Greville, not remembering that excess of love may cause lack of care, "they began the cure, and continued some sixteen days with such confidence of his recovery as the joy of their hearts overflowed their discretion, and made them spread the intelligence of it to the Queen and all his noble friends in England, where it was received not as private but as public news." "All the worst days be passed, as both surgeons and physicians have informed me," Leicester wrote to Walsingham on the 2d of October, the tenth day, " and he amends as well as is possible in this time ; and he himself finds it, for he sleeps and rests well, and hath a good stomach to eat."

But Sidney himself was at no time sanguine. On being removed from Zutphen, he was heard to whisper thanks to God for not taking him at once, but rather leaving him a little space in which to prepare for death. On the 30th of September he sent for his friend George Gifford, an eminent divine, who wrote an interesting if over-wrought account of the sick-bed experiences. "Although he had professed the Gospel, loved and favoured those that did embrace it, entered deeply into the concerns of the Church, taken good order and very good care for his family and soldiers to be instructed and to be brought to live accordingly," says Gifford, "yet, entering into deep examination of his life now, in the time of his affliction, he felt those inward motions and workings of a spirit exciting him to a deep sorrow for his former conduct." He professed grief and repentance at much that he had done, and much that he had failed to do, in his short life. "All things in my former life have been vain, vain, vain," he declared; and he asked that "The Arcadia" might be destroyed.

He wrote a short poem, "La Cuisse Rompue," which was set to music, and sung to him. He also wrote to his learned friend Belarius, "a large epistle, in very pure and eloquent Latin," a copy of which, we are told, "for the excellency of the phrase, and the fittingness of the matter," was transmitted to Queen Elizabeth. Neither letter nor poem remains for us to read.

On the 30th of September he made his will, to which a codicil was added a fortnight later. This document, as Fulke Greville considered, "will ever remain for a witness to the world that those sweet and large, even when dying, affections in him could no more be contracted with the narrowness of pain, grief, and sickness, than any sparkle of immortality can be buried in the shadow of death."

To his father-in-law, Sir Francis Walsingham, and his brother Robert, or either of them, he gave authority to sell so much of his property in the counties of Lincoln, Sussex, and Southampton, as was necessary to pay his father's debts and his own; which latter were heavy in consequence of the expenses he had been put to in helping the war in the Netherlands. To his wife, Dame Frances Sidney, he bequeathed, during her lifetime, half the income arising from all the manors, lands, tenements, rents, rights, and reversions he had lately inherited from his father or otherwise acquired. In trust for his daughter Elizabeth he left £4,000 as a marriage portion, suitable provision being made for her education and maintenance until she was entitled to receive the principal. To his younger brother Thomas he assigned lands to the value of £100 a year, to be selected from any part of his estates, except Penshurst. That, with all the rest of the present income, save certain other small bequests, and reversion of the whole property, were left to the other brother, Robert.

Several of the minor bequests are noteworthy. To his " dear sister," the Countess of Pembroke, he left " my best jewel, beset with diamonds." To his uncles, the Earls of Leicester and Warwick, and to his wife's parents, Sir Francis and Lady Walsingham, he left £100 apiece, " to bestow in jewels for my remembrance." For his aunt, the Countess of Sussex, another aunt's husband, the Earl of Huntingdon, and his brother-in-law, the Earl of Pembroke, he desired that three gold rings, set with

large diamonds and all exactly alike, might be
fashioned ; and to his aunt, Lady Huntingdon, and
the wives of his uncles, the Earls of Warwick and
Leicester, he appointed " every one of them a jewel,
the best I have." To his " dear friends," Edward
Dyer and Fulke Greville, he left all his books ; to
another, Sir William Russell, his best suit of armour ;
to Edward Wotton, his companion in Vienna in
1574, an annual present of a buck from Penshurst.
Every servant was remembered, from the old and
faithful Griffin Madox, who had been his steward
ever since their return from foreign travel, and to
whom he assigned an annuity of £40, down to the
humblest in his employment, who were to receive £5
apiece. To the surgeons and divines who were waiting upon him during this his last illness gifts of £30 in
one case and of £20 in the others were to be made.

On the 6th of October the Earl of Leicester
wrote hopefully about his nephew. " He feeleth no
grief now but his long lying, which he must suffer."
But Sir Philip knew that he was dying. On the 8th
he discovered, what the surgeons had not noticed
and now denied, that mortification of his shattered
limb had commenced. His only fear was that the
pains he was enduring, and concealing from such un-
observant eyes as Leicester's, might spoil the vigour
of his mind before the body was at rest. " I do
with trembling heart, and most humbly," he said,
" intreat the Lord that the pangs of death may not
be so grievous as to take away my understanding."

On the evening of Sunday, the 16th, after he had
been ill for four and twenty days, Sidney suddenly

raised himself in his bed, and, resting his elbow on the pillow, called for a piece of paper. In a fitful gleam of hope, perhaps, he wrote this touching little note to his friend John Wier, the chief physician of the Duke of Cleves, and the famous pupil of Cornelius Agrippa : " Mi Wieri, veni, veni. De vita periclitor, et te cupio. Nec vivus, nec mortuus, ero ingratus. Plura non possum, sed obnixe oro ut festines. Vale. Tuus Ph. Sidney."

But death came more quickly than the physician. Before daybreak on Monday, the 17th, Gifford walked gently to the bedside and asked Sidney how he was. " I feel myself more weak," he replied. " I have not slept this night." He was troubled in his mind, doubting whether his prayers had been answered and his sins forgiven. Gifford comforted him with texts and pious assurances. Sidney then, lifting up his eyes and hands, exclaimed, " I would not change my joy for the empire of the world."

He called for his will, had it read over to him, and dictated and signed the codicil, by which, among other bequests, he left his best sword to the Earl of Essex, and the next best to Lord Willoughby. That done, he asked that the poem he had written two or three weeks ago might be chanted to him for the last time. During the next three or four hours he conversed at intervals on matters proper to the occasion. Whenever there was a long pause and his friends kept silence, thinking he might be asleep, he asked them to talk on : " I pray you speak to me still."

About noon he became visibly weaker, and he took leave, one by one, of his sorrowing friends.

One of the last to be addressed was his brother
Robert, knighted ten days before for his bravery at
Zutphen.   " Love my memory," said Sir Philip;
"cherish my friends; their faith to me may assure
you they are honest.   But above all, govern your
will and affections by the will and word of your
Creator; in me beholding the end of the world with
all her vanities."

A little later, at about two o'clock in the afternoon
of this memorable Monday, the 17th of October,
1586, as he lay with closed eyes, Gifford said to him:
" Sir, if you hear what I say, let us by some means
know it; and if you have still your inward joy and
consolation in God, hold up your hand."   Straightway he raised not one hand alone but both, and set
them together on his breast, with joined palms and
fingers pointing upwards, in attitude of prayer.

Thus died Sir Philip Sidney.

SIDNEY'S TREE

CHAPTER XIX.

SUPPLEMENTARY.

IR," wrote the Earl of Leicester to Sir Francis Walsingham on the 25th of October, eight days after Sir Philip's death, " the grief I have taken for the loss of my dear son and yours would not suffer me to write sooner of those ill news unto you, especially being in so good hope, so very little time before, of his good recovery. But he is with the Lord, whose will be done. What perfection he was born unto, and how able he was to serve her Majesty and his country, all men here almost wonder. For mine own part I have lost, beside the comfort of my life, a most principal stay and help in my service here, and, if I may say it, I think none of all hath a greater loss than the Queen's Majesty herself. Your sorrowful daughter and mine is with me here at Utrecht, till she may recover some strength; for she is wonder-

fully overthrown through her long care since the beginning of her husband's hurt; and I am the more careful that she should be in some strength ere she take her journey into England, for that she is with child, which I pray God send to be a son, if it be His will; but, whether son or daughter, they shall be my children too." Neither son nor daughter, however, came into the world alive. Lady Sidney's wifely zeal had interfered with her parental responsibilities, and her child was still-born. "The Lord hath inflicted us with sharpness," Leicester said in another letter.

"I go no whither," Fulke Greville wrote to a fellow-mourner soon after the news of his friend's death reached him. "The only question I now study is whether weeping sorrow or speaking sorrow may most honour his memory that I think death is sorry for. What he was to God, his friends, and country, fame hath told, though his expectations went beyond her good. Give me leave to join with you in praising and lamenting him, the name of whose friendship carried me above my own worth, and I fear hath left me to play the ill poet in mine own part." *

All England went into mourning for the dead Sidney. "It was accounted a sin," we are told, "for any gentleman of quality, for months after, to appear at Court or city in any light or gaudy apparel." On the day when the corpse was landed in England for burial Queen Elizabeth sent a message to Sir Francis Walsingham, saying she would have visited

---

* Hatfield MSS.; Fulke Greville to Archibald Douglas, (October,) 1586.

him in person that morning but for fear that their meeting would have redoubled both his and her grief at the loss of Sir Philip.* The Queen's grief seems to have shown itself in rough ways. Naunton, in his " Regalia," tells how, some time after, young Lord Mountjoy having stolen away from Court and joined Sir John Norris's company, Elizabeth had him brought home by special messenger, and, " when he came into the Queen's presence, she fell into a kind of reviling, demanding how he durst go over without leave." " Serve me so once more," quoth she, " and I will lay you fast enough for running. You will never leave it until you are knocked on the head as that inconsiderate fellow Sidney was."

On Monday, the 24th of October, the hero's body, having been suitably embalmed, was removed from Arnhem to Flushing, there to remain for another week. On the 1st of November it was conveyed to the water's edge, followed by twelve hundred of the English soldiers, walking three abreast and trailing their swords and muskets in the dust, and by a vast concourse of Dutch burghers. As they marched solemn music was performed. Rounds of small shot were thrice fired by all the men present, and from the great ordnance on the walls two volleys were discharged as the corpse was taken from the shore. It was placed in *The Black Pinnace*, Sir Philip Sidney's own vessel, its sails, tackle, and other furniture being all of black stuff, and was accompanied out of port by several other ships, all in mourning.

---

* State Papers, Domestic, Elizabeth, vol. cxcv., No. i.; Davison to Walsingham, 5 November, 1586.

23

The people of the Netherlands were loth to part with the remains of him who had died in their service. The States entreated that the honour of providing for his burial might be conferred on them ; if so, they would pledge themselves, they averred, to erect for him as fair a monument as had ever been set up for any king or emperor in Christendom ; " yea, though the same should cost half a ton of gold in the building." But England claimed her own.

On Friday, the 5th of November, the mournful cargo was landed at Tower Hill, on the Thames, and thence borne to a house in the Minories, where it waited three months for interment.

The reason for this unusual delay is curious. "Sir Philip Sidney hath left a great number of poor creditors," Walsingham wrote to Leicester on this 5th of November. "What order he hath taken by his will for their satisfaction I know not. It is true that, immediately after the death of his father, he sent me a letter of attorney for the sale of such portion of land as might content his creditors ; but there was nothing done before his death. I have paid and must pay for him about £6,000, which I do assure your lordship hath brought me into a most desperate and hard state, which I weigh nothing in respect of the gentleman who was my chief worldly comfort." When the will in which Sidney had made arrangements for payment of his father's debts reached England informalities were found in it, and there were legal difficulties in its execution owing to the son's death having followed so quickly on the father's. " I have caused Sir Philip Sidney's will to be considered by some gentlemen learned in the law," Walsingham wrote in another letter, "and I find the same imperfect touching the sale of his land for the satisfying of his poor creditors ; which, I assure your lordship, doth greatly afflict me, that a gentleman that hath lived so unspotted a reputation, and had so great cares to see all men satisfied, should be so exposed to the outcry of his creditors. This hard estate of this noble gentleman maketh me stay to take order of his burial until your lordship return. I do not see how the same can be performed, with that solemnity that appertaineth, without the utter undoing of his creditors, which is to be weighed in conscience."

The Earl of Leicester would not or could not find means for the burial of his nephew. Therefore it was postponed either until the lawyers' hindrance had been removed, or, as is more probable, until Sir Francis Walsingham had saved enough money to defray the expenses out of his own pocket. It was commonly reported at the time that the thing was being done at his individual cost, and purely out of regard for his son-in-law's memory. At any rate, we may be sure the funeral was honestly paid for ; and it was a more splendid funeral, perhaps, than had ever yet been given to any English subject.

Thursday, the 16th of February, 1587, four months all but a day after Sidney's death, was appointed for the ceremony, and no pains were spared to make the pageant worthy of the hero. Upwards of seven hundred mourners took rank in the procession, which contained representatives of every class of English society, duly betokening the grief felt by all England.

Two and thirty poor men, one for each year of Sidney's life led the way, in long mourning gowns, with their short hats pressed tightly over their heads, and long staves in their hands. Next followed officers, fifers, and drummers of foot, and captains, corporals, and trumpeters of Sidney's regiment of horse, all with their truncheons reversed, and with ensigns, bearing the mottoes *Semper eadem* and *Pulchrum propter se*, trailing in the dust.

After these came an uplifted standard, Sidney's own, showing the cross of St. George, the Sidney crest—a porcupine, collared and chained, between three crowned lions' heads—and the device *Vix ea nostra voco*. It was borne by Mr. Richard Gwyn, who was followed by sixty of Sidney's gentlemen and yeomen, of all ages and sizes, but clothed alike in sombre garb and walking in pairs. By themselves were the dead man's chief physician and surgeon, Dr. James and Mr. Kell; and a few paces behind was Griffin Madox, his loving steward. Next walked, in pairs, sixty of his kindred and friends, among them being Sir Francis Drake and Sir William Herbert, Edward Waterhouse and Thomas Perrott. The preacher chosen for the day, attended by two chaplains, parted these latter from the bearer of a pennant on which were embroidered Sidney's arms, and which introduced a separate portion of the procession.

The hero's war horse, richly furnished, was led by a footman and ridden by a little page in whose hand was one half of a broken lance, the other half being trailed on the ground ; and following it was a barbed horse, caparisoned with cloth of gold, ridden by another little page who supported a reversed battle-axe on the saddle. Next appeared a great banner, carried by Henry White and attended by five heralds, in whose hands were badges of Sidney's knighthood. Portcullis held his spurs and his gloves, Blue-Mantle his gauntlets, Rouge-Dragon his helmet, Richmond his shield, and Somerset his tabard, while Clarence King-at-arms walked sedately in the rear.

All these served as ushers of the coffin, which at length approached. Shrouded in rich black velvet, and adorned with the Sidney arms, it was lodged on two long poles, each resting on the shoulders of seven yeomen. Four youths of the family held up the family banners, and the pall-bearers were Sir Philip's four especial friends, Fulke Greville, Edward Dyer, Edward Wotton, and Thomas Dudley ; one being at each corner, and all clad in long gowns and close-fitting hoods.

Sir Robert Sidney, dressed in the same garb, walked as chief mourner, and at a little distance were four knights and two gentlemen of the Sidney and Walsingham households, Thomas Sidney being foremost. After them rode in pairs the Earls of Leicester and Huntingdon, the Earls of Pembroke and Essex, the Lords Willoughby and North ; and there were seven gentlemen from the Low Countries, one representing each of the United Provinces.

Finally, a long cavalcade was headed by the Lord Mayor of London, in his purple robes, and by his aldermen, sheriffs, and recorder, twenty in all. A hundred and twenty unarmed citizens were in attendance, and about three hundred citizens trained for war, all holding their weapons reversed.

The company, thus ordered, started from the Minories and proceeded slowly to St. Paul's Cathedral, through streets so crowded that it was difficult to pass at all. The inside of the church was draped with black. When the coffin was placed upon a pile, the words inscribed upon it, and made the preacher's text, " Blessed are the dead who die in the Lord," found an echo in the hearts of all the thousands present. The sermon being over and the service read, the body was interred under the Lady Chapel, at the back of the high altar—all which, of course, was destroyed by the great fire of 1666; and a double volley of shot from the churchyard informed the world outside that Sir Philip Sidney had been buried.

Death was busy with Sidney's kindred after as well as before the year in which his own life was prematurely ended. Both his father and his mother had passed away in the summer of 1586, the brilliant career of his most famous uncle, the Earl of Leicester, a bad man in many ways, but not without some redeeming qualities, was closed in 1588, and in 1590 his other uncle, the Earl of Warwick, passed from a world in which he had dwelt much less pompously, but much more worthily. In 1590, too, England lost one of its ablest and most honest statesmen, and the Sidney family its best friend, in

Sir Francis Walsingham, who died in his fifty-fourth year, so poor that it was needful to bury him at night time in St. Paul's Cathedral, where he lay in the same tomb as his honoured son-in-law.* The amiable and talented Countess of Pembroke lived on in widowhood till 1621, and was the patron of Shakespeare and many other famous men of letters unknown to fame in her brother Philip's day. Of her youngest brother Thomas we lose trace. The other brother, Robert, inheriting both the Sidney property and the wealth left by his uncle the Earl of Leicester, was created Baron Sidney of Penshurst in 1603, Viscount de L'Isle in 1604, and Earl of Leicester in 1618, and lived until 1626. To him in 1615 reverted the property of his niece Elizabeth, Sir Philip's only child, who at the age of fifteen was married to Roger Manners, fifth Earl of Rutland, and who died without issue when she was thirty. Her mother survived her. In 1590 Sir Philip's widow became the wife of the young Earl of Essex, and, after his execution, accepted as a third husband Richard de Burgh, Earl of Clanricarde.

Spenser and the other poets, following Sidney's lead, and speaking in fictitious terms of Lady Rich as Stella, sometimes applied the title to Dame Frances Sidney also. It is worthy of note that the true

---

* This was hidden from view in 1591, when, as Stow tells us in his "Survey of London," the body of Sir Christopher Hatton was buried close by, "under a sumptuous monument where a merry poet wrote thus :

    "'Philip and Francis have no tomb,
    For great Christopher takes all the room.'"

Stella, the object of Sidney's homage in verse, was the daughter of Walter Devereux, the first Earl of Essex, and that her brother, Robert Devereux, the second Earl of Essex, had Sidney's widow, the other Stella, for his wife. Thus the two Stellas were closely linked, in different relationships, to the three men who stand out most prominently as types of English chivalry in the Elizabethan age.

The earliest of the three, the first Earl of Essex, unfortunate in nearly all the events of his life, died before he was thirty-five, and after Queen Elizabeth had been eighteen years on the throne.

The latest of the three, the second Earl of Essex, was Queen Elizabeth's prime favourite, and the most conspicuous exemplar of chivalrous life, such as it was and could be then, during thirteen years before she caused him to be beheaded, when his age was not yet thirty-four.

Between these two, and greater and worthier than either, in some ways the pupil of the one, in some ways the tutor of the other, was Sir Philip Sidney, whose short term of brilliant eminence was in the middle period of Queen Elizabeth's reign, and was closed by death when he lacked six weeks of being thirty-two years old.

It is not necessary here to catalogue or largely quote from the praises and lamentations uttered in prose and verse by hundreds of Sir Philip Sidney's contemporaries, and the tributes to his worth offered by other hundreds living after him. Unlike as Hamlet is to Sidney, with some remarkable resemblances in particulars, it is not mere guessing to assume that Shakespeare, who settled in London and joined the Earl of Leicester's company of players while all the world was talking of Sidney's life and its heroic ending, had him in his thoughts when he made Ophelia speak of Hamlet as

> The courtier's, scholar's, soldier's eye, tongue, sword,
> The expectancy and rose of the fair State,
> The glass of fashion and the mould of form,
> The observed of all observers.

How Sidney was regarded by men who could not have been blamed had they shut their eyes to his merits may be learned from one of the "Four Sonnets to Sir Philip Sidney's Soul," written by Thomas Constable, the Papist who had to divide much of his life between exile and imprisonment on account of his religion, yet had nothing but tenderness and reverence for one who was a foremost champion of Protestant supremacy.

> Give pardon, blessed soul, to my bold cries,
>   If they, importunate, interrupt the song
>   Which now, with joyful notes, thou sing'st among
> The angel-choristers of heavenly skies !
> Give pardon, eke, sweet soul, to my slow cries,
>   That since I saw thee now it is so long,
>   And yet the tears that unto thee belong
> To thee as yet they did not sacrifice !
> I did not know that thou wert dead before :
>   I did not feel the grief I did sustain.
> The greater stroke astonisheth the more :
>   Astonishment takes from us sense of pain :
> I stood amazed when others' tears begun,
> And now begin to weep when they have done.

"This is that Sidney," wrote William Camden of the friend he had lost, "who, as Providence seems to have sent him into the world to give the present a specimen of the ancients, so it did on a sudden recall him and snatch him from us as more worthy of Heaven than of earth." But the true-hearted student of men's thoughts and actions was too wise to grieve or repine. "Rest, then, in peace, O Sidney," he added. "We will not celebrate your memory with tears, but admiration. Whatever we loved in you, whatever we admired in you, still continues and will continue in the memories of men, the revolutions of ages, and the annals of time. Many, as inglorious and ignoble, are buried in oblivion : but Sidney shall live to all posterity. For as the Grecian poet has it, 'Virtue 's beyond the reach of fate.' "

But our record of Sir Philip Sidney's life, his chivalrous aims and chivalrous achievements, must be closed with words written by his comrade and kinsman, Fulke Greville, afterwards Lord Brooke, the man who knew him intimately from childhood, and who, outliving him by two and forty years, caused the title, "Friend to Sir Philip Sidney," to be inscribed upon his tomb.

"Indeed," Fulke Greville wrote, "he was a true model of worth ; a man fit for conquest, plantation, reformation, or what action so ever is the greatest and hardest among men ; withal, such a lover of mankind and goodness that whosoever had any real parts in him found comfort, participation, and protection to the uttermost of his power ; like Zephyrus, he giving life where he blew. The universities abroad and at home accounted him a very Mæcenas of learning, dedicated their books to him, and communicated every invention or improvement of knowledge with him. Soldiers honoured him, and were so honoured by him, as no man thought he marched under the true banner of Mars that had not obtained Sir Philip Sidney's approbation. Men of affairs in most parts of Christendom entertained correspondence with him. But what speak I of these, with whom his own ways and ends did concur? since, to descend, his heart and capacity were so large that there was not a cunning painter, a skilful engineer, an excellent musician, or any other artificer of extraordinary fame, that made not himself known to this famous spirit, and found him his true friend without hire, and the common rendezvous of worth in his time. Besides, the ingenuity of his nature did spread itself so freely abroad as who lives that can say he ever did him harm? whereas there be many living that may thankfully acknowledge he did them good. Neither was this in him a private but a public affection; his chief ends being not friends, wife, children and himself, but above all things the honour of his Maker, and the service of his prince and country."]

INDEX.

A

Aid, the, Queen Elizabeth's ship, employed in Frobisher's expedition, 156, 157

Alençon, Francis, Duke of. *See* Anjou, Francis, Duke of

Alexander, Sir William, editor of "The Arcadia," 264

Alva, Duke of, his persecution of the Netherlanders, 78

Amadas, Captain, his voyage to Virginia, 298

American colonisation, attempted by Frobisher, 156, 157, 161; Sidney's plans for, 296, 297; Raleigh's expeditions, 298, 299

Anjou, Francis, Duke of, the project of his marriage with Queen Elizabeth in 1572, when he was Duke of Alençon, 57, 59, 64; revival of the project in 1579, 177; Sidney's opposition to it, 178, 223; Sidney's letter to the Queen about it, 182–185; the French embassage to Queen Elizabeth in furtherance of the project in 1581, 231; further marriage negotiations, 250, 251; his visit to England, 251; at Antwerp in 1582, 251–253; his death, 300, 301

Anjou, Henry, Duke of. *See* Henry III. of France

Anne, daughter of Philip II. and widow of Maximilian II., Sidney's visit to, at Prague, 121, 122

Antonio, Don, claimant of the crown of Portugal, Sidney's friendship with, 317

Antwerp, Sidney at, 86, 115, 127, 251–253; Languet at, 222, 253; the siege of, 312, 325

"Apology for Poetry," Sidney's. *See* "Defence of Poesy"

"Arcadia," Sanazarro's, 260

"Arcadia," Sidney's, 67, 68, 203, 206, 207, 213–218, 225, 247, 255–257, 259–271, 274, 346

Areopagus, Sidney's and Spenser's 199–203, 206, 254, 256, 257, 269, 292

Arnhem, 336, 339; Sidney's illness and death at, 344–350, 353

Arran, Earl of, 307, 308

Arundel, Earl of. *See* Howard, Philip

Ascham, Roger, 40; on Venice, 72; Sidney's debt to, 189, 190

Ashton, Thomas, founder of Shrewsbury School, 26, 31, 37

"Astrophel and Stella," Sidney's, 206, 224, 225, 236, 237, 240, 241, 243–245, 247, 255, 256, 269, 272–274

Athlone, Sidney at, 106

24

ImTheStory.com

Lightning Source UK Ltd.
Milton Keynes UK
UKOW06f1312171115

262912UK00018B/677/P